COLLECTED STUDIES
IN
GREEK AND LATIN SCHOLARSHIP

COLLECTED STUDIES
IN
GREEK AND LATIN SCHOLARSHIP

BY

A. W. VERRALL, Litt.D.
KING EDWARD VII PROFESSOR OF ENGLISH LITERATURE
AND FELLOW OF TRINITY COLLEGE, CAMBRIDGE
HON. LITT.D., DUBLIN

EDITED BY

M. A. BAYFIELD, M.A.

AND

J. D. DUFF, M.A.

Cambridge:
at the University Press
1913

CAMBRIDGE
UNIVERSITY PRESS

University Printing House, Cambridge CB2 8BS, United Kingdom

Published in the United States of America by Cambridge University Press, New York

Cambridge University Press is part of the University of Cambridge.

It furthers the University's mission by disseminating knowledge in the pursuit of education, learning and research at the highest international levels of excellence.

www.cambridge.org
Information on this title: www.cambridge.org/9781107643000

First published 1913
First paperback edition 2014

A catalogue record for this publication is available from the British Library

ISBN 978-1-107-64300-0 Paperback

PREFACE

THIS volume contains a selection of articles which seemed to deserve publication in a permanent form, collected from the numerous contributions made by the author to classical periodicals during the last thirty years; six papers not hitherto published, and one essay which originally formed part of *Studies in Horace*, a book now out of print. The selection was made by Dr Verrall, in compliance with the suggestions of friends, in the spring of 1912, and it was confirmed by the present editors, by whom the essays have been revised and prepared for the press. In only one or two places do the editors think that the author might have wished to make modifications which seemed beyond their competence.

In the case of republished articles, the names of the Journals and Reviews in which they originally appeared are given in the Table of Contents, and where the date of publication of a particular essay seemed to be of importance a footnote giving this has been added *ad loc.* The dates of composition of the hitherto unpublished papers are not known with precision; some of them are fairly recent, while others were written a good many years ago. Most of them were probably read at meetings of the Cambridge Philological Society, or of some other.

For permission to republish, our thanks are due to the Classical Journals Board for papers from the *Classical Review*; to the Council of the Society for the Promotion of Hellenic Studies for essays from the *Journal of Hellenic Studies*; and to Messrs Macmillan & Co. for those from the *Journal of Philology*, and for the reprint from *Studies in Horace*.

We have also to thank Mrs Verrall for valuable assistance.

Footnotes added by the editors are printed in square brackets.

M. A. B.
J. D. D.

May 1913

TABLE OF CONTENTS

CORRIGENDA

On p. 208, *for* ἐπαινῷ (*bis*) and Ἐπαινῷ *read* ἐπαίνῳ and Ἐπαίνῳ.

TYRTAEUS. I

THE history of poetry, says Horace[1], begins with the various lore attributed to such half-mythical personages as Orpheus and Amphion, and presents to us next the famous names of Homer and of Tyrtaeus, 'whose verses made sharp for battle the souls of men.' It is implied by the context that this conjunction, though partly suggested by community of spirit between the poet of the *Iliad* and the military bard of Lacedaemon, is also justified by chronology; and in fact, if we accept the tradition which ruled in the Roman schools and still rules in modern manuals, the elegiacs and anapaests composed by Tyrtaeus for the encouragement of the Spartans in their struggle to recover Messenia were the earliest pieces of literature, strictly historical and datable, which the Greeks possessed. According to the story, presented to us in its entirety by Pausanias, and accepted in substance by all writers of the Roman age, the original subjugation of Messenia was accomplished in two episodes, a first conquest and a rebellion, separated by an interval of about one generation. The central date is B.C. 700. The activity of Tyrtaeus was assigned, since he expressly

[1] *Ars Poetica* 401.

describes his war as a war of recovery, not to the first of these contests but to the second, and his date therefore stood about B.C. 680. The modern speculations, which would bring it a little lower, assuming for the moment that they work on a substantial foundation, would still make no essential difference. If we place Tyrtaeus at any time before 650, we put him as high as we can with assurance put any extant Greek literature, except the primitive Epos or portions of it: and if in that age or near it his elegiacs, being what they are, were current and popular in Laconia, their importance to history in many respects is such as we cannot easily overrate. The object of this paper is to overturn this hypothesis completely, not by any speculative argument, but by direct testimony, the full, plain, and conclusive statement of the principal and only trustworthy witness who speaks to the point.

The adventures of Tyrtaeus in the 'second Messenian war' of the seventh century, as admitted or partly admitted by modern historians, are the remnant of an elaborate 'house on the sands,' some time since flooded and ruined by the rain of criticism. All, I believe, are now agreed, and it is therefore needless to argue, that about these primeval conflicts between the Spartans and Messenians the ancients had no solid information, except what they might rightly or wrongly infer from the poems of Tyrtaeus. To support that long romance,—all omens, oracles, desperate amours, miraculous feats, and hair-breadth escapes,—which is reproduced in detail by Pausanias, no authority is even pretended, except writers, the chief of them a poet, separated by four centuries from the events supposed: and if Rhianus of Crete and Myron of Priene troubled themselves about the evidence for their novels any more than Scott troubled himself about the evidence for *Ivanhoe*, they must have found that evidence in such oral tradition as may have been propagated in Messenian cabins during the dark ages of oppression, ready to emerge and expand after the deliverance effected in the fourth century by Epaminondas. But for that deliverance, as Grote remarks, we should probably have heard little or nothing about the original resistance. The historians or quasi-historians of the third and later centuries would probably then have left the events of the 'first and second Messenian wars' in that general oblivion which seems to cover them down to the age of Aristotle. In these circumstances scientific criticism had a simple task. Aristomenes, the protagonist of the alleged Messenian insurrection, belongs to that class of popular heroes whose history is naught and their very existence not unquestionable. He may stand possibly above Tell or Vortigern, but not with William Wallace or Llewelyn, perhaps on a level with Hereward the Wake. For serious writers it is now enough to mention his name[1].

[1] See for example Beloch, *Gr. Geschichte*, vol. 1, p. 284. Those who (as Prof. Holm and Mr Abbott) condescend to repeat the narrative of Pausanias do so under reservations effectually destructive; and in fact there is no controversy about the matter.

If therefore these same writers treat on a totally different footing the connexion of this same episode with the life of Tyrtaeus, if for the 'second Messenian war' they use the fragments of Tyrtaeus as confidently as Aeschylus for the battle of Salamis, they do so, not because this proceeding is countenanced by Pausanias, nor out of deference to any witness who can have been influenced by the transfiguration performed upon the history of Messenia in the romances of the third century. Pausanias, and in general all the writers of later antiquity, accepted and circulated so much about primitive Messenia which no one would accept now, that we should concern ourselves little, if that were the question, with what they allege about Tyrtaeus. But in fact the poems of Tyrtaeus, and his story, complete in all essential features, can be traced, not indeed into the seventh century, but well above the level of Rhianus or Myron[1]. Already in the fourth century both he and his works were known and had admirers at Athens. He is cited and some points in his life are noticed by Plato in the *Laws*; he is extolled by the orator Lycurgus, who also narrates at length the circumstances in which his elegies were composed. And more significant than all upon the question of his historical validity, Aristotle, in the *Politics*, adduces without scruple the witness of his poem entitled *Eunomia*, or *The Blessings of Order*, as to the

[1] The date of Myron cannot be fixed, but that he was an author of the same kind and standing as Rhianus is plain from the account and treatment of him in Pausanias.

effect of external pressure in producing a particular kind of political discontent. It is upon the strength of these names, which certainly make together as strong a body of evidence as could be desired, that historians now accept what can be learnt from or about Tyrtaeus as affording a glimpse at least of 'the second Messenian war.' Rhianus cannot have seduced Plato; Lycurgus had not read Myron; Aristotle had probably never heard, and certainly did not depend upon, any fireside anecdotes that may have run loose in Messenia. If all three are agreed—and they are—in accepting a certain belief about Tyrtaeus, it was probably in the main well founded. But the question remains, What was it?

Of the three, the fullest and most explicit statement is that of the orator. The allusions of Plato and Aristotle, though they support that statement so far as they go, and are significant when read in the light of it, contain but little information, and upon the vital point are in themselves uncertain. The account of Lycurgus, which words could hardly make plainer or more definite than it is, puts everything, if we believe him, beyond question. In reading it we should bear in mind that the speaker was in his day perhaps the very first figure in the literary world of Athens, not so much for his actual production, which is and was always reckoned imperfect, as for his political and social character, his zealous and somewhat ostentatious interest in educational matters at large. If there is any person from whom we may accept the assurance that at Athens in the latter part of the fourth century a certain piece of Athenian history was unquestioned, that person is Lycurgus, who shall now be quoted at length. He is dilating upon the beauty and praises of patriotism, which he has illustrated from Euripides; and he continues the subject as follows[1].

Another authority whom I would commend to your approbation is Homer: a poet of whose merit your forefathers had so high an opinion, that they appointed his works by law to be recited, solely and exclusively, at the quadrennial celebration of the Panathenaea, as an advertisement to Hellas that the noblest of actions were the chosen ideal of Athens. And in this they did well. Laws in their brevity command what is right, but do not teach it: it is the poets, with their pictures of human life, who select the noblest examples, and also by reason and demonstration recommend them to men. Take for instance the patriotic exhortation which is addressed to the Trojans by Hector,

'Fight to the ships, fight on: and whoso meets
Perchance from sword or spear the fated death,
E'en let him die! To die defending Troy
Mis-seems him not; and for his wife and babes,
They are saved, and safe his homestead and his fields,
If but the foeman's navy homeward fly.'

This, gentlemen, is the poetry to which your ancestors used to listen; and the ambition of deeds like these wrought in them such a valour, that not for their own city only, but for Hellas also, our common fatherland, they were ready to lay down their lives, as was seen when the army of Marathon gave battle to the foreigner and defeated the host of Asia, imperilling themselves to win security for the whole Greek brotherhood, and proud not of their glory but of the deeds by which it was deserved. They had made Athens the champion of Hellas and mistress over the national foe, because their manly virtue was not exercised in

[1] Lycurgus, pp. 162–163, *c. Leocr.* §§ 102–109.

phrases, but exhibited to the world in act. And therefore so excellent, both as a body and as individuals, were the men by whom our city was in those days administered, that when the Lacedaemonians, who in earlier times were first in martial qualities, had a war with the Messenians, they were commanded by the oracle to take a leader from among us, and were promised victory, if they did so, over their opponents. And if to the descendants of Heracles (for such have been ever the kings of Sparta) the Delphian god preferred a leader from among us, it must be supposed that the merit of our countrymen was beyond all comparison. It is matter of common knowledge that the director whom they received from Athens was Tyrtaeus, with whose help they overcame their enemies, and also framed a system of discipline for their youth, a measure of prudence looking beyond the peril of the moment to the permanent advantage of the future. Tyrtaeus left to them elegies of his composition, by the hearing of which their boys are trained to manliness: and whereas of other poets they make no account, for this one they are so zealous as to have enacted that, whenever they are under arms for a campaign, all should be summoned to the king's tent, to hear the poems of Tyrtaeus; nothing, as they think, could so well prepare the men to meet a patriot's death. It is good that you should listen to some of these elegiacs, and thus learn what manner of poetry obtained the approval of Sparta.

'He nobly dies who, foremost in the band,
Falls bravely fighting for his fatherland;
But beggared and expelled, to utter woes
From town or happy farm the exile goes,
With all his dearest vagabond for life,
Old sire, sweet mother, babes, and wedded wife.
No loving welcome waits him in the haunt
Where need may drive him and the stress of want.
His birth to stain, his person to deface,
All vileness cleaves to him, and all disgrace.
If, then, the wanderer pines in such neglect,
And all his seed are doomed to disrespect,

Fierce for our country let us fight to death,
And for our children fling away our breath.
Stand firm, young gallants, each to other true;
Let never rout or scare begin with you.
Stout be your hearts within, your courage high,
And fighting, reck not if ye live or die.
Your elders there, whose limbs are not so light,
Betray not ye their honour by your flight.
What shame it were, upon the field to find
The wounded, age in front and youth behind;
To see the hapless senior, hoar and gray,
Gasp in the dust his noble soul away,
His hands the bleeding entrails holding in—
O sight to taint the very eyes with sin!—
His body bare!...But nothing misbeseems
The lad, whose youth in him yet lovely teems:
Eyes, hearts adore him, while he draws his breath;
And falls he vanward, fair he is in death.
So plant you each one firmly on the land
With open stride, set tooth to lip,—and stand.'

Yes, gentlemen, they are fine verses, and profitable to those who will give them attention. And the people, therefore, which was in the habit of hearing this poetry, was so disposed to bravery, that they disputed the primacy with Athens, a dispute for which, it must be admitted, there was reason on both sides in high actions formerly achieved. Our ancestors had defeated that first invading army landed by the Persians upon Attica, and thus revealed the superiority of courage above wealth and of valour above numbers. The Lacedaemonians in the lines of Thermopylae, if not so fortunate, in courage surpassed all rivalry. And the bravery of both armies is therefore visibly and truly attested before Hellas by the sepulchral inscriptions, the barrow at Thermopylae bearing the lines,

'Go tell to Sparta, thou that passest by,
That here obedient to her laws we lie.'

while over your ancestors it is written,

> 'Foremost at Marathon for Hellas' right
> The Athenians humbled Media's gilded might.'

Such is the passage which—the fact may appear astonishing, but it shall presently be accounted for—is constantly mentioned in histories and books of reference, as part of the evidence for the current assertion that Tyrtaeus lived and wrote two hundred years before the Persian war. Is it not surely manifest beyond all possibility of debate, if only we raise the question, that on that supposition the whole narrative and argument of Lycurgus would be nonsense? Lycurgus assumes, and calls it a 'matter of common knowledge,' that Tyrtaeus flourished about a hundred years before his own time, *between the Persian war and the Peloponnesian*, and that the Messenian war in which Tyrtaeus served the Lacedaemonians was that of our fifth century, now dated about 464–454 B.C. The preference, he says, given by the Spartans with divine sanction to Tyrtaeus, an Athenian, over their own countrymen, was a *consequence* and *attestation* of the virtue displayed by Athens in the defeat and conquest of the Persians. And again, the teaching of Tyrtaeus, by restoring and elevating the Spartan character, encouraged and enabled the Spartans to dispute the pre-eminence which (according to the orator) in the times immediately following the deliverance of Hellas had belonged without question to Athens. How can this be understood, or what can it mean, if Tyrtaeus had lived and done this work, had strengthened the Lacedaemonian arms and improved the Lacedaemonian schooling, two hundred and fifty years before Athens and Sparta contended for the hegemony, and a full century or more before that public adoption of Homer by Athens as the basis of an improved education from which the orator (rightly, though not perhaps exactly on the right grounds) deduces, as an effect, the primacy of Athens, and the greatness displayed by his city at Marathon, at Salamis, and in the development of the Confederacy of Delos? Athens became so pre-eminent about B.C. 475, that she bestowed a teacher upon Sparta—in 680? Sparta from about B.C. 445 began to dispute that pre-eminence of Athens, by virtue of an education adopted—in 680?

The meaning of Lycurgus is so plain, and so plainly stated, that we hardly know how to suppose it to have been overlooked. But it is at any rate the fact that, in the best and most recent expositions which I can discover, the early date of Tyrtaeus is taken as constant, without a hint that, according to one at least of the oldest witnesses adduced, that date is wrong by a trifle of two centuries. And there is a possible reason for this, which is itself not the least curious part of the case. It is not indeed possible, as I think, to read the whole passage of Lycurgus, with a mind awake to the question, 'At what date does he put Tyrtaeus?', without arriving at the right answer. But it is easy (I may perhaps say so, as I have done it several times myself) to inspect the place, or even to glance through the paragraph, under the presumption that Lycurgus adopts the common date, without perceiving that he does not. It happens that, exactly at the point upon which a student 'verifying the reference' would chiefly fix his attention, accident has prepared for a mind so preoccupied the possibility of mistake: *τοιγαροῦν*—so begin the sentences which mention Tyrtaeus—*οὕτως ἦσαν ἄνδρες σπουδαῖοι καὶ κοινῇ καὶ ἰδίᾳ οἱ τότε τὴν πόλιν οἰκοῦντες, ὥστε τοῖς ἀνδρειοτάτοις Λακεδαιμονίοις ἐν τοῖς ἔμπροσθεν χρόνοις πολεμοῦσι πρὸς Μεσσηνίους ἀνεῖλεν ὁ θεὸς παρ' ἡμῶν ἡγεμόνα λαβεῖν κ.τ.λ.* The words *ἐν τοῖς ἔμπροσθεν χρόνοις* are in themselves, as a relative term, open to ambiguity, and in this place may be affected by different punctuations; so that there are not only three ways of understanding them, all consistent with the general sense of the passage, but even a fourth, which is not. Either we may read them with the verbs of the sentence, *πολεμοῦσιν* and *ἀνεῖλεν*, '...that, when the martial Lacedaemonians had in former times a war with the Messenians, they were commanded...': in that case *former*, by the context, must be relative to the date of the speech, and the point (as in *οἱ τότε τὴν πόλιν οἰκοῦντες*) is to contrast the ancient consideration of Athens with her enfeeblement, so bitterly felt by the orator, in his own days. Or else—which seems preferable, and even perhaps necessary to make the description *τοῖς ἀνδρειοτάτοις* significant in itself and harmonious with the rest—we may take together *τοῖς ἀνδρειοτάτοις*

Λακεδαιμονίοις ἐν τοῖς ἔμπροσθεν χρόνοις[1], '...that, when the Lacedaemonians, *who were in former times first in martial qualities,* had a war with the Messenians': in this case *former* may be relative to the times of which the orator has been speaking, and the meaning then is that, before the contest with Persia and rise of Athens, Sparta in military spirit had been unquestionably first: this, which is true, he notes in order to enhance the compliment paid to the new rival when Sparta borrowed Tyrtaeus from Athens. Or again, while adopting this second construction, we may refer *former* to the date of the speech: in that case the contrast will be between the ancient might and present feebleness of Sparta. Between these three the choice is open and unimportant.

But again fourthly, by taking ἐν τοῖς ἔμπροσθεν χρόνοις with the verbs of the sentence, and also assuming that *former* is relative to the events narrated, it is easy, *currente oculo,* to read this particular clause as if the 'war with the Messenians' preceded the Persian wars of which Lycurgus has been speaking. Consideration will indeed show that

[1] As to the order of the words see Kühner *Gr. Grammar* § 464, 8. The example would fall under his class *d*, τὸν ῥέοντα ποταμὸν διὰ τῆς πόλεως (Xen. *Hell.* 5. 2. 4), ὁ δυσμενέστατος ἄνθρωπος τῇ πόλει (Demosth. *Crown* 197), etc. Two other arrangements would have been possible (1) τοῖς ἀνδρειοτάτοις ἐν τοῖς ἔμπροσθεν χρόνοις Λακεδαιμονίοις, and (2) τοῖς ἐν τοῖς ἔμπροσθεν χρόνοις Λακεδαιμονίοις ἀνδρειοτάτοις, but the first is cumbrous, and the second, though otherwise natural, was to be avoided from the cacophony of τοῖς ἐν τοῖς.

this interpretation deprives of meaning even the sentence in which the words occur, to say nothing of the general argument. Nevertheless, if we bring to Lycurgus the presupposition about Tyrtaeus which would have been brought, as we shall see, by Strabo, Diodorus, Pausanias, Athenaeus, Justin (supposing that any of them consulted him on the point), and which has been brought there by every modern, we may well go away with the same supposition unquestioned, and justified, as we imagine, by fresh authority. In this way, arguing perhaps presumptuously from my own repeated error, I am inclined to account for the citation of Lycurgus by Grote—and by others who must be supposed to have verified the reference—among the witnesses for the presence of Tyrtaeus at the 'second Messenian war' as related by writers both ancient and modern. But be the explanation what it may, the error is, I venture to say, patent and indisputable. Lycurgus dates Tyrtaeus not in the seventh century B.C., but in the fifth.

Now it would be strange indeed if important events, assigned by a man like Lycurgus, upon 'common knowledge,' to the century preceding his own, were nevertheless placed at the distance of three centuries by such contemporaries and countrymen of his as Plato and Aristotle. But Aristotle agreed with him, and so, for anything that appears to the contrary, did Plato. Aristotle cites Tyrtaeus apparently once, on the point that in aristocracies disturbances may arise from any cause, war being the most common, which makes in the governing body a very rich class and a very poor class. 'This also,' he says, 'occurred in Lacedaemon in connexion with the Messenian war, as appears from the poem of Tyrtaeus entitled *The Blessings of Order*. Some, who were reduced to distress by the war, demanded a redistribution of the land[1].' Now would it be natural, or even intelligible, thus to refer an event to '*the* Messenian war,' if history, as conceived by Aristotle, had presented three 'Messenian wars,' three conflicts between Sparta and Messenia, distant from his own time about 100, 300, and 350 years respectively? It would be as if an English political writer should now say 'an illustration of this may be found in *the Crusade*,' leaving us to choose between the nine. But the truth appears to be that in the time of Aristotle there was no fixed and accredited history of any 'Messenian war' except one, and that was of course the war mentioned by Lycurgus, the war of the fifth century described in outline by Thucydides. About the earlier, primeval conflicts, though there were tales very recent for the most part in notoriety[2], serious students did not yet

[1] *Politics* 5 (8). 7, συνέβη δὲ καὶ τοῦτο ἐν Λακεδαίμονι ὑπὸ τὸν Μεσσηνιακὸν πόλεμον· δῆλον δὲ [καὶ τοῦτο] ἐκ τῆς Τυρταίου ποιήσεως τῆς καλουμένης Εὐνομίας κ.τ.λ. In the second clause καὶ τοῦτο is not explained by the context as it stands, since Tyrtaeus has not been cited before. It has perhaps slipped in from the preceding clause, where it is explained by a reference to Lacedaemonian history shortly preceding.

[2] The extant allusions are, with hardly an exception, not earlier than Leuctra: they begin immediately after this, with Isocrates.

pretend to know anything definite: the 'first war' and the 'second,' with their dates and episodes, were among the many events of remote antiquity about which the historians of the decadence were so much better informed than their authorities. That the words of Aristotle in themselves compel us to this view, I would not say; but reading them in connexion with what Lycurgus gives as the 'common knowledge' of his time, which was also the time of Aristotle, we cannot reasonably refuse an interpretation which not only brings the two into accord but is also most natural in itself. It may be added that, as scientific evidence, the *Eunomia* of Tyrtaeus much better deserved the attention of Aristotle, if known to date from the daylight age of Cimon and Pericles, than if it had been supposed to descend from the twilight of 680 B.C.

As for Plato, his references to Tyrtaeus do not import, so far as I can discover, any opinion about his date, unless indeed we choose, for the credit of Plato himself, to see such an indication in his remarking, as if it were a fact well-known and ascertained, that Tyrtaeus 'was born an Athenian and became a Lacedaemonian[1].' If Tyrtaeus was born in the eighth century, it is more than unlikely that any sound evidence about such biographical particulars was attainable; nor is it, I think, the habit of Plato thus to expose himself to criticism without reason. It is otherwise, if Tyrtaeus belonged to the generation of Sophocles. In another place[2]

[1] *Laws* 629 A. [2] *Ib.* 858 E.

the phrase 'Homer, Tyrtaeus, and the other poets,' read by itself, might seem to suggest a remote antiquity; but any reader of the *Laws* will be aware that Homer and Tyrtaeus are joined here for the same reason which brings them together in the passage already quoted from Lycurgus. Plato, like the orator, is comparing literature with legislation in respect of its moral and educational effect; and Tyrtaeus at Sparta, as Homer at Athens, was pre-eminently the poet of the schools. It is however not improbable that the conjunction thus originated, which re-appears, as we saw, in the *Ars Poetica*, helped to countenance, though it had really nothing to do with chronology, the chronological error which we shall presently trace[1].

Such is our oldest evidence, our only evidence which relatively to the matter can be called ancient, respecting the date of Tyrtaeus; and such was the opinion of Athens in the fourth century. It remains to consider, whether that opinion was right, or whether, counting heads, we should prefer the strangely different opinion which in Roman times prevailed, so far as appears, without dispute.

Now in the first place, as against anything short of a proved impossibility, the statement of Lycurgus, considering the nature of the subject and the

[1] It is perhaps worth notice that the passage about Tyrtaeus given in the *scholia* to the *Laws* is itself, like the text, perfectly consistent with his true date. Probably this is accidental; but it is not impossible that the note, which bears no certain mark of modernity, is as old as the *Laws* or indeed—for it has no special bearing on Plato—even older.

circumstances of the speaker, ought surely to be taken as conclusive. The public speakers of Athens, even in formal orations carefully revised, were inaccurate in matters of history, and sometimes deceptive; but surely there were limits. It is not quite easy to suggest an adequate modern parallel to the folly of Lycurgus in composing and deliberately uttering his remarks about Tyrtaeus, if there was any possibility of doubt whether the Athenian poet, whom he places only two or three generations before himself, did really live then, and not (if we may borrow the phrase) in the Middle Ages. Imagine the Earl of Shaftesbury or the Earl of Halifax, at a debate in the presence of Charles the Second, reminding his audience of 'the important missions which, as Your Lordships will all be aware, were entrusted to the poet Chaucer by Queen Elizabeth,' and printing it afterwards in a pamphlet! A highly accomplished Athenian of the fourth century, alleging in public assembly that another Athenian, 'as every one knows,' lived and played a public part in the fifth, can scarcely be refuted, let us repeat, by anything less than the intrinsic impossibility. Where then is the intrinsic impossibility, or improbability, that the poems of Tyrtaeus, and the story told of him, referred to the Messenian war of 464 B.C.? The extant fragments consist almost entirely of commonplace, equally applicable to any war; and from the few references to person or place nothing can be gathered but that the war in question was being waged by Sparta for the recovery of Messenia.

Moreover we happen to know, and shall have occasion presently to remember, that in this respect the fragments fairly show the character of the whole poems, as possessed by the ancients. For Pausanias reports, and on this point is a competent witness, that Tyrtaeus did not mention the names even of the contemporary kings of Sparta[1]. About earlier history, or rather legend, we do learn a little from the fragments, among other things that the original conquest of Messenia occupied a round twenty years, and that it was achieved by 'our ancestors' ancestors'—or 'fathers' fathers,' whichever word we prefer[2]—that is to say, 'in the old, old days.' But there is nothing whatever in the way of statement or allusion which marks the seventh century as the time of writing, or excludes the fifth. As little is there of antique note in the language, which is in the main the regular hackneyed *lingua franca* of Greek elegiac verse at all periods from Simonides downwards. Whether it could have been written in B.C. 680 may be questionable, but let that stand by; it could certainly have been written in B.C. 460.

As for the story related about Tyrtaeus, so far from requiring a date in the seventh century, it becomes intelligible and credible only when restored to its place in the fifth. Taken apart from rhetorical colour, the facts, as alleged by Lycurgus, are these.

[1] 4. 15. 1.

[2] Frag. 3 πατέρων ἡμετέρων πατέρας. The attempt to make out of this phrase something definite in the way of chronology is properly abandoned by Beloch, *Gr. Gesch.*, vol. 1, p. 285 (n.).

Tyrtaeus was an Athenian of some literary talent, who, having become associated with the Lacedaemonians at a time when they were distressed in war against Messenia, rose to high consideration among them through the popularity of his martial and patriotic poetry, which not only served for the moment to rouse and restore the national spirit, but also, after the victory, was adopted by Spartan authority, with his help and direction, as permanent material for an improved education. To this account, of which the latter part, relating to education, is supported by Plato, and the former part, the connexion with the Messenian war, by Aristotle, we should perhaps add, as derived (if we can trust indirect evidence) from respectable Athenian authority later by one generation, that the Attic home of Tyrtaeus was Aphidnae[1]. Referred to the seventh century, all this is justly thought open, not only to various objections of detail, but to one comprehensive objection, that the narrators had no means of knowing it. Referred to the fifth century, it is perfectly probable and warrantable. That the Lacedaemonians then sought and received aid from Athens against the revolt of the Messenians, is a fact. The Athenian troops were, in memorable circumstances, abruptly sent back; but that a certain individual Athenian emigrated, and achieved by means happily

[1] Philochorus, with Callisthenes and others (according to Strabo). For the birthplace they are cited distinctly; what more, if anything, comes from them we cannot say, and indeed it would be unsafe to assume that Strabo cites at first hand.

suited to the occasion what is described by Lycurgus and more soberly by Plato, is not only credible, but ought on such evidence to be without hesitation believed. In particular the educational function of Tyrtaeus, a mere absurdity if attributed to the Sparta of 670, when even in Attica there was not yet, and was not to be for another century, any 'plan of education' or so much as a school, becomes, with the date 450, significant and interesting. At that time Sparta, in regard to the cultivation of the popular intelligence, was much behind the age, and at an immense distance behind her new rival on the Piraeus. Nothing is more likely than that the humiliations of the Messenian war, and specially the humiliation of having petitioned, even temporarily, for the aid of Athenian wits, awakened the Spartan government to this among their other deficiencies, and that they employed to mend it an Athenian who had shown his power of pleasing their countrymen. That the educator gave to his own works a dominant place in the curriculum is a pleasing touch of nature, and indeed in the circumstances it was probably the best thing that he could do. One thing only Lycurgus alleges to which we must demur, that Tyrtaeus was adopted by the Spartans directly in obedience to the Delphic oracle. And even this is nothing but what they themselves must have said and believed *ex post facto*. That they procured an oracle for their application to Athens is proved by the application itself: in the politics of Sparta the sanction of Apollo was common form. The result was disappointment, and also unexpected success. The Athenian general and his army gave offence and were dismissed; while an Athenian of no likelihood helped to rehabilitate Sparta by ways unforeseen. That 'Apollo' thereupon disclaimed the failure and claimed the triumph, by identifying the destined 'leader' with Tyrtaeus, and that piety subscribed, all this is matter of course.

And the true date also dissolves another mystery: why it is near the middle of the fourth century, and not before, that Tyrtaeus is brought to our notice. If his works had been extant in Lacedaemonia, and had exercised their influence there, ever since the alleged time of 'the second Messenian war,' it is strange that three centuries of silence should cover documents of such peculiar interest. Specially remarkable is the neglect of Plato, who certainly wanted not interest in the antiquities either of poetry, or of education, or of Sparta. In the *Republic* and elsewhere are many places which, given the now prevailing notion about Tyrtaeus, must suggest his name to the mind. Yet we find it nowhere before the work of Plato's last years. But the fact is that, although the career of Tyrtaeus is worth curiosity, his poetry, divested of its fictitious date, is not remarkable. It is clear and spirited, correct in sentiment and diction, but wonderfully verbose and platitudinous. I speak of the elegiacs; of the anapaestic marches we have not enough to estimate, but they seem to have been essentially of the same quality. At Athens, amid the sunset of Aeschylus and the dawn of Sophocles, a reputation could no more have been made by such verses than now by correct and well-sounding heroic couplets. Hundreds could do it, if not as well, nearly as well; and indeed it is part of the tradition that in his native city Tyrtaeus was of no account. Lacedaemonia was a different field, and he hit, both as man and as writer, the Lacedaemonian taste. But this would not serve him elsewhere: it was not to Lacedaemonia that people went for literary fashions, and least of all the Athenians, who dictated them. For two generations we hear nothing of him, and probably little was said. But about that time circumstances changed somewhat in his favour: after Aegospotami the foreign communications of Sparta were of necessity somewhat enlarged; and Leuctra did much to remove the barrier between the country of his birth and the country of his adoption. At any rate he began to have readers even in Athens. To Plato, a theorist on education, the poems were interesting in their moral aspect as a school-book, but they 'bored' him nevertheless, as he reveals by one of those delightful touches of drama, which in the *Laws* are only too rare:

The Athenian. For example, let us bring before us Tyrtaeus, who was born an Athenian but adopted by the country of our friends from Lacedaemon. No one has insisted more strenuously on the importance of martial qualities. 'I would not name, nor reckon in the list,' he says, a man, though he might be ever so wealthy, though he were endowed with various advantages (of which the poet names perhaps all that there are), who did not on every occasion distinguish himself in war. May I presume that you (*to Cleinias the Cretan*) have heard these poems? Our friend has no doubt had enough of them.

The Lacedaemonian. Yes, indeed.

Cleinias. Oh, they have reached us in Crete; they were imported from Lacedaemon[1]!

Few perhaps, except Plato, could have marked so neatly the special vice of tediousness in elegiacs, the tendency, produced by the form, to make every point separately, similarly, and at the same length. Ovid is notoriously liable to it. In Tyrtaeus it is so persistent (see for example even the extract selected by Lycurgus) that a volume of him would be scarcely tolerable, except as an alternative for the cane. And we may note by the way that, if the works of Tyrtaeus had been older than Archilochus, it would have been odd in Plato's Athenian to doubt whether a man of learning was acquainted with them, and ridiculous surely to doubt whether they had reached Crete. In reality it may be doubted rather whether indeed they had, though Plato, for the sake of his jest, chooses to suppose so. However, Plato read them; Aristotle read them, as he read everything, to make notes; and by some other Athenians it began to be thought, especially since Sparta was no longer the prime object of Athenian jealousy, that to have furnished their ancient rival with her favourite poet and educator, to have produced the Spartan Homer, should be counted to their city's credit. This is the sentiment played upon by Lycurgus. Also Tyrtaeus was thought good for

[1] *Laws* 629 B.

the young, as was natural in societies which laid so much stress on military patriotism, though Plato naturally is dissatisfied with him even as a moralist, and 'examines' him very pertinently. But there is no sign (and indeed Plato goes to prove the contrary) that in the judgement of those times Tyrtaeus held any conspicuous rank. To this he was not advanced until it came to be known that his elegiacs and anapaests were nearly as old as the *Works and Days.* The manner of which remarkable discovery we will show, as briefly as possible, by way of conclusion.

It is by no means clear—and in such a case we ought certainly to give the benefit of the doubt—that the originator of the falsehood, about whose work, though lost, we happen to have uncommonly full information, meant it to be taken seriously. The form and contents of his composition were such as in themselves to absolve him from responsibility to those who, pretending to write history, chose at their peril to borrow from him[1]. The 'Aristomeneïs,' as Grote appropriately calls the

[1] On the materials for the 'first' and 'second' Messenian wars, see Grote, Part II, chap. vii. Apart from Tyrtaeus, the only remark to which we may demur is that the account of Diodorus was 'very probably taken from Ephorus—though this we do not know.' Ephorus undoubtedly did much mischief to genuine history, but the fictions admitted by the compilers of the Roman period are in this case so wild that no one, I think, should be accused of a part in them without positive evidence The only 'authorities' certainly traceable are Rhianus and Myron, both of whom appear to have been simply 'novelists,' and scarcely deserve to be brought into court.

poem of Rhianus, was upon the face of it a mere romance, and if the author chose to enrich it with a figure called Tyrtaeus, chronology and science had really no claim to interfere. The only 'sources' which could be of much use to him in such a composition would be, as was said before, the popular tales of Messenia; and that his 'Tyrtaeus' came thence is at any rate probable, for the adviser of Sparta was made ridiculous both in person and character[1]. If in such tales, as may be presumed, the personages of legend and history were jumbled together with that fine freedom which belongs to the genus, it was not the business of a poet to sift or to correct them. To pronounce however a sure and just sentence on Rhianus, we should need the text of his poem. What concerns us now is that, with or without excuse, he did as a fact illumine his picture of the olden times with hints reflected or refracted from the real history of the fifth century. And of this, as it happens, there is evidence quite apart from the introduction of Tyrtaeus. According to Rhianus, at the time when Aristomenes lived and fought, the king of Sparta was *Leotychides*[2]. But here, as Pausanias gravely remarks, it was impossible to follow him, inasmuch as Leotychides, the successor of Demaratus, did not reign until many generations later. In fact, as Grote bids us observe, his reign almost extended, and his life may have actually extended, *to the so-called 'third' Messenian war*,

[1] Pausanias 4. 15. 6; 4. 16. 1.

[2] Paus. 4. 15. 1.

since he was banished about B.C. 469. It seems scarcely dubitable that this is the explanation of the phenomenon which perplexed Pausanias[1]; and wherever or however Rhianus came by his 'contemporary king Leotychides,' there and so he naturally found his 'Tyrtaeus.' His fiction was not history, but it was innocent enough, and it should have been harmless.

Unfortunately it was with such materials as this that in later ages, when fifth century and seventh were faded alike into objects of mere curiosity, the compilers of 'universal history' filled up the gaps in their scheme of fanciful chronology. At the present time, though it is but lately, their methods are well understood; and, bit by bit, much of their pretended restoration has been stripped from the scanty and broken masonry within. To discriminate the stages and dates of the plastering is not often possible, and is not so in the case before us. At the commencement of the Roman Empire, to which we must next descend, the epoch of Tyrtaeus was already fixed, as we see from Horace and Strabo, in accordance with Rhianus. Nor is this surprising. The tale of Rhianus seems to have been attractive; there is interest even in the bare abstract. Above all, it was a 'full' authority. Moreover, in regard to Tyrtaeus, it invested his extant poems with the

[1] Pausanias is content simply to discard this particular trait of Rhianus, and to discover another 'contemporary king' on principles of his own. Others (see the spurious genealogy inserted in Herodotus 8. 131) preferred, it seems, to invent an earlier Leotychides.

fascination of a primeval document. With such a bribe, before such a tribunal as that of Diodorus, Rhianus might well have beaten Thucydides; but probably there was no contest and no adversary. The Spartans were not commonly historians; and by any one except a Spartan the 'third' Messenian war may well have been related, as it is by Thucydides, without mention of Tyrtaeus' name. A real search, no doubt, must have raised the question, and a sound criticism must have instantly decided it. The statement of Lycurgus stood where it stands now, and might probably have been reinforced by others now lost, though in those times not much, it seems, was thought of Tyrtaeus, and presumably not much said. Nor did it matter what had been said. Methodical history, seen in a glimpse between Thucydides and Aristotle, had long been lost again; among the notices of Tyrtaeus in late authors not one, I believe, cites even Lycurgus—whom indeed they might have actually read, as we have seen, without being much the wiser. Rhianus therefore and suchlike had it their own way, with the result that a versifier, whose real part in the development of Greek poetry is about as important as that of Mason in our own, was elevated to an antiquity not venerable merely but miraculous.

For although, to clear the way, we have hitherto acquiesced in the assumption that the Spartans in the seventh century used, or might have used, marches and elegies like those of Tyrtaeus, the evidence for that assumption is nothing more, or at least better, than the error about Tyrtaeus himself.

To follow this matter, with all the subsidiary misconceptions, to the bottom would take us too far; but, for myself, I should as soon believe that *The Hind and the Panther* was written by Gavin Douglas, as that in Lacedaemonia, a century before Solon, popular audiences were regaled with the full-formed classic style, neither archaic, nor personal, nor provincial, developed out of the Ionic epos by that 'greater Ionia' which included Athens. It is not certain that in B.C. 680 elegiacs had been written anywhere; but, if anywhere, it was in Ionian Asia, and there, we must suppose, not in a pruned, castigated, conventional vocabulary like that of Tyrtaeus. And indeed upon this head some passing scruples do seem to have visited the scholars of the Empire, and to have produced the eccentric hypothesis reported by Suidas, that Tyrtaeus was a native of Miletus; which however, if true, would not appreciably affect their problem. But for most minds there was no problem. Tyrtaeus, as we have noted, seems to have dealt mostly in commonplace, and scarcely at all with contemporary individuals, and therefore did not trouble Pausanias with anachronisms of positive fact, such anachronisms as were likely to trouble Pausanias. That the whole thing, in phrase and fashion, was one monstrous anachronism, could naturally not be suspected by men who were accustomed to relate and to read how, three hundred years before Solon, and about one hundred years (was it?) after Homer, the *Iliad* was brought to Sparta by her first legislator and appointed for recitation—one might suppose, at the Panathenaea.

TYRTAEUS. II

It may perhaps be expected by readers of the *Classical Review*, and by the critic[1] of my former article, that I should state here, whether I am convinced or moved by the observations on my treatment of this subject which he has done me the honour to make. To the proposition which formed the base or kernel of my previous paper, that the orator Lycurgus associated the story of Tyrtaeus with the Messenian war of the fifth century (*circa* 464–454 B.C.), my critic gives a single paragraph, and concludes that the contrary is manifest. It would seem at this rate that I ought to have little difficulty in recognizing my mistake; and silence could hardly be taken otherwise than as an ungracious acknowledgement. As a fact, the paragraph leaves me (I say it with all respect) precisely where I stood before. It does not affect, because it does not touch at all or pretend to touch, that part of Lycurgus' exposition, by which, as I thought and think, his opinion on the date of Tyrtaeus is made clear. The paragraph deals only with another part, which by itself would prove nothing precise upon the point, being dependent

[1] Dr R. W. Macan, in *Classical Review*, vol. XI, p. 10.

for its chronological definition on that part which the paragraph ignores.

But as the purpose of discussion is to promote agreement, and not to accentuate differences, let me first note with pleasure the impression which has evidently been made upon the writer by my remarks on the impossibility of assigning to the date of the supposed early 'Messenian wars,' and to an origin in Sparta at that time, the poetry which bears the name of Tyrtaeus. For it should be observed that, in this respect at least, all of it stands on the same footing. In language, form, and style all the extant fragments are similar, nor is there (so far as I am aware) the slightest indication that the fourth century B.C., or any other age, claimed to possess any 'Tyrtaeus' of a different quality,—that is to say, any Tyrtaeus which, as a matter of fact, could have been composed for the Lacedaemonian public, or popular among Lacedaemonians, in 680 B.C. or anywhere near that date. Of all important Hellenic peoples the Lacedaemonians were, according to general testimony, the last to acquire such a diffused popular culture of the intelligence as would be needed for the general appreciation of literature cast in foreign forms and a foreign dialect. The very passage of Lycurgus which we are to consider shows that, even down to the fourth century, that great classical literature which ruled in Athens and elsewhere had still no general vogue in Lacedaemonia, and that the public there, in spite of Tyrtaeus and his educational reforms, still went, in 'the poets' recognized by Athens, little beyond the Lacedaemonian school-book, the compositions of Tyrtaeus himself. In the early part of the seventh century, if the average warriors of Lacedaemonia took interest (which may be doubted) in any poetry at all, the military songs which they heard and sang must have been songs in their own language, something resembling in style, but with more of local colour and archaism, the most 'Laconian' of the fragments attributed to Alcman, or the fictitious Laconian of Aristophanes. That then, or for many generations later, they cheered their fights and watches with classical elegiacs, we should believe as soon as that 'Come if you dare, our trumpets sound' was a favourite in the camp of Robert Bruce. If Tyrtaeus flourished in 680 B.C., or near that time, then what Strabo and Pausanias knew as his works were all, on the face of them, spurious—a conclusion which there would be no difficulty in accepting. Indeed, Strabo at least was aware that the genuineness of his quotations might be questioned, and makes some remarks on the subject; which however show, as might be expected, an imperfect conception of the arguments which should be brought to bear. Before his time it had become practically impossible that, by the learned of Graeco-Roman society in general, the question should be seen in a true light. We will return to this presently.

If the alleged works be spurious, it makes, so far as concerns the authenticity of what is called the 'history' of the early Messenian wars, little or no difference whether we do or do not suppose 'the real Tyrtaeus' to have lived in the age to which these wars are assigned. The claim of that 'history' to be better accredited than other legends or traditions respecting times before continuous record has hitherto rested, not on the name or story of Tyrtaeus, but on the supposed existence, in this one instance, of these wonderfully early documents. If the framers of the story had some genuine documents, then they, or their authorities, might well have had others of equal authenticity. But if Tyrtaeus, however real a person, left nothing properly certified except his name, which served as a peg upon which to hang sundry forgeries, then we cannot hope to win trustworthy information by sifting the poetic fables which gathered around it and them.

But the hypothesis of forgery is one which at this stage it would be premature to entertain. *Prima facie*, and until the contrary is proved, the works of Tyrtaeus, presented to us with the invariable statement that they were composed for Lacedaemonians, and conquered the admiration of the Lacedaemonian public, are themselves evidence that Tyrtaeus lived at a time when such works could have had this origin and history. Our business is therefore to examine, and to examine without prejudice, the statements of our authorities on the date of Tyrtaeus the man, and to see whether they really support that early date which would raise a difficulty, and call in the hypothesis of forgery as an explanation. This ground we will not now traverse again, but will turn at once to the cardinal authority, the passage of Lycurgus (*Leocrat.* §§ 102–109). I am still unable as ever to see how that passage can be understood at all on any other supposition than that Tyrtaeus, according to Lycurgus, lived and composed in the fifth century B.C.

The passage, of which a complete version is given in my previous paper, shall here be recapitulated briefly. It begins with a reference to Homer, to the public adoption of his works by the Athenians, as evidenced by the legal establishment of the recitations at the Panathenaea, and to the improvement in Athenian character which thereupon ensued. To this cause is attributed the excellent spirit displayed by Athens in the delivery of Hellas from the Persians, and in particular at the battle of Marathon. Such, continues the orator, were the Athenians of that age that the Lacedaemonians themselves, being at war with the Messenians, took a leader from Athens in the person of Tyrtaeus, who not only brought them victory, but also aided them in framing an improved education for their youth, based upon the teaching of his own patriotic poetry in elegiacs; and from these a long extract is cited. So efficient was this poetry in stimulating the spirit and patriotism of the Lacedaemonians, that they disputed with Athens the 'hegemony' or leadership in Hellas.

That part of the original which corresponds to my last sentence runs as follows:

οὕτω τοίνυν εἶχον πρὸς ἀνδρείαν οἱ τούτων (the

poetry of Tyrtaeus) ἀκούοντες, ὥστε πρὸς τὴν πόλιν ἡμῶν περὶ τῆς ἡγεμονίας ἀμφισβητεῖν. εἰκότως· τὰ γὰρ κάλλιστα τῶν ἔργων ἀμφοτέροις ἦν κατειργασμένα. οἱ μὲν γὰρ πρόγονοι τοὺς βαρβάρους ἐνίκησαν οἳ πρῶτοι τῆς Ἀττικῆς ἐπέβησαν, καὶ καταφανῆ ἐποίησαν τὴν ἀνδρείαν τοῦ πλούτου καὶ τὴν ἀρετὴν τοῦ πλήθους περιγιγνομένην. Λακεδαιμόνιοι δ' ἐν Θερμοπύλαις παραταξάμενοι ταῖς μὲν τύχαις οὐχ ὁμοίως ἐχρήσαντο, τῇ δ' ἀνδρείᾳ πολὺ πάντων διήνεγκαν. These are the words to which my critic, in the paragraph which he gives to *The Date of Tyrtaeus*, confines his remarks, and of which he says, very truly, that they do not demand for Tyrtaeus a date after the Persian wars. But neither do they demand a date before them. Taken by themselves, they leave for the date so wide a choice, as to be almost insignificant upon the question. We learn from them only that the time when Tyrtaeus, as previously narrated, established his works as the material of education in Lacedaemonia, was before the time when Sparta 'contended against Athens for the hegemony'; and not so long before (I think we must add) but that, at the time of the 'contention,' the national performances of the Lacedaemonians might be attributed mainly and essentially to his reforms. This upward limit is vague, but not absolutely indefinite. An educational force or an educational system, however permanent, could not naturally be cited as the main and true cause of what was done at a particular epoch by the people subject to it, if at that epoch it had been acting for more than a moderate space of time, a generation, let us say, or two at the most. With lapse of time the effect of this single cause must become so entangled with those of other causes, that to trace so precise and particular a connexion would be irrational. The English character, and therefore all the acts of England, are deeply affected to this day, and long will be, by the educational revolution of the sixteenth century, the diffusion of Protestantism and of the English Bible. Yet no one could reasonably say that the Reformation showed its effect in the stand made by England against Napoleon. On the other hand the stand against Philip, and the formation of the Puritan party, of course could and would be properly traced to this particular cause. This would give us for Tyrtaeus some sort of a *terminus a quo*, and one which, vague as it is, would scarcely admit the seventh century, to say nothing of 680 B.C. But what is the *terminus ad quem*? When was it that the Lacedaemonians 'contended against Athens for the hegemony'? I suppose that by a liberal interpretation, without actual violence, the words might apply to almost any time from (say) the middle of the sixth century to near the middle of the fourth, the age of Lycurgus himself. I took them and take them still (for reasons which will presently appear) to refer to the last half of the fifth century, the Peloponnesian war and what led up to it. And surely if any one were asked 'When did Athens and Sparta contend for the hegemony?', 'In the Peloponnesian war' would be the first and most obvious answer. As for the immediate context, the passage already cited in the original, it neither proves this particular reference, nor excludes it:

> And the people, therefore, who were in the habit of hearing this poetry, were so disposed to bravery, that they disputed the primacy with Athens, a dispute for which, it must be admitted, there was reason on both sides in high actions formerly achieved. Our ancestors had defeated that first invading army landed by the Persians upon Attica, and thus revealed the superiority of courage above wealth and of valour above numbers. The Lacedaemonians in the lines of Thermopylae, if not so fortunate, in courage surpassed all rivalry....

My critic would take the words *οἱ μὲν γὰρ πρόγονοι τοὺς βαρβάρους ἐνίκησαν κ.τ.λ.* as referring back to *περὶ τῆς ἡγεμονίας ἀμφισβητεῖν*, translating them (I presume, and it is a perfectly legitimate translation) 'Our ancestors *defeated*' etc. He thus deduces that the 'dispute for the primacy,' or, to speak with more technical accuracy, for the 'hegemony' of Hellas, consisted in the rival exploits of Athens at Marathon and Sparta at Thermopylae. Whether the term 'contest for the hegemony' applies to those battles quite as naturally as to the Peloponnesian war, may be open to question; I am not sure whether *a priori* one would naturally say that the Spartans at Thermopylae were 'contending against Athens for the hegemony.' Also it does not appear, what precisely, on this reading, were the supreme exploits which, before the 'contest for the hegemony,' that is *ex hypothesi* before Marathon and Thermopylae, 'had been achieved' (*ἦν κατειργασμένα*) by the rivals respectively, or why these previous exploits are brought into view. However I am quite ready to admit the interpretation, so far, as possible. But necessary it is not. If, upon other grounds, we see reason to think that by the 'contest for the hegemony' the speaker means the Peloponnesian war, then we shall of course refer the words οἱ μὲν γὰρ πρόγονοι κ.τ.λ., with at least equal justification, not to the more remote ἀμφισβητεῖν, but to the clause which immediately precedes them, τὰ γὰρ κάλλιστα ... κατειργασμένα, translating, as in the version above, 'Our ancestors *had defeated*...,' not 'Our ancestors *defeated*...,' the aorist ἐνίκησαν admitting either version equally, and being in fact the only tense which, on either hypothesis, could naturally and idiomatically be employed. Marathon and Thermopylae, on this reading, were not the 'contest for the hegemony,' but previous exploits which justified both rivals, the Lacedaemonians no less than the Athenians, in claiming the first place, and in pressing their claims to the arbitration of war. The orator, who throughout speaks of the Lacedaemonians with a friendly feeling, after glancing at the great duel of Athens and Sparta and at the passions of a time passed away, returns, by a dexterous transition, to the more congenial topic of their achievements against the common enemy.

From this then, and if we took this part of Lycurgus' remarks by itself, we could learn, as to his opinion respecting the date of Tyrtaeus, not indeed nothing, but nothing precise. It would appear that at all events he did not agree with the opinion established in later times, and did not put Tyrtaeus anywhere near 680 B.C. The sixth century, and the latter part of it rather, would be the earliest epoch naturally admissible; but anywhere from 550 to 450 would be a date which, so far, we might accept.

But I did not see before, and do not see now, why we should be at the pains to consider what would be the effect of this particular portion taken separately, when the point which (as we will assume) it would leave in doubt has been already determined by what precedes. Lycurgus, after reminding his hearers that their fathers had established Homer as the legalized poet of Athens, and referring in this connexion particularly to the recitations at the quadrennial Panathenaea, deduces, from the educational effect of Homer upon such habitual hearers, the public spirit and Hellenic patriotism displayed by Athens in the repulse of Persia, and specially the battle of Marathon. He then continues thus:

τοιγαροῦν οὕτως ἦσαν ἄνδρες σπουδαῖοι καὶ κοινῇ καὶ ἰδίᾳ οἱ τότε τὴν πόλιν οἰκοῦντες, ὥστε τοῖς ἀνδρειοτάτοις Λακεδαιμονίοις ἐν τοῖς ἔμπροσθεν χρόνοις πολεμοῦσι πρὸς Μεσσηνίους ἀνεῖλεν ὁ θεὸς παρ' ἡμῶν ἡγεμόνα λαβεῖν καὶ νικήσειν τοὺς ἐναντίους....[1]τίς γὰρ οὐκ οἶδε τῶν Ἑλλήνων ὅτι Τυρταῖον στρατηγὸν ἔλαβον παρὰ τῆς πόλεως, μεθ' οὗ καὶ τῶν πολεμίων ἐκράτησαν καὶ τὴν περὶ τοὺς νέους ἐπιμέλειαν

[1] The words omitted merely dwell on the splendour of the compliment thus paid to Athens, and have no bearing on the question of date. It is unnecessary to repeat here what was said in the previous essay upon the ambiguity of ἐν τοῖς ἔμπροσθεν χρόνοις. My critic, I am glad to see, agrees with me that these words determine nothing, and that, of the many admissible ways of construing and interpreting them, more than one is consistent with my general view.

συνετάξαντο, οὐ μόνον εἰς τὸν παρόντα κίνδυνον ἀλλ' εἰς ἅπαντα τὸν αἰῶνα βουλευσάμενοι καλῶς; κατέλιπε γὰρ αὐτοῖς ἐλεγεῖα ποιήσας, ὧν ἀκούοντες παιδεύονται πρὸς ἀνδρείαν, καὶ περὶ τοὺς ἄλλους ποιητὰς οὐδένα λόγον ἔχοντες περὶ τούτου οὕτω σφόδρα ἐσπουδάκασιν ὥστε νόμον ἔθεντο κ.τ.λ.

and so we go on to a long citation from Tyrtaeus himself, and finally to the effect of his influence and training upon the Lacedaemonians, as set forth in the passage previously cited.

And therefore so excellent, both as a body and as individuals, were the men by whom our city was *in those days* administered, that when the Lacedaemonians, who in earlier times were first in martial qualities, had a war with the Messenians, they were commanded by the oracle to take a leader from among us, and were promised victory, if they did so, over their opponents.... It is matter of common knowledge that the director whom they received from Athens was Tyrtaeus, by whose help they overcame their enemies, and also framed a system of discipline for their youth....

This is the passage of which I said, and must still say, that the only date which it allows for Tyrtaeus (in the opinion of Lycurgus, of course) is the Messenian war of 464–454 B.C. The Athenians, from among whom Tyrtaeus emigrated, were the Athenians *of those days*, **οἱ τότε τὴν πόλιν οἰκοῦντες**. The speaker has just dwelt at length upon the great achievements of the Athenians in the Persian wars. Unless the adoption of Tyrtaeus by the Lacedaemonians took place at the same time or some closely approximate time, what can it have to do with the subject, or how could it prove the excellence attained by the Athenians *in those days*? And if we take the speaker to be proceeding in a proper order, if we do not arbitrarily assume that he here suddenly reverses the natural course of thought, we must suppose that he places Tyrtaeus near *and after* the Persian wars, not near and before them. I will even make bold to say that, if we had only Lycurgus to deal with, no other idea would ever have been suggested. Nor will it make any difference if, forcing his arrangement, we extend *those days* backward so as to cover the time near, but prior to, the Persian wars. For in any case, and on pain of destroying his whole argument, they must be *posterior to the legal establishment of Homer as the state-poetry and educational literature of Athens.* To trace the sequel and effect of that educational advance, the most momentous thing, taken with its consequences, in all Greek history and perhaps in the history of the world, is the speaker's whole design. That the change took place, not in a day of course, but gradually, during the central part of the sixth century, all, I believe, are agreed: our authorities assign it sometimes to Peisistratus, sometimes to his sons, sometimes (but this under suspicion of prejudice) to Solon. But we should know of it, and could date it, without any express authority. We should know it by its effects. The tragedy of Aeschylus, and all the public literature which followed it, the ecclesia of Cleisthenes, and all that made its fate so different from that of other democratic experiments, the larger thoughts and wider sympathies which within a score of years converted (as Lycurgus indicates) a mere canton into the conscious centre of a nation, and made in fact a new Hellas—the whole story of Athens is but one commentary on the fact that towards the close of the sixth century there arose in Athens a generation of men far exceeding all predecessors and contemporaries in respect of diffused intelligence. Lycurgus, when he deduces the repulse of the barbarian from 'the recitations at the Panathenaea,' is referring in the accustomed form to this unparalleled development and its educational causes. That he should bring into his story, as part of the effect, something which happened before the new education could have produced any fruits, or before it was even begun, I took and take to be impossible. On no narrow or technical construction therefore, but on the plain purport of the whole passage, I assume 530 (or, if any one pleases, 540) to be the very earliest date to which any part of the story (Tyrtaeus included) can be carried back. But if so, we need not ask whether the speaker does or does not give us other reasons for placing Tyrtaeus after the Persian wars; it is enough for the purpose that he places him after Pisistratus. For starting thence we must still come down to 464 to find any time to which the story could be fitted, to find a 'Messenian war.' At least so I supposed. If this is not so, if some hitherto unknown 'Messenian war' can be fixed (say) about 520, I shall be ready to admit that Lycurgus might have linked Tyrtaeus with that war and date; though I should still think that, in that case, his arrangement of his matter would be perverse, and should still therefore prefer the date 464, as not raising needless objections. As things are, 464 seems not only obvious, but inevitable; it also satisfies all the other conditions of the context, following near after the Persian wars (as it should) and preceding (as it should) by about one generation that unique and special 'contest for the hegemony between Athens and Sparta' which is commonly called the Peloponnesian war.

Thus much as to the opinion of Lycurgus. Whether he was right is another matter; I see no reason to doubt it, but will refer to my previous paper. As however I do not wish to return to the subject again, I should like to add one consideration which was before not very clearly brought out. The mere fact that Lycurgus attributes to Tyrtaeus the composition of commonplace, flowing, and classical elegiacs, would be of itself a grave reason for thinking that he cannot have dated Tyrtaeus as he was dated by Strabo, Pausanias, and others of those later times. I mean that the wild error as to the date of the style, though possible in the days of Augustus or Caracalla, and quite of a piece with much that was then calmly narrated and believed, cannot with equal propriety be attributed to an Athenian statesman of the fourth century B.C. Whether Strabo or Lycurgus would have judged better in a case where knowledge was equal, we need not inquire; in this case knowledge, vital and efficient knowledge, could not be equal, and the advantage was greatly with Lycurgus. What makes the account of Strabo impossible (given for Tyrtaeus the date which he asserts) is the deep and wide difference in language, linguistic affinity, taste, habit, and tradition, which existed between Athens and Sparta until long after the era assigned, and which at that era, so far as we can conjecture, had not even begun to be bridged. Now to educated men in the age of Augustus, or even in the age of the Diadochi, distinctions of this kind, between Greek and Greek, had almost no practical importance, and were known only as matters of history, erudition, or literary fancy. The process of amalgamation, the process of which the introduction of Tyrtaeus and his works to Sparta was one, not unimportant, stage, had been accomplished, and all dialectical or local peculiarities merged, so far as concerned the ordinary life of educated men, in one common language, which flattered itself that it was Athenian. Compared with the actual state of the world, the fifth century was almost as remote and unreal as the seventh; and there was nothing to prevent a confusion between the two but the weak barrier of acquired science. Altogether different was the position of an Athenian statesman in the fourth century, of such a man as Lycurgus. To him the moral and mental difference between Attica and Lacedaemonia was not a matter of historical or literary learning; it was a fact of vital importance in common life and current politics. The process of assimilation between the peoples, and the creation of a common medium, had by no means yet been brought so far as to put out of sight the time when it had been begun and the stages by which it had been carried on. In the very passage before us Lycurgus, as we have seen, shows himself perfectly aware that even then, in his own day, Lacedaemonia, as a whole, was a field practically closed against that literature which was being studied, admired, and enlarged by Athens. Of all that made the story of Tyrtaeus and his elegiacs, as Lycurgus tells it, possible for the middle of the fifth century, but impossible for the beginning of the seventh, Lycurgus could not, as it would seem, be ignorant. For this reason, as well as others, I take him to mean the simple, natural, and reasonable thing which he appears to say. And since his account is contradicted by no one who, on such a point, is entitled comparatively or positively to consideration, I accept it, as at present advised, without hesitation as true.

HERODOTUS ON THE DIMENSIONS OF THE PYRAMIDS

I VENTURE, though neither archaeologist nor Egyptologist, to ask the attention of those who are such to a few remarks on the topic proposed above, because there seems to be at this time some danger that the gain of their rich discoveries may be turned unnecessarily to an indirect loss, in depreciating, or rather destroying at all points, the credibility of an author upon whom, after all, we depend for much information not to be had from hieroglyphs. The interpretation of what Herodotus says about the size of the Pyramids is disputable; it is perhaps open to fresh light; but of this at least I am sure, that if we must accept the interpretation which appears to content some recent investigators, the testimony of Herodotus is universally worthless. He is convicted of that 'crass negligence' which, in its effect upon the value of a witness, is as damaging as deliberate fraud.

Describing first the larger of the two great pyramids, the Pyramid of Cheops, Herodotus says (II 124) that 'every way each face of its square is 8 *plethra*,' τῆς ἐστὶ πανταχῇ μέτωπον ἕκαστον ὀκτὼ *πλέθρα, ἐούσης τετραγώνου.* Describing next the smaller of the two, the Pyramid of Chephren, he says (*ib.* 127) that 'it does not come up to the dimensions of the other's pyramid, for those of this one we[1] measured ourselves' (*ἐς μὲν τὰ ἐκείνου μέτρα οὐκ ἀνήκουσαν· ταῦτα γὰρ ὦν καὶ ἡμεῖς ἐμετρήσαμεν*), and that 'in laying his first foundation (made of variegated Aethiopian marble) Chephren came 40 feet short of the other, and then built it so as in the same size to keep near the big one': *ὑποδείμας δὲ τὸν πρῶτον δόμον λίθου Αἰθιοπικοῦ ποικίλου, τεσσεράκοντα πόδας ὑποβὰς τῆς ἑτέρης, τὠυτὸ μέγαθος ἐχομένην τῆς μεγάλης οἰκοδόμησε.* The last words are not clear and perhaps corrupt. But they are clear enough for our present purpose; and if we make allowance for a colloquial writer not provided with mathematical science, they may appear not incapable of complete explanation. That *ἐχομένην τῆς μεγάλης, near to the big one,* means something more and other than that the second pyramid stood near the first, appears from the relation of these words to the context. The proximity of the two monuments in position is separately mentioned in the next sentence, 'they stand both on the same hill,' *ἑστᾶσι δὲ ἐπὶ λόφου τοῦ αὐτοῦ ἀμφότεραι.* The nearness marked by *ἐχομένην* must therefore be a metaphorical proximity, a proximity in size; and indeed, unless we understand it so, Herodotus, after assuring us that he actually took the dimensions of

[1] The plural probably includes some guide or companion; of himself Herodotus habitually speaks in the singular.

the lesser pyramid, incomprehensibly omits all indication of them, except as to the size of the base. The metaphor seems to be that of a follower who, starting at a certain distance behind another, *ἔχεται αὐτοῦ* 'keeps with him,' or maintains the same distance throughout. So Chephren, or his pyramid, beginning with a slightly smaller base, 'kept,' so to speak, 'the same size near to' the model which it followed. The accusative *τὠυτὸ μέγαθος* (if correct) gives the definition or measure of the proximity denoted by *ἐχομένην*, as when one thing is said *τοσούτους πόδας ἀπέχειν*, *to be so many feet distant* from another. That is to say, in such more appropriate and technical language as would be used by a modern writer or a Greek of scientific times, the two pyramids were similar in figure, but with a difference, relatively small, in scale. If necessary (though I think otherwise), we may suppose that before *τὠυτὸ μέγαθος* we should insert *κατὰ*, or make some other correction in the same sense. This question however, for our present purpose, may be set aside. Since at any rate Herodotus notes the small difference of size in the bases, and notes no other such difference, distinct from the difference mentioned and not connected with it, he clearly meant to give upon the whole an impression approximately such as we have deduced, that the pyramids were similar in shape and proportions, and were nearly of the same bulk.

Now in all this, his representation, within such limits of accuracy as he leads us to expect, is true;

indeed it has more exactness than, all things considered, we should look for. The use of so large a unit as the 100-foot *plethron* marks at once that Herodotus speaks in round numbers, and makes no pretence to a precision which was probably beyond his means and opportunities. As to the form of the pyramids he is right, and as to their size and scale he is nearly right. To the pyramid of Cheops he gives a base of 800 *Greek* feet (*i.e.*, about 776 English feet) square; to that of Chephren a base of 760 Greek feet square. The present measurements appear to be, in *English* feet, about 755 and 706 respectively[1]. At the most Herodotus is out by about 20 feet in '8 *plethra*,' and allowing for the uncertainty of restoration, his error may probably be less. So far then, he is at least as good as his promise.

But in the description of the larger pyramid there are three words which we have not yet cited. 'Every way,' he says, 'each face of its square is 8 *plethra, and the height equal*,' *τῆς ἐστὶ πανταχῆ μέτωπον ἕκαστον ὀκτὼ πλέθρα, καὶ ὕψος ἴσον.* Taking these last words with the rest of his description, what sense are we to put on them? Recent Egyptology, as represented by the elaborate and useful commentary of Alfred Wiedemann[2], seems content to say that, according to Herodotus, the *vertical height* of Cheops' pyramid was equal to the side of

[1] Flinders Petrie, *Pyramids of Gizeh*; Wiedemann (cited below).

[2] Leipzig, Teubner, 1890.

its base, *i.e.* 800 Greek feet. The present vertical height is given as 481⅓ English feet, and the original height, in the feet of Herodotus, cannot have much exceeded 500. We are to believe then that Herodotus, while giving the measure of the base with fair accuracy, has, roughly speaking, *doubled* the height.

Now the point upon which I would insist is this. If Herodotus meant to combine this statement with the rest of his statements about the matter, then not any statement of his about anything deserves attention in respect of its truth. The objection has been considered by many (Rawlinson, Blakesley, and Stein), but has not perhaps been presented with full effect. As a mere error in judging a great vertical height, the discrepancy would be pardonable, though excessive. We might excuse also, though surely with some difficulty, the utterly false picture of the object, which would result from the proportions alleged. We might perhaps suppose that Herodotus had not formed, and could not form, any notion of how a pyramid would look, if its vertical height were equal to the side of its square base. But what shall we say of his consistency with himself? If he allowed himself to think that the greater pyramid (of Cheops) had 8 *plethra* of vertical height, then *what, in the face of his own words, did he suppose to be the height of that of Chephren?* The two are nearly of the same height, as any observer must see. In fact Chephren's, 'The Great Pyramid,' *stands* a little the higher by advantage of ground, and only measurement can discover that it is really less, a discovery which the generality of spectators do not make[1], though Herodotus did. Now he says that he did 'measure the dimensions' of the lesser pyramid, and happens to be supported[2], if he needed it, by a statement of Diodorus, that this one was accessible to ascent. The dimensions which he measured, in such fashion as he could, were necessarily the external dimensions, the principal lines of the monument. He knew then approximately, upon his own showing, that its measurement *along the angle, from base to summit*, was what it was, that is to say, *a little less than* 800 *of his feet.* Yet in the face of this he is to tell us that the *vertical height* of the greater pyramid was 800 such feet; and therefore, that the *vertical height* of Chephren's (being, as he could see and gives us to understand, but little less) was little less than 800 such feet, the rule by which he calculates being apparently that *the vertical height of a climbable hill is about equal to the length of the climb!* What reason have we to suppose, that such was the measure of his intelligence?

Perhaps few readers, had the case been fully stated, would have been content so to suppose. And even the alleged discrepancy between Herodotus and fact has encountered a fair suspicion. It has been suggested (by Rawlinson, Stein, and others), in order to diminish this discrepancy, that by 'height' he means 'height of the side,' *i.e.*, the length of an imaginary perpendicular drawn *upon the face* from base to summit. It must however be admitted that

[1] Wiedemann *ad loc.* [2] Stein *ad loc.*, Wiedemann *ad loc.*

to this, the only conciliation proposed[1], there are serious objections. One, founded upon the 'Greek usage' of the word ὕψος, is perhaps answerable; it shall be considered presently. But two others, I think, are not easily answerable. *First*, as a defence of Herodotus, the conciliation is inadequate and scarcely serviceable. Even in 'the height of the side,' the pyramid of Cheops did not much exceed 600 Greek feet; and therefore that of Chephren also, in fact and according to Herodotus, was in this dimension not far from 600, and not anywhere near 800. For a length which in any fashion he 'measured,' the discrepancy is still gross; and, what to my mind tells more, it is strangely different from his approximations in the measurement of the two bases. *Secondly*, the 'height of the side' is a fictitious line, not suggested by the object itself; and to measure the pyramid by this would be an artificial method, agreeable neither to nature nor to science. Science would measure by the vertical, the perpendicular from the summit to the plane of the base; while to an unscientific observer, like Herodotus, the obvious things to measure were the real, visible, and palpable lines, that of the base and that of the solid angle.

And surely this consideration justifies us in giving the one simple interpretation which reconciles Herodotus both with himself and (so far as he claims it) with fact, to the words τῆς ἐστὶ πανταχῇ μέτωπον ἕκαστον ὀκτὼ πλέθρα ἐούσης τετραγώνου, καὶ ὕψος

[1] Wiedemann *ad loc.*

ἴσον. By the height 'of the pyramid' Herodotus means the actual ascending line of the pyramid, the line of the solid angle. What he says, translated into later language, is, that the two pyramids are similar, having each a square base and four faces, each face an equilateral triangle, and that the lines of the two respectively measure in round numbers 800 Greek feet and 760 Greek feet. A calculation, which any one can now make from the foregoing *data* (and which even in the fifth century B.C. could have been made by a professional man of science, though by Herodotus possibly not), will show that all this is as near the truth as in such a brief, unprofessional description could be expected; and in fact, for common purposes it might well stand even now. As a fact, the pyramids were apparently not *exactly and scientifically* similar, and in neither were the triangular faces *exactly* equilateral, the ascending lines in each being something, but relatively little, less than the base. Taken rigorously, Herodotus must be held to say that in the edge of the lesser pyramid, which he measured, he found 760 of his feet. He should apparently have found less; precisely how much less, in the uncertainty of the most scientific restoration, it is impossible to say. We do not know, for instance, how the pyramid was finished off or crowned. By the most unfavourable assumptions his error in measurement of the angle or edge cannot, I think, be made greater than 50 of his feet; while upon favourable and not unreasonable assumptions it may come but to about 20 such feet.

At the utmost the error, for the purpose of picturing the pyramid and forming a conception of the labour spent upon it (and Herodotus, of course, aims at no more), is quite immaterial. All this we may say, if we take him rigorously. But in truth it is not fair so to take him, and he does not commit himself to the assertion that his measurement of the lesser pyramid gave him 760 feet. His whole history of both pyramids, including the description and measurements, is given avowedly from information received, and even written mostly in the form of quotation. The part relating to Chephren runs thus: "It is said that Chephren, as in other things he used the same fashion as Cheops, so likewise he made a pyramid, which does not come up to the dimensions of the other's, for those of the smaller we measured ourselves (nor has it indeed subterranean chambers below it, nor is there a channel from the Nile, bringing a stream into it as into the other, which stream, passing in by a builded conduit, surrounds an island, wherein, as they say, is laid Cheops himself). In laying his first foundation of Aethiopian marble, he came below the size of the other pyramid by 40 feet, and then built it so as [in the same size?] to keep near the big one. Both stand upon the same hill, which is somewhere about 100 feet high." *Καὶ τοῦτον δὲ τῷ αὐτῷ τρόπῳ διαχρᾶσθαι τῷ ἑτέρῳ τά τε ἄλλα καὶ πυραμίδα ποιῆσαι, ἐς μὲν τὰ ἐκείνου μέτρα οὐκ ἀνήκουσαν· ταῦτα γὰρ ὦν καὶ ἡμεῖς ἐμετρήσαμεν· οὔτε γὰρ ὕπεστι οἰκήματα ὑπὸ γῆν, οὔτε ἐκ τοῦ Νείλου διῶρυξ ἥκει ἐς αὐτὴν ῥέουσα·*

δι᾽ οἰκοδομημένου δὲ αὐλῶνος ἔσω νῆσον περιρρέει, ἐν τῇ αὐτὸν λέγουσι κεῖσθαι Χέοπα. ὑποδείμας δὲ τὸν πρῶτον δόμον λίθου Αἰθιοπικοῦ ποικίλου, τεσσεράκοντα πόδας ὑποβὰς τῆς ἑτέρης, τὠυτὸ μέγαθος ἐχομένην τῆς μεγάλης οἰκοδόμησε. ἑστᾶσι δὲ ἐπὶ λόφου τοῦ αὐτοῦ ἀμφότεραι, μάλιστα ἐς ἑκατὸν πόδας ὑψηλοῦ. Attention should be given to the manner and place in which the writer introduces the remark that he himself took measurements. So far from founding upon this remark his account of Chephren's building, he does not even attach the remark to the figures. It is remarkably and rather oddly detached from them, and tacked to the limited statement that *the dimensions of Chephren's pyramid are less than the* (*alleged*) *dimensions of Cheops'*. Surely the purpose and effect of this arrangement are unmistakable. What Herodotus proved to himself by his 'measuring,' the difficulty and imperfection of which, when applied to objects so vast and peculiar, he must have known, was just this, that assuming Cheops' pyramid to be of the size alleged, that of Chephren, *though it looked higher*, certainly was, as it was said to be, somewhat smaller. And for this much his means may well have been sufficient. As to the figures, he doubtless thought it enough if, measuring as best he could, he came pretty near them, and therefore found no reason for not accepting them as round numbers. That the pyramids were exactly symmetrical was naturally the common belief, seeing how little, in proportion to their bulk, they came short of being so. Indeed it is scarcely possible to repress a suspicion, perhaps irreverent, that the builders meant them so to be, and thought they were, but missed the intended perfection by a minute error in the angle of elevation. Herodotus makes them symmetrical, on the authority of his informant, and is as right as he pretends to be, that is roundly and approximately.

It remains to consider whether this interpretation of his meaning, although it makes sense and truth out of self-contradictory falsehood, must be rejected on the ground that to describe the edge of a pyramid as its ὕψος is not consistent with the 'usage' of the Greeks, which takes ὕψος, as we should in such a case, for the vertical height of the solid. This objection has been brought against interpreting ὕψος as the 'height of the side[1],' and might therefore, I suppose, be alleged against referring it to the line of the angle. But I confess that I see no force in it. It depends on attributing to Herodotus and his age a scientific habit of mind and language which did not belong to them. The authority produced for limiting the use of ὕψος, as we in the like case should now, is Euclid. Certainly no scientific writer, such as Euclid, nor perhaps any writer in an age when scientific conceptions were widely diffused, would allow to pass, in a matter of exact measurement, an expression so ambiguous as *height* for the length of a slope. But in the language of popular description, such as that of Herodotus, it is still so used frequently, the ambiguity being determined by the context.

[1] Wiedemann *l.c.*

'The *height* of that hill is about half a mile' is surely not a phrase that would surprise our ears. To my ear it is rather more natural than *length.* If Herodotus might not call the length of the pyramid's edge a ὕψος, by what term in his repertory was he to designate it? Nor *in this case* would it even appear ambiguous to him. It is so to us only because to us it is natural to think, in such a case, of the vertical height, the perpendicular to the plane of the base. But we think of this, and expect to hear of its measurement, only because we know that it can be easily measured. Herodotus possibly did not know, certainly most of his readers did not, any way in which it could be measured. Why then should he think of it in connexion with measuring, or expect any such connexion in the minds of his readers? Here therefore I see no objection; but even if there be, and if Herodotus is chargeable with an ambiguity which he could and should have avoided, this and no more is the extent of his offence. Of what he means there is not, upon his whole statement together, room for reasonable doubt.

To establish this interpretation however is not our principal object, but rather to deprecate that attitude towards Herodotus which appears in the facile acceptance of the other. In the valuable commentary to which I have chiefly referred, it seems to be too often assumed, that (since we know so much better) what Herodotus said or meant is really of little consequence: of course he is wrong, and how far wrong, or with how much or little justification, we need not inquire. And the like spirit has appeared too frequently elsewhere. Even Stein, though on the whole free from prejudice, must describe as 'self-laudatory' (*selbstberühmend*) the author's remark, that of the lesser pyramid he 'actually took measures'; and Stein is echoed by Wiedemann. Yet in what simpler or less pretentious language could he possibly state a thing which, if true, it would have been absurd to omit? The account which he gives, professedly at secondhand, of the works under the pyramid of Cheops, the subterranean moat and the conduit from the river, has perhaps no element of truth, and the modern explorations tend to prove this, though they have not proved it yet. But it is needless and prejudicial to discuss the way in which Herodotus 'may have been led to his idea[1].' There is nothing to show that it was his idea. He gives it simply as the statement of his informants, which, as the thing was plainly possible, he was entitled, if not bound, to do, without affecting his personal credit. But he was not at liberty so to assert that the pyramid of Cheops had 800 feet of vertical height, because, upon his own statements, he must have known that this could not possibly be true. To some therefore it will be a pleasure to notice that, as a fact, he does not assert this, and generally that his description is not only the best, in spite of its early date, which has descended to us from the Graeco-Roman world, but also, to such a degree as he indicates, true and correct.

[1] Wiedemann *l.c.*

THE SITE OF PRIMITIVE ATHENS

In his brief account of primitive Athens Thucydides writes as follows (II 15):—

ἐπειδὴ δὲ Θησεὺς ἐβασίλευσε, γενόμενος μετὰ τοῦ ξυνετοῦ καὶ δυνατὸς τά τε ἄλλα διεκόσμησε τὴν χώραν, καὶ καταλύσας τῶν ἄλλων πόλεων τά τε βουλευτήρια καὶ τὰς ἀρχὰς ἐς τὴν νῦν πόλιν οὖσαν, ἓν βουλευτήριον ἀποδείξας καὶ πρυτανεῖον, ξυνῴκισε πάντας, καὶ νεμομένους τὰ αὑτῶν ἑκάστους, ἅπερ καὶ πρὸ τοῦ, ἠνάγκασε μιᾷ πόλει ταύτῃ χρῆσθαι, ἣ ἁπάντων ἤδη ξυντελούντων ἐς αὐτὴν μεγάλη γενομένη παρεδόθη ὑπὸ Θησέως τοῖς ἔπειτα· καὶ ξυνοίκια ἐξ ἐκείνου Ἀθηναῖοι ἔτι καὶ νῦν τῇ θεῷ ἑορτὴν δημοτελῆ ποιοῦσιν. τὸ δὲ πρὸ τούτου ἡ ἀκρόπολις ἡ νῦν οὖσα πόλις ἦν, καὶ τὸ ὑπ' αὐτὴν πρὸς νότον μάλιστα τετραμμένον. τεκμήριον δέ· τὰ γὰρ ἱερὰ ἐν αὐτῇ τῇ ἀκροπόλει καὶ ἄλλων θεῶν ἐστί· καὶ τὰ ἔξω πρὸς τοῦτο τὸ μέρος τῆς πόλεως μᾶλλον ἵδρυται, τό τε τοῦ Διὸς τοῦ Ὀλυμπίου καὶ τὸ Πύθιον καὶ τὸ τῆς Γῆς καὶ τὸ ἐν Λίμναις Διονύσου, ᾧ τὰ ἀρχαιότερα Διονύσια τῇ δωδεκάτῃ ποιεῖται ἐν μηνὶ Ἀνθεστηριῶνι, ὥσπερ καὶ οἱ ἀπ' Ἀθηναίων Ἴωνες ἔτι καὶ νῦν νομίζουσιν· ἵδρυται δὲ καὶ ἄλλα ἱερὰ ταύτῃ ἀρχαῖα· καὶ τῇ κρήνῃ τῇ νῦν μὲν τῶν τυράννων οὕτω σκευασάντων Ἐννεακρούνῳ καλουμένῃ, τὸ δὲ πάλαι φανερῶν τῶν πηγῶν οὐσῶν Καλλιρρόῃ ὠνομασμένῃ, ἐκείνῃ τε ἐγγὺς οὔσῃ τὰ πλείστου ἄξια ἐχρῶντο, καὶ νῦν ἔτι ἀπὸ τοῦ ἀρχαίου πρό τε γαμικῶν καὶ ἐς ἄλλα τῶν ἱερῶν νομίζεται τῷ ὕδατι χρῆσθαι· καλεῖται δὲ διὰ τὴν παλαιὰν ταύτῃ κατοίκησιν καὶ ἡ ἀκρόπολις μέχρι τοῦδε ἔτι ὑπ' Ἀθηναίων πόλις.

Attention and controversy have recently been drawn to this passage by the excavations and theories of Dr Dörpfeld, which have brought into doubt the identification of the sites mentioned. It seems worth while therefore to examine the text upon the assumption that these sites are unknown, and to ascertain as far as possible, without reference to anything now disputed, what is the view propounded by the historian respecting the limits of primitive Athens. In certain points the current interpretation still seems to require correction.

The description proper is contained in a single sentence: 'before this,' that is, before the concentration under Theseus, 'the *acropolis*, which is now, was the city, together with τὸ ὑπ' αὐτὴν πρὸς νότον μάλιστα τετραμμένον.' The term *acropolis*, as appears from the next sentence, which speaks of sanctuaries '*in* the acropolis itself' (ἐν αὐτῇ τῇ ἀκροπόλει), is used first in the strict sense, for the precinct at the top of the hill. To this we are to add, as comprised in the city, τὸ ὑπ' αὐτὴν (τὴν ἀκρόπολιν) πρὸς νότον μάλιστα τετραμμένον. These words give us no circumscribing line, and not much information of any kind. Something however may perhaps be inferred from the shape of the sentence. The additional area, the τὸ ὑπ' αὐτήν, seems to come in as a detail, almost as an after-thought, appended to the statement that ἡ ἀκρόπολις ἡ νῦν οὖσα πόλις ἦν. We should therefore naturally figure it as not only subordinate to the acropolis but in some way closely incorporated with it. In relation to the acropolis this additional area, to justify the arrangement of Thucydides, should be a part neither large nor independent.

His supporting arguments are indicated with such excessive brevity, that there is scarcely one sentence of which the natural bearing is perfectly clear. There is however one such sentence. Καλεῖται δὲ, he says in conclusion, διὰ τὴν παλαιὰν ταύτῃ κατοίκησιν καὶ ἡ ἀκρόπολις μέχρι τοῦδε ἔτι ὑπ' Ἀθηναίων πόλις: 'and because of the ancient settlement here, the acropolis, as well (as the present city), is still to this day called by the Athenians πόλις.' He alleges, as a thing explained by his theory and therefore supporting his theory, the fact that the acropolis bore in his day the name πόλις. Now whatever he may have intended, there is not room for dispute respecting the true and natural bearing of this fact as an argument upon the ancient topography of Athens. It is possible to argue from it, not perhaps conclusively, but with force, that what the acropolis was still called, that the acropolis once actually was; that 'the city' of some former time was the acropolis *and nothing more.* So it might be argued, and correctly, from the present application of the name *city* to a certain area in London, that this area once was London. And the inference must be this or nothing; if the later usage of the name πόλις be not held to prove that the acropolis was once itself the πόλις, then it can prove nothing for topography whatever. We thus get a strong light upon ἡ ἀκρόπολις ἡ νῦν οὖσα πόλις ἦν, καὶ τὸ ὑπ' αὐτὴν κ.τ.λ. The form of this statement, we said, suggests that τὸ ὑπ' αὐτήν is something subordinate and supplementary. We now see that this must be true to the utmost conceivable extent. If the supporting argument is to be relevant, τὸ ὑπ' αὐτήν must be so strictly subordinate, so mere a supplement, that in a looser way of speaking, it might be included as part of the acropolis itself. If Thucydides' ancient πόλις was the citadel *plus* something, it was also the citadel simply.

The explanation of this inconsistency—for a verbal inconsistency there is—has been properly sought in the features of the site. It is plain that the *acropolis* in the narrow sense, the summit-fortress, never could have been occupied alone. The western end was and is not difficult of access: and modern researches have proved that of the southern face also a portion, the western portion, was in its natural state of no impracticable slope. An outer enclosure securing these slopes would be at once a necessary *addition* to the citadel proper, and, in a looser way of speaking, a necessary *part*. Taking then the expressions of Thucydides together, something of this sort we should suppose to be in his mind[1]. We will now see how far his other arguments seem to be reconcilable with this conception.

Τεκμήριον δέ· τὰ γὰρ ἱερὰ ἐν αὐτῇ τῇ ἀκροπόλει καὶ ἄλλων θεῶν ἐστί. This clause has not been treated with sufficient accuracy. First, a needless doubt has been raised about the reading. Since the expression ἄλλων θεῶν, '*other* deities,' does not explain itself, it is suggested that we should 'complete

[1] So Dr Dörpfeld and his supporters, to whose arguments so far I have little to add.

the sense' by inserting καὶ αὐτῆς τῆς Ἀθηναίας or the like—'in the acropolis itself are the sanctuaries *of Athena herself* and other deities.' But the suggestion is gratuitous. The goddess of the Acropolis has been mentioned, under her proper title ἡ θεός, in the clause next but one before this, καὶ ξυνοίκια ἐξ ἐκείνου Ἀθηναῖοι ἔτι καὶ νῦν τῇ θεῷ ἑορτὴν δημοτελῆ ποιοῦσιν. In such a context, no obscurity can attach to the phrase 'other deities also have their sanctuaries in the acropolis,' and the proposed insertion would be technically indefensible, even if true to the meaning[1].

But secondly—and this is a point of great importance to the general interpretation—the insertion is not true to the meaning. Even those who do not alter the text, appear generally to alter the sense, by treating the sentence *as if* it contained the words καὶ αὐτῆς τῆς Ἀθηναίας or the like, and signified accordingly 'in the acropolis itself are the sanctuaries *of Athena and* of other deities also.' The sentence of Thucydides refers not at all to any 'sanctuaries of Athena,' but only to those of other gods, respecting which it asserts that *these* are

[1] Mr L. Whibley has pointed out to me that the contrast between ἡ θεός (Athena) and οἱ ἄλλοι θεοί was actually familiar to the official language. The treasurers of Athena were ταμίαι τῶν τῆς θεοῦ or ταμίαι τῆς θεοῦ, and there was a similar board of ταμίαι τῶν ἄλλων θεῶν. See the decree of Callias, *C.I.A.* I 32, and compare *C.I.A.* I 194. Such a use would greatly aid in interpreting Thucydides' ἄλλοι θεοί to the ear, even if it were not clear in itself. The decree of Callias also exemplifies the alternative use of πόλις and ἀκρόπολις.

in the acropolis, as well as those of Athena, and not those of Athena only.

To change the sense is to thrust upon the author a proposition irrelevant to his purpose. From the general statement that the acropolis contained ancient sanctuaries, those of Athena and others, what could be inferred? The common assumption appears to be that it is intended to prove the antiquity of the acropolis. This would be a strange piece of reasoning. The acropolis being the manifest nucleus and first cause of the city, its primitive antiquity would naturally be assumed, not proved,—as in fact it is assumed by Thucydides. But if we will suppose a disputant so sceptical as to require proof, it would be idle to offer proof from the monuments. With far less temerity, with far less absurdity, he would deny the antiquity of these, and the argument, thus conducted, must revolve in a circle.

But Thucydides is not guilty of any such paralogism. His proposition, which is neither designed to prove the antiquity of the acropolis, nor capable of proving it, is simply that *in the acropolis itself there are the sanctuaries of deities other than Athena*: and the question is, what inference, respecting the ancient limits of Athens, he can draw from that. It is by no means obvious, and our answer must be tentative. We may perhaps find the way by asking first, why he should regard the presence in the acropolis of other sanctuaries than those of Athena as noticeable at all. Why should they not be there? Because (shall we not answer?), as the acropolis was regarded in the Periclean age, as it had then long been regarded, the Παλλάδος ὄχθος belonged to Pallas so entirely and absolutely, that no worship not connected with her seemed to have a natural place there. By the recent reconstruction, by the Parthenon, Erechtheum and Promachos, the conception of the citadel as the sanctuary of 'the goddess' had been developed to the utmost capacity of art. It seems therefore not unreasonable to suppose that in that age the introduction of other worships there would have seemed an anachronism, and therefore the presence of other worships there would seem a relic of antiquity, a fact demanding historical explanation. If we may suppose this, and remember that Thucydides aims (as we have seen) at proving the citadel to have been once itself the city, the bearing of this argument will become clear. 'The citadel,' Thucydides argues, 'is and immemorially has been appropriated to Athena; it is natural to suppose that, ever since it became a citadel merely, the central point of a large surrounding city, it must have been reserved, as we should and do reserve it now, for the patron goddess only, and that other worships would be accommodated elsewhere. Why then do we actually find in the citadel other sanctuaries? It is because, before Theseus and his συνοικισμός, the citadel was itself the city; and the 'other deities,' if not admitted there, would have been excluded from Athens altogether. These sanctuaries therefore record, and are evidence for, the fact of such a former limitation.'

Καὶ τὰ ἔξω (ἱερὰ), proceeds the argument, *πρὸς τοῦτο τὸ μέρος τῆς πόλεως μᾶλλον ἵδρυται, τό τε τοῦ Διὸς τοῦ Ὀλυμπίου κ.τ.λ.* 'and the sanctuaries outside are situated towards this part of the city rather, as that of Zeus Olympios,' etc. Here it was until recently taken as obvious that *πρὸς τοῦτο τὸ μέρος τῆς πόλεως* refers to *πρὸς νότον*, the 'part of the city' meant being identified with *τὸ ὑπ' αὐτὴν πρὸς νότον μάλιστα τετραμμένον.* And obvious, in the proper sense, this may be; that is to say, it is a supposition which, from the form and disposition of the clauses, would readily suggest itself; and if it was not the intention of the author, he has run some risk of mistake. But it will hardly be maintained that Thucydides never wrote ambiguous sentences; and the question is, not whether this interpretation is obvious, but whether it is correct.

Be it noted first, that in supposing it obvious, modern readers have been guided partly by an assumption certainly erroneous, the assumption that the preceding clause, referring to the sanctuaries within the acropolis, is intended as a proof that the acropolis was *part* of the ancient city,—as an argument for the first half of the proposition that 'the ancient city consisted of (1) the acropolis, and (2) *τὸ ὑπ' αὐτὴν κ.τ.λ.*' Assuming this, it was perhaps inevitable to connect our present clause with the second half of that proposition. But in reality, as has been shown, the clause relating to the sanctuaries within the acropolis will not bear either the sense or the inference which has been put upon it. The supposed connexion therefore fails: the argument upon the sanctuaries *without* is totally distinct from the argument on the sanctuaries *within* (it should be divided from it not by a comma, but by a colon); and thus a relation between πρὸς τοῦτο τὸ μέρος τῆς πόλεως and τὸ πρὸς νότον is no longer presumable.

Further, it should be remarked that if there is indeed an intended correlation between the two uses of πρός, the author is inaccurate in the latter use. The monuments (he must have meant to say) lie 'in' or 'about' (ἐν, κατά) the southern part of the city, not 'towards' that part. In writing πρός 'towards,' he must have been unduly influenced by the feeling that 'this part' meant 'the part *towards* the south.' Such an inaccuracy is indeed conceivable, but it is not to be disregarded in weighing the merits of the interpretation.

But a graver objection remains. Thucydides is contending that the ancient city was limited to a certain portion of the later city, that it comprised this and no more; and he would prove this (as is supposed) by the existence of very ancient monuments within the portion prescribed. Now such an argument would be precarious, and would do little credit to the logic and sagacity of the author. It is of course true that the appearance of ancient monuments in a certain quarter tends to prove ancient occupation; but it is not at all true that, in estimating the antiquity of occupation in different quarters, the non-appearance of ancient monuments necessarily disproves ancient occupation. We have first to eliminate or allow for the possibly unequal effects of time and change; and from certain remarks which Thucydides makes elsewhere[1], we should suppose that he could not have been blind to this consideration, and would not have rushed lightly to the conclusion, that the ancient dimensions of a city can be limited off-hand by drawing a line round the visible ancient monuments.

For these reasons, and especially for the last, this interpretation appears, if not inadmissible, so unsatisfactory that we ought to prefer a suspension of judgement. Our purpose is to ascertain what Thucydides can tell us, on the assumption that the sites which he mentions are unknown. And the sentence *τὰ ἔξω ἱερὰ πρὸς τοῦτο τὸ μέρος τῆς πόλεως μᾶλλον ἵδρυται* ought, on this assumption, to be marked as uncertain. The interpretation which might suggest itself superficially is seen upon consideration to be untenable. No other, as I think, would occur naturally; and a prudent reader would therefore await further information, supposing that the topographical data, the sites of the monuments, if they could be recovered, would explain the brief and vague indication which without them is not sufficient.

A similar difficulty rests upon the remaining argument, drawn from the fact that in the time of the author it was 'still the custom, in consequence of the antique (habit), to use before weddings and for other sacred purposes the water' of a fountain

[1] See Thuc. I. 10.

called Enneacrounos, or *Nine-spouts*, the history of which, so far as necessary for the purpose, is given in the same brief elliptical style as the rest. The *Nine-spouts*, he says, derives its form and name from the operations of the Peisistratidae, and covers the natural spring or springs which bore the name Callirrhoé. This spring 'was near, and they used it for the most important purposes,' ἐκείνῃ ἐγγὺς οὔσῃ τὰ πλείστου ἄξια ἐχρῶντο[1]. The arrangement of the words is odd and characteristic, but he seems clearly to assume and imply, that his ancient city was ill-supplied with water, having no other source but Callirrhoé both conveniently near and good enough 'for the most important purposes'; and further, that the yield of Callirrhoé itself was scanty. Fresh water easily accessible would naturally be used for all purposes, so far as it would go; and the destination of it to 'the most important' is intelligible only as the effect of necessity. As to *Enneacrounos*, the very name and form seem to import a large use and supply; and it therefore appears that the operation of 'the despots' not merely absorbed the old source, but greatly increased it by supplies from elsewhere. Indeed it is for this reason that Thucydides, who is least of all mortals a gossip, refers to the history of the fountain at all. His point is this: the

[1] The change of ἐκείνῃ to ἐκεῖνοι is mistaken and obscures the point, which is, that because *Callirrhoé* (ἐκείνῃ) was once naturally or necessarily used in a certain way, therefore the water of *Enneacrounos*, its successor and representative, is still used in a similar way, though in the altered state and circumstances such a use is no longer natural.

water of Enneacrounos is now sought by Athenians for certain sacred purposes; in the present condition of the city and the fountain there appears no cause for this, the water being quite ordinary; it is explained by the fact that Enneacrounos replaces and represents Callirrhoé, which for primitive Athens was necessarily a special and reserved water, the city as then limited having only this supply both near and good, and that not adequate for all purposes. The present use of Enneacrounos, therefore, is evidence for the ancient limitation of the city. How Callirrhoé was used by those who lived near it, he takes to be known; as doubtless it was, since the alteration of the fountain was almost within memory. All this is interesting, but until we know the site of Enneacrounos (which is one of the points in dispute), does not help to determine the intended limitation of the city.

To sum up, then, what can be learned from Thucydides himself respecting his 'Athens before Theseus,' we find that (1) it might be identified with the acropolis, if that name were taken largely; (2) the portion of it which was external to the acropolis proper, comprised the south-western slope by which the citadel was approached; and (3) this external portion can in no case cover any ground which might not, in a loose and popular way of speaking, be regarded as actually pertaining to and included in the acropolis itself.

It does not belong to the plan of this paper to identify the disputed sites. But whatever may be right, the view prevalent until lately appears, as an explanation of Thucydides, manifestly impossible. The long acceptation of it can be taken only as one instance among many of the facility with which, where the facts are supposed to be known, a text, especially if at all obscure, will be strained to accord with them. This explanation started from the assumption that the 'sanctuary of Zeus Olympios' and the 'Pythion' mentioned by Thucydides are the unfinished temple of Peisistratus and a precinct of Apollo adjoining it. These lie S.E. of the citadel, more than a quarter of a mile from its nearest point. Thucydides was therefore taken to mean that Athens 'before Theseus' comprised, together with the citadel, an area extending southwards of it to this distance or thereabouts. Now this will explain the words *τὰ ἔξω (ἱερὰ) πρὸς τοῦτο τὸ μέρος τῆς πόλεως μᾶλλον ἵδρυται*, if we put upon them the superficial interpretation which has been above discussed. It will explain this clause, so taken, and it will explain nothing else. In particular it conflicts with the plainest of the author's assertions, that he accounts for the application of the name *πόλις*, in a narrower sense, to the acropolis itself. The former existence of a *πόλις* comprising, with the citadel, an external area to the south having a radius of 500 or 600 yards, *i.e.* many times as large as the citadel itself, could no more account for that application of the name than the plan of the Periclean city could account for it. One might as well explain the narrower sense now sometimes given to the name 'city of London,' by the fact that London once extended no further west than St James's Square.

Dr Dörpfeld's plan, which draws the outer wall of the archaic city close round the S.W. of the acropolis hill, is at least in general accord with the representation of Thucydides as a whole: it gives, as he rightly maintains, a πόλις practically limited to the citadel and so explaining the origin of the name. He claims, as I understand, to have found some slight traces of such a wall. He has certainly discovered, near the foot of the hill on the west, a place to which water was conveyed by an elaborate and still existing water-course, the construction of which can (he says) be dated by the character of the work in the sixth century, the age of 'the despots.' There he would place *Enneacrounos*. It has been made an objection that such traces of a spring, as have been found there, indicate a small and scanty source, which now seems to have failed and disappeared; and further that the surrounding ground was always without fountains, as appears by the numerous wells. All this seems, on the contrary, to accord with Thucydides, and actually to be required for the Enneacrounos of his story[1].

[1] There is evidence (late) for an *Enneacrounos* by the Ilissus and near the Peisistratean temple of Zeus Olympios; but this, supposing it trustworthy, raises no difficulty, as there is not the slightest reason for presuming that the name was unique. The word *enneacrounos* is, strictly speaking, rather a description than a proper name; and if 'the despots' or their engineers gave such a form to a fountain in one place, they may well have done so in another or in others; or again the type may have been imitated

Close by, on the other side of the ancient road to the acropolis from the west, Dr Dörpfeld claims to have found the precinct of Dionysus ἐν Λίμναις. Here also I see no objection, though the actual evidence is, so far as I can judge, less strong than for his Enneacrounos[1].

The 'sanctuary of Gé' is easily found, on the testimony of Pausanias, immediately before the gate of the acropolis. Evidence, slight but sufficient, shows that the title *Pythios* was connected with a sanctuary at or near the cave of Pan, on the N. face of the acropolis and near the W. end, and the title of *Zeus Olympios* (probably) with a sanctuary adjoining it. These Dr Dörpfeld supposes to be those named by Thucydides.

Now these sites would suit the general purport of Thucydides very well. If the city once consisted of the acropolis only, it might be expected from the nature of the case, that sanctuaries would be found crowded about what was then the only gate and approach; and Thucydides will be indicating that they were so found, naming four and adding that

in later times. Dr Dörpfeld would suppose a transference of the name from his original site to the other, but his explanation seems, though possible, artificial, and is in any case not necessary.

[1] Nothing can be argued from the title ἐν Λίμναις. Inferences from the apparent meaning of proper names, of which the history is beyond investigation, are useless and misleading. The name may have changed its sense, or may be a mere corruption. The sanctuary ἐν Λίμναις may have had no more connexion with any *marsh* than *Burnham Beeches* with any *beech*, or *Sandiacre* with any *sand*.

there were others. In the collective description of these sites as lying πρὸς τοῦτο τὸ μέρος τῆς πόλεως μᾶλλον, we must take τοῦτο τὸ μέρος τῆς πόλεως as signifying that portion of the (later) city which has been previously marked off as the content of the ancient city, that is to say, the acropolis and its outwork, the acropolis in the larger sense. This is Dr Dörpfeld's supposition, and it gives a natural sense, so far, to the words. But what then exactly is meant by πρός? Dr Dörpfeld, if I understand him rightly, takes πρός to mean *on the ascent to*, on *the slope of*, citing the description of Torone (Thuc. 4. 110) as οὔσης πρὸς λόφον, *lying up hill*; where however the notion of ascent is given not by πρός but by λόφον. With such a phrase as *this part of the city*, πρός can hardly signify more than *towards*. But is not this enough? Is not *towards*, in a description so very brief, a sufficient equivalent for *on and about the approach to*? What Thucydides must (*ex hypothesi*) wish to indicate is, that if you approached his 'ancient city' by the only way in which it could be approached, you would find ancient sanctuaries lying, as they should lie, especially thick about the entrance. It seems a not unnatural way of putting this in compressed form, to say that they lay *towards* his ancient city *more* than anywhere else. And we have thus a point and reason for the word μᾶλλον, which ought not to be superfluous. Sanctuaries very ancient there probably, indeed certainly, were in other parts of the later city. Nor does the argument deny this, depending only on the fact that 'towards this part of the city' there was a special aggregation of them.

It must of course be frankly admitted, as was said before, that Thucydides, if this was his meaning, has exposed himself to be misunderstood by readers not acquainted with the facts. The proximity of the words *πρὸς τοῦτο τὸ μέρος τῆς πόλεως* to *πρὸς νότον*, and the appearance of a relation between them, is, if in fact there is no relation, a flaw in composition which would not have been passed by a pupil of Isocrates. But to Thucydides such a standard is surely inapplicable. Facility was not even his aim; and in such a context as this he may well have been more than commonly blind to an ambiguity. At all events the clause must bear some meaning consistent with the passage as a whole, and can lend no countenance to the identification of his 'sanctuary of Zeus Olympios' with the temple of Peisistratus. That Athens should have contained more than one such sanctuary, and more than one *Pythion*, is as little surprising as that in a mediaeval city there should be more than one church of St Mary. The caprice of ruin, which has made the Peisistratean foundation so signally conspicuous, seems to have been the chief cause of a supposition not reconcilable either with the natural course of the city's development or with the general purport of the historian.

ON A LOST WORD IN HOMER

πολλοὶ δ' ἐν τάφρῳ ἐρυσάρματες ὠκέες ἵπποι
ἄξαντ' ἐν πρώτῳ ῥυμῷ λίπον ἅρματ' ἀνάκτων.
Il. 16. 370.

Μυρμιδόνες δ' αὐτοῦ σχέθον ἵππους φυσιόωντας,
ἱεμένους φοβέεσθαι, ἐπεὶ λίπεν ἅρματ' ἀνάκτων.
v. l. λίπον. *Ib.* 506.

THE commentaries on these passages (see Leaf, *ad locc.*) bring us to two conclusions, both of which seem, as far as they go, to be sound and incontestable. (1) The two are connected by some conscious or unconscious reminiscence on the part of the composer or one of the composers. The words in which they agree, *λίπον* (or *λίπεν*) *ἅρματ' ἀνάκτων*, are apparently not a commonplace; and in the former passage we have the phenomenon, characteristic and continually characteristic of the Homeric style, that a whole verse is framed of tags or recollections, since *ἄξαντ' ἐν πρώτῳ ῥυμῷ* is found also in Z 40. (2) Each passage, read and construed in the received fashion, presents great if not insoluble difficulties of grammar. In the first we have, breaking into a row of plurals, the strange dual participle *ἄξαντε*. For this we are offered the justification (Monro, *Homeric Grammar*, § 170) that the *many horses* are many *pairs* of horses, and that the words ἄξαντ' ἐν πρώτῳ ῥυμῷ refer to a single pair, 'breaking *each pair* its chariot, at the pole-joint.' But in calling this construction 'extremely harsh,' Dr Leaf does not go beyond the mark. Let it be granted on the dubious authority of E 487 (see notes there) that if it is specially desired that a multitude of things should be thought of in pairs, we may speak of them with a dual participle and a plural verb. That will not account for the solitary appearance of a dual, where a whole continuous line of plurals shows that the speaker is *not* thinking of objects in pairs, and where in fact there is no point in such a distribution. And the dual here is solitary, for as Dr Leaf truly observes, the singular ἐν πρώτῳ ῥυμῷ gives no support to it. With the correct and regular plural ἄξαντες, the singular (not ἐν πρώτοις ῥυμοῖς) would still be regular, not to say necessary. Just so it is perfectly natural and regular to say ἀνατείνοντες τὼ χεῖρε of many persons who hold up each his two hands, or ἀνατείνοντες τὴν χεῖρα, if each holds up one, but these common locutions are no help to the supposed ἄξαντε, which can in truth be defended only by the candid assumption of certain ancients, that the dual may be used 'for the plural.'

In the second passage (507) the objections are still more cogent. Of the two variants, λίπεν—λίπον, the former is 'the best attested' (Leaf) and would be exclusively acceptable, even if this were not the case. With this reading, the plural ἐπεὶ λίπεν ἅρματ' ἀνάκτων, signifying 'when he (the dying

Sarpedon) quitted the chariot (ἅρματα?) *of the lords*,' is no better than nonsense. On the other hand λίπον, suggested by its occurrence in the parallel passage (371), makes a facile correction, 'when they (the horses) quitted the chariot of their lords';—a facile and also a futile correction, for 'the meaning evidently is that the Myrmidons capture chariot and horses: if the horses had broken away from the chariot we must have been told so' (Leaf), whereas the preceding verse expressly marks that there was not even time or opportunity for such a thing. With λίπον therefore, a palpable and inadmissible conjecture, we have no concern, and the only question is, whether we can construe λίπεν. Aristarchus, characteristically honest and clear-sighted as to the critical *data*, and also characteristically insensible to any consideration not reducible to rule, endeavoured, it seems, to do this, by supposing that λίπεν is here equivalent to ἐλίπησαν: the horses set themselves to flee, 'since the chariots of their lords *were deserted*.' But it is hard to take this seriously. Even if we get rid of the irrelevant plural (for there is only one chariot concerned, that of Sarpedon and his companion) by assuming that ἅρματα, in spite of the plural verb, really means ἅρμα, *the chariot*; and if, further, we remove the feeble addition 'of their lords,' by taking ἀνάκτων, without Homeric warrant (Leaf), as dependent upon λίπεν, 'parted from its lords,' that is, 'was quitted by them'; and if, further, we grant that Aristarchus might have reason, though we have not, for thinking that the aorist ἐλίπην was a form in use, and that a Homeric bard could use it instead of his regular passive ἐλιπόμην;—even if we swallow all the objections of form, there will remain the fatal objection, that men do not think in grammatical riddles, and bards even less than others. The supposed phrase has to be construed *a posteriori* by the ingenious application of rules, and could not have been originally evolved by process of nature. It is a hollow darkness, an elaborately ambiguous nothing, such as happily human brains do not as a matter of fact produce. Nor would it therefore be any help to suppose with some (see Leaf), that the sentence, with perhaps some of the context, is an 'interpolation.' The problem remains unaffected by any question of authorship. Whoever wrote the verses, it is equally to be presumed that he meant something, and that his words had some intelligible relation to his meaning.

We come then to this, as the result of the previous investigations, that of the two passages the first is barely construable, and for the second no tolerable construction has been discovered. Now before we go further in this direction, before we look for yet other possible ways of grammatical or quasi-grammatical distortion, should we not ask whether, upon the facts, it is credible that in either passage the text which we are straining is correct? To me it seems a logical impossibility. The passages have in common a certain special turn of phrase, λίπον (λίπεν) ἅρματ' ἀνάκτων. What strange witchcraft is there, or could there be, in this form of words, to account for the fact that in two places a poet, in using them, should fall into obscure, difficult, unconstruable grammar? The passages agree in their wording; they also agree in being ungrammatical, and this, be it noticed, in different and unconnected ways. To suppose such agreement accidental, is contrary to reason. The common phenomenon must have a common cause; and from the nature of the case this common cause can be nothing but an *error*, common to both texts and traceable to the same origin. It is useless therefore to seek translations which, if they were otherwise passable, must still be rejected *a priori*. What is the common error in the texts? That, as it seems to me, is the only question open to us.

From this point of view our attention, in regarding the phrases common to both, will fix itself readily upon the word ἀνάκτων, and for this reason: in both passages this possessive is superfluous, and in the second it is, as we have partly seen, worse than superfluous. Let us take the context, beginning from the last words of the dying Sarpedon:

ὣς ἄρα μιν εἰπόντα τέλος θανάτοιο κάλυψεν
ὀφθαλμοὺς ῥῖνάς θ'· ὁ δὲ λὰξ ἐν στήθεσι βαίνων
ἐκ χροὸς ἕλκε δόρυ, προτὶ δὲ φρένες αὐτῷ ἕποντο·
τοῖο δ' ἅμα ψυχήν τε καὶ ἔγχεος ἐξέρυσ' αἰχμήν.
Μυρμιδόνες δ' αὐτοῦ σχέθον ἵππους φυσιόωντας,
ἱεμένους φοβέεσθαι ἐπεὶ λίπεν ἅρματ' ἀνάκτων.

Now the supposed ἄνακτες here must of course be the Lycian prince and his charioteer. And it is of course true that Sarpedon had a charioteer, whose death has been briefly mentioned some forty lines before (465). But it is none the less inappropriate that in describing what happened upon the fall of Sarpedon, the forgotten charioteer should be suddenly dragged into view by this idle reference to *the lords*, even if we assume (against 464 ὅς ῥ' ἠῢς θεράπων Σαρπηδόνος ἦεν ἄνακτος) that ἄνακτες is a proper Homeric description of such a pair. There is thus, apart from all other difficulties, an intrinsic defect in the word ἀνάκτων here; and the flaw, though in itself not worth mentioning among such an arsenal of objections, serves to clinch the conclusion that this word is the peccant spot.

Looking closer at it, we see that it contains one doubtful letter; one letter, I mean, about which our MSS. can convey no certain information. An ω in Homer is an ambiguous testimony, telling us only that tradition gave either this letter itself or an ο. Let us try the alternative in both our passages:

> **Μυρμιδόνες δ' αὐτοῦ σχέθον ἵππους φυσιόωντας,**
> **ἱεμένους φοβέεσθαι ἐπεὶ λίπεν, ἅρμα τ' ἄνακτον.**

'And the Myrmidons caught on the spot the snorting steeds, who, when he abandoned them, were starting to flee, and got (captured) the chariot unbroken.' A keen interest in the spoil is a marked and constant note of battle as described by the Homeric bards. It is the note of this passage, which describes the promptitude by which the Myrmidons secured a valuable piece of booty which, if they had lost a moment, would have been snatched from them or ruined. If the horses had been allowed to bolt, they would have done one of the two things which in similar circumstances occur elsewhere. Either they would have carried off the chariot into the Trojan lines, or they would have wrecked it, burst away, and left the wreck behind them. But the Myrmidons, by seizing them 'on the spot,' get both them 'and the chariot unbroken.' In transference from the horses to the chariot the word σχέθον is slightly changed in sense, or rather colour, but the 'zeugma' is hardly worth notice. As for ἄνακτος, from ἀγ- *break*, it is of a type peculiarly Homeric, the type of ἄβλητος *not hit*, ἄρεκτος *not done*, ἀνούτατος *not wounded*, etc. The pristine form would, I suppose, have been ἄϝακτος, but in Homer the root has commonly no initial consonant (*e.g.* Π 801).

Upon this passage by itself the evidence for ἄνακτον would be strong, but it becomes something more than strong when we find that with the same word we can with equal simplicity mend the fault of the other passage, and thus solve not only the separate difficulties, but also that problem of the connexion between them which lies at the root of the whole matter.

πολλοὶ δ' ἐν τάφρῳ ἐρυσάρματες ὠκέες ἵπποι
ἄξαν τ' ἐν πρώτῳ ῥυμῷ λίπον ἅρμα τ' ἄνακτον.

'And in the fosse many swift chariot-steeds either broke the chariot in the pole or left it behind unbroken.' The point which the describer here wishes to make is that in the wild flight across the ditch many chariots were parted from their horses. There were many ways in which this might happen. One, perhaps more likely than any in so frantic an attempt, was an actual break in the chariot itself, most probably in the pole, which was part of it. But without any such break, without any injury to the ἅρμα itself, there were many ways, such as the breaking of the yoke, or of the pin or the ring by means of which the yoke was attached to the pole, and others needless to specify. All such, in antithesis to the breaking of the chariot (ἄξαν τε ἅρμα), are summed up in the contrasted phrase 'or get quit of it without breaking' (λίπον τε ἅρμα ἄνακτον). The *either* and *or* of the English are represented in Greek as usual by τε...τε, and indeed could not be expressed otherwise. The place of the second τε after ἅρμα is not a mere licence for metre, though as such it would be familiar and unobjectionable; it is actually advantageous where, as here, the common object (ἅρμα) of both clauses is expressed in the second only, and therefore, being as it were overdue, has a natural tendency to push forward. The singular ἅρμα corresponds to the singular ἐν πρώτῳ ῥυμῷ, and is admissible, or rather preferable, in Greek as in English, for the same reason.

The history and connexion of the passages thus becomes clear. The earlier of the two is probably that on the death of Sarpedon. It was plainly the word ἄνακτος, probably not very common, which fixed the sound of λίπεν ἅρμα τ' ἄνακτον in the ear of the poet who describes the flight over the fosse.

By instinct, rather than conscious borrowing, he has linked the phrase to his other reminiscences from Book VI. To a Greek of the historical age, such a word as ἄνακτος, *not broken*, was of course no longer alive; indeed the root ἀγ-, with all its derivatives, lost ground to other forms and inventions, and was restricted to a narrow field. On the other hand the letters ανακτον were in old books familiar, but as the script for ἀνάκτων. Accordingly, as a matter of course, ἀνάκτων expelled ἄνακτον from both passages, but with the natural result that both became unintelligible.

DEATH AND THE HORSE

(κλυτόπωλος, κλυτός, ἕλιξ etc.)

Did the Greeks, and in particular did the Homeric poets, associate Death with the Horse? The great importance, in the archaeology of art and religion, of all associations connected with the grave, will perhaps give interest to a somewhat full discussion of this question, or rather of the single piece of evidence upon which, so far as concerns Homer, the question seems to turn. Did the poets describe Hades, lord of Death, as 'lord of the goodly steeds'? Is this what they meant by κλυτόπωλος? It is the purpose of this paper to show that they did not, that this interpretation is involved in difficulties and impossibilities three-fold and four-fold, has for it neither reason nor authority, and must, with all that depends upon it, be given up.

The first and perhaps sufficient objection is this. Before the epithet κλυτόπωλος could be referred to the horse, πῶλος, it is plain, must have signified *a horse.* Now it is quite certain, though apparently not recognized, that to the composers of the *Iliad* and *Odyssey* no such word as πῶλος *horse* was known.

They used, it is true, the word to which, by a stretch of meaning and for convenience, that sense was given by their imitators and successors; but they knew it only and strictly in what seems to have been its primitive and etymological sense, *a foal*, a young horse *under the mother*. 'Chestnut horses (ἵππους) a hundred and fifty, all mares and many with their foals (πῶλοι) at their feet' says Nestor in Λ 681: and see also Υ 222, 225. Against πῶλος *horse* the evidence is overwhelming. If these poets had known at all a word so irresistibly convenient as a synonym for ἵππος beginning with a consonant, they must have used it, in the extant poems, not once but scores of times. This estimate is no mere conjecture: it is proved by experiment. The composers of the *Hymns*, imitators of 'Homer' but differing much in language and feeling, did, like the Attic poets, know πῶλος (*young horse*) in a sense nearly equivalent to ἵππος, and accordingly with them horses are πῶλοι twice (those of Ares in 8. 7, and those of Selene in 32. 9), that is to say about once for ten times that the animal is mentioned. Now at this rate the *Iliad* alone should have given us πῶλος *horse* about forty times or more[1]; yet it does not once. Nor does the *Odyssey*. We read, it is true, in ψ 246 how Athena 'detained at Oceanus the golden-throned Morn, and would not let her yoke

[1] ἵππος is found there about 400 times; see Ebeling's *Lexicon*, *s.v.* My references and statistics are largely taken from this book, though I may mention perhaps that I have read both *Iliad* and *Odyssey* through with this subject in mind.

the swift-foot steeds that bring light to men, Lampos and Phaethon, the πῶλοι that draw Morn.'

Ἠῶ δ' αὖτε
ῥύσατ' ἐπ' Ὠκεανῷ χρυσόθρονον, οὐδ' ἔα ἵππους
ζεύγνυσθ' ὠκύποδας, φάος ἀνθρώποισι φέροντας,
[Λάμπον καὶ Φαέθονθ', οἵτ' Ἠῶ πῶλοι ἄγουσι].

If we suppose this last verse to be of the true 'Homeric' age, we must translate it according to the use of that age, and must take the poet to mean, what is perhaps not inconceivable or unnatural, that the car of the young Morning is drawn by a team of *foals*. But it is an obvious and more probable supposition, that the verse is a mere note, satisfying that passion for names to which poet-scholars were liable but bards were not, and that the author of the verse, using πῶλοι as synonymous with ἵπποι, simply betrays thereby his later date. To invent for this single passage a sense of πῶλος which *Iliad* and *Odyssey* combine to reject and disprove, is not permissible; and it remains therefore true that by the composers of these poems πῶλος *horse* was not used, which in the circumstances is equivalent to 'not known.'

If therefore in κλυτόπωλος, as used in the *Iliad*, πῶλος meant *horse*, it is a case of survival. We should have to assume that πῶλος had once borne this meaning, as it did again in later poetry, and that in the compound, as a traditional epithet, this sense held its ground, although the corresponding sense of the simple word had suffered in the age of 'Homer' an odd eclipse. Let us see whether the application of the compound admits this supposition.

That application is extremely peculiar. It is restricted not merely to Hades, but to Hades in one single phase and function, as receiver of the warrior's parting soul:—

'And for thee I say that slaughter and black Death shall come about here at my hands; vanquished by my spear, thou shalt yield to me my glory, and thy life to Hades *klytopōlos*'

εὖχος ἐμοὶ δώσειν, ψυχὴν δ' Ἄϊδι κλυτοπώλῳ[1].

Now when the poets so used κλυτόπωλος, surviving, *ex hypothesi*, from a time when it meant *of the goodly steeds*, of what sense in it, if any, were they conscious? Or could they use it traditionally, without any question of the sense? Surely not. They may have so used, and probably did, διάκτορος ἀργεϊφόντης, as a description of Hermes. But then these words, or rather names, were free, for them, from any connexion of etymology. They do not, on the face of them, signify anything in the Greek of Homer; they are not in appearance formed from any elements to which separately Homer gives a sense. But κλυτόπωλος is. Of one meaning in Homeric language it was manifestly capable: it could mean 'of the famous *foals*.' How then, unless the elements of the word were capable of some other meaning, should this meaning be ignored; or how could the compound continue to be used in a

[1] E 654, and similarly Λ 445, Π 625.

connexion where, in its natural meaning, it was plainly absurd? The epithet χρυσηλάκατος, 'of the golden *arrow*,' was retained by the Homeric poets in its traditional connexion with Artemis, although to them, by a restriction in the sense of ἠλακάτη, it had come to signify 'of the golden distaff' (δ 122, 131); because the new sense was in this connexion, though less appropriate, at least not impossible. And similar was the history of Ζεὺς τερπικέραυνος, transformed from the *hurler* of the thunder into the *delighter* in it. But when πῶλος *horse* had 'come to mean' *foal*, and *foal* only, then Ἀΐδης κλυτόπωλος, as an expression significant but now absurd, would naturally die. That it did not die is *prima facie* proof that it was not connected, and was not supposed to be, with the πῶλος which for Homer meant *foal*; and that in attributing to this πῶλος, by pure hypothesis, a use earlier than Homer, but for Homer extinct, in the sense of *horse*, we are on a wrong track.

Now in these circumstances it is instructive, and it should not be surprising, to find that, although to the Greeks of the classic and later times no other word πῶλος was known, as a term in use, except that which primarily meant *foal* and subsequently also *horse*, nevertheless among students of Homer the best tradition affirmed that the termination of κλυτόπωλος (Ἀΐδης) had an origin and meaning totally different. Aristarchus, according to several witnesses[1], connected it with πωλεῖσθαι, *to range, haunt, visit*. The explanations of the epithet which

[1] See note on p. 90.

the witnesses deduce from this etymology are certainly incredible, indeed preposterous. But this only goes to prove that the etymology itself, which they could not use, was not invented by them (nor by Aristarchus, if he is responsible for the explanations), but was a genuine inheritance from times when the language of the rhapsodists was not yet dead. And whether this was so or not, the etymology, as an etymology, is possible, correct, and Homeric. The verb *πωλέομαι* is Homeric, and to *πωλέομαι* the adjectival termination *-πωλος* stands in the same relation as *-πολος* (in *οἰοπόλος*, *τρίπολος*, *δικασπόλος*, *ἀμφίπολος*) to the parallel, cognate, and synonymous *πολέομαι*. Before therefore, in order to interpret *κλυτόπωλος*, we assume a sense of *-πωλος* which Homer does not warrant, we are bound to try whether, with or without the assistance of Aristarchus, we can interpret it by the warranted sense.

The truth appears to be, that the little group of Homeric adjectives in *-πωλος* (for *κλυτόπωλος* is not unique) are all connected not with *πῶλος* *foal*, and certainly not with *πῶλος* *horse*, to Homer a *vox nihili*, but with the root *πωλ-* *range*, which appears in *πωλέομαι*. The position in Homer of the nominal stem from this root, *πωλο-*, is exactly parallel to that of *πολο-*; that is to say, neither appears in Homer as an independent substantive, though *πόλος* had elsewhere in Greek a long and illustrious descent; and both appear in Homer as terminations in a group of compound adjectives. The particular use of *πωλέομαι* from which the most familiar of these adjectives originally came, is that which, as was indicated (according to the witnesses) by Aristarchus[1], survives in the compound ἐπιπωλέομαι, when connected with activity on the battle-field:—

αὐτὰρ ὁ τῶν ἄλλων ἐπεπωλεῖτο στίχας ἀνδρῶν 'then went he elsewhere ranging the warrior-ranks' (Λ 264). It refers to that rapid and incessant motion from place to place which, in the loose, desultory, and undisciplined method of Homeric fighting, made so large a part of the fighter's power and efficiency. When all depended, as it does in Homer, on catching your man in the instant of isolation or exposure, to be *quick of movement, nimble in range* was among the first of warlike qualities; and this is the quality which is claimed for the Phrygians (in general), when they are called αἰολόπωλοι (Γ 185, etc.), and for the Danaoi (in general), and the Myrmidons (in general), when they are called ταχύπωλοι. Even if it were legitimate and Homeric (which, let us repeat once more, it is not) to assume for these adjectives the element πῶλος *horse*, that assumption would still be excluded by the use of them. The men of Agamemnon and Achilles, as a class or people, could not possibly be known or noted for their *swift horses*; for with few exceptions they had no horses at all. But as fighters they are noted for their *quick range*, their nimble movements in the field.

From the same stem probably came ἐύπωλος, the

[1] See Ebeling *s.v.* κλυτόπωλος.—ὁ Ἀρίσταρχος ἐπὶ τοῦ κλυτοπώλῳ ἀκούει κλυτὴν ἐπιπόλησιν (*sic*) κ.τ.λ.

traditional epithet of *Ilios*, though here a doubt arises, which for ταχύπωλος and αἰολόπωλος is not entertainable. It is possible to derive εὔπωλος from πῶλος *foal*, and to connect it with the famous legend of the *twelve foals*, begotten by Boreas upon the mares of Erichthonios, son of Dardanos (Υ 220 foll.); and this we may even take to be so far true, as that the epithet, so interpreted, gave a likely suggestion for the legend. But that the legend produced the epithet is not likely, for then it would naturally have linked itself in poetic tradition with *Dardania*, which was the name of the place where the foals were born, and not with *Ilios*, which (according to the legend itself, Υ 216) did not then exist, but was built, according to the prevalent account, long after, for Laomedon son of Ilos. As a fact, though *Dardania* is ἐύπωλος in the *Lesser Iliad*, only *Ilios* is so called in the *Iliad* and *Odyssey*; nor is the legend required to account for the phrase Ἴλιος ἐύπωλος, which meant originally just 'Ilios, the pleasant haunt,' (from πωλο-, πωλέομαι, as οἰοπόλος χῶρος 'a solitary haunt') and signified, like ἐὺ ναιόμενος etc., that the place was 'good to visit' and 'good to frequent,' in short, a country agreeable for human habitation. And indeed the tradition of ancient scholarship preserved an obscure memory of this, when ἐύπωλος (see Ebeling, *s.v.*) was translated, not incorrectly, by εὔγεως 'a pleasant land,' and the like.

Apart from proper names, such as Ἐχέπωλος, which may mean anything or nothing, these are, I think, all the words in -πωλος which Homer supplies, except κλυτόπωλος itself. This, if it was really known and used by the poet or poets of the *Iliad*—we shall see presently the reason for the doubt—cannot be separated from αἰολόπωλος and ταχύπωλος. Hades, as κλυτόπωλος, must be 'Death, the famous *ranger* (of the battle-field)': and since, in fact, it is always the soul of the warrior slain upon the field which this Hades receives, the conception is one which we may well accept as, at any rate, a stage in the history of the phrase. Compared with the irrelevant and impossible *horses*, it is no less superior on the poetic side than on the linguistic. But it seems that we ought to look yet further.

For *first*, although from αἰολόπωλος and ταχύπωλος it is not hard so to interpret κλυτόπωλος, it was not perhaps equally natural and obvious upon these lines to invent it. Both αἰολο- and ταχυ- are terms of motion, like πωλο- itself. Not so κλυτο-, and the coalition is thus less easy. Nor have we a perfectly satisfactory analogy in εὔπωλος or οἰόπολος, which, strictly speaking, would justify only the rendering 'Death, famous for his haunt,' famous, that is, for the place which he *ranges* or *visits*, an idea neither so clear as might be wished, nor so much to the purpose. *Secondly*, how does it come about, that this 'famous ranger' of the field is never so described when the breadth and rapidity of his range would be illustrated by the circumstances, never in scenes of wide, swift massacre, such as are so often presented, but only at the side of the single fallen man, over whom his enemy stands exulting?

A 'fixed epithet' may be often misapplied, but it should scarcely be so always. These objections do nothing to help in the 'horses,' to which the second applies even more strongly than to the 'range'; indeed it is impossible, as I think, to explain why, if κλυτόπωλος had really referred to horses, it should never be linked by Homer to any of the numerous personages who are with him 'famous for horses,' and only to Hades, who, so far as appears, was not. But the objections justify a suspicion that we are not yet at the bottom of the matter; and since the capacities of πωλο- seem to be exhausted, it remains to see whether anything more can be made of κλυτο-, an examination which, as few Homeric words are more characteristic and important than κλυτός, will be interesting for its own sake.

In general the Epic use of κλυτός is simple and well defined.

(1) It is applied, according to the etymology, to persons, places, and the like, which are properly and literally 'heard of,' *famous, renowned.* So Agamemnon, Argos, etc., etc. Even in this class, however, it appears, upon a more careful inspection, that some selective feeling, not apparent in the etymology, has affected the choice of objects. Not all renowned persons are in fact κλυτοί, nor those chiefly, or indeed at all, who are most plainly renowned; females, for example, hardly ever, neither goddesses nor women, not Penelope, not Helen, though more 'famous,' one would think, than all the male sex together; of the gods some only, and those

repeatedly, but chosen, if 'fame' were the question, with strange caprice.

(2) What the selective principle is, by what association the word was attracted and confined, appears plainly in the *things*, the objects not capable of personification, to which it belongs. It is said or implied in *Lexica* that κλυτός *renowned* is extended in Homer to the general sense of *beauteous* or *goodly*; but this statement is so inexact as to be practically false. How ill such large and vague expressions correspond with Homeric feeling about the word, might appear sufficiently from the fact that Homer, using κλυτός incessantly, knows no such expression as, for example, κλυτὸς ἵππος. Even the limitation that 'Homer uses it especially of the works of human skill' (Liddell & Scott), though mainly true, is both too wide and too narrow. When the word does not mean simply and literally *renowned*, it is applied *solely* to works of art, or rather to works of *craft*, human or divine, and among works of craft almost exclusively to a small and peculiar class. *Arms* (and more rarely *clothes* in general) are everywhere κλυτά, κλυτὰ τεύχεα, κλυτὰ εἵματα; *houses* are everywhere κλυτά, κλυτὰ δώματα; and so are, here and there rarely, one or two other things of the same kind, that is to say, *products of craft which directly manifest the power, dignity, and security of the person by whom the craft is possessed or commanded.* The feeling which, whether known to the poets by observation or divined by imagination, the word expresses, is the

admiration, respect, and worship attaching, in the rudimentary stage of civilization, to *craft* and its possessors, to the empire of the metals, and the powers which depend upon it, good smith-work, good masonry, and good carpentry. That is why, with rare and dubious exceptions[1], *males* only are κλυτοί; why Ἥφαιστος (or Ἀμφιγυήεις) and Ἐννοσίγαιος (not *Poseidon* as such), who would be patrons, one of the smithy and the other, in his *subterranean* office, of the mine, are conspicuously κλυτοί; and lastly, why the instances of κλυτὰ τεύχεα (εἵματα) and κλυτὰ δώματα are more numerous than all other κλυτά together. So also the objects, when specified, by which persons are entitled to the epithet, are almost always works of craft, and apparently never products of nature: κλυτόεργος, κλυτοτέχνης, κλυτότοξος, ναυσίκλυτος, δουρίκλυτος. It is in later poetry, not in Homer, that we find such expressions as κλυτόδενδρος.

It is worth while, since this topic lies deep in the sources of Homeric feeling, to dwell for a moment upon the signal illustration of it offered by four pictures in the *Odyssey*, all intended to create wonder, and in a certain sense admiration: the dwellings of Calypso, of Circe, of the Phaeacians,

[1] Even the very rare examples of a feminine κλυτός are not beyond suspicion (Β 742, ε 422): κλυτή apparently does not occur, a significant fact. In ε 422 the unique κλυτὸς Ἀμφιτρίτη may be an error (suggested by κλυτὸς Ἐννοσίγαιος in the next line) for θεὸς Ἀμφιτρίτη or the like. In Β 742 it is easy to restore a masculine κλυτῷ, and to account for the corruption of it.

and of the Laestrygons. If κλυτός, to Homeric ears, had signified only that sentiment of vague and general admiration which belongs to the terms which we have to put for it, to *beauteous*, *noble*, *goodly*, *glorious* and the like, then, among these homes and their occupants, the epithet must belong plainly and conspicuously, though with some difference perhaps in the shade of it, to Calypso and to Circe; it must apply also to the Phaeacians, less strongly perhaps, but not much less; while to the Laestrygons it must be altogether refused. The abode of Calypso is painted as the very ideal of natural goodliness, that of Circe as consummate in the luxuries of magic, Phaeacia as exquisite in art; but the land of the Laestrygons, where was no tillage, 'no signs of the labour of men and oxen, only we saw the smoke curling upwards from the land,' is as dreary and repulsive as its people. But quite other, for Homer, are their claims to be κλυτοί. That is a matter not of beauty, but of craft. Calypso is not κλυτός, nor her cave, trees, waters, nor any of the fair things that belong to her. Neither (which might more surprise us) is Circe; no, not though she has a house, a true palace (κ 210 and *passim*), and that full of magnificent wonders. But this, if we have once felt the Homeric feeling about κλυτός, is intelligible enough and quite right. Magic may be superior to 'craft,' but it is not the same thing. Houses of men, and of gods too, when and because they are the works of craft, are κλυτὰ δώματα: but the chambers of a witch, who could create serving-maids out of the fountains and streams (κ 350), need not be the product of craft at all; and accordingly the δώματα Κίρκης, though mentioned repeatedly and adorned with various epithets (τετυγμένα, καλά, even ἱερά or *mystic*), receive not once the familiar and regular Homeric epithet κλυτά: nor does anything which the witch possesses. The Phaeacians upon the same principle are of course κλυτοί, and their works κλυτά, κλυτοί, ἀγάκλυτοι, and περίκλυτοι, themselves, their dress, houses, sanctuaries, etc., etc.; not because they are 'goodly,' but because they are in all things artists, and their dwelling-place full of wonderful art. For the Laestrygons and their works, though assuredly not 'goodly,' 'beautiful,' or attractive in any way, are κλυτοί and κλυτά no less, and indeed in this quality have a marked pre-eminence. The whole account of them and their country fills but 50 verses, as the Odyssean voyagers scarcely enter it and barely escape. Yet the epithet occurs three times (κ 87 λιμένα κλυτόν, 112 κλυτὰ δώματα, 114 κλυτὸν Ἀντιφατῆα), and is the first note, as it were, of Odysseus' impressions. And the reason, upon Homeric principles, is obvious. It is the 'artificial basin,' with its plumb walls and projecting piers of wrought stone, which excites this awe in the beholders, and in Odysseus a salutary fear. It is the 'smooth road' and the 'high buildings' (103, 111), and the formidable weapons (121, 124), which show that Antiphates, king of the Laestrygons, commands to a supreme degree the resources of craft, and therefore, though cannibal, is emphatically κλυτός. Indeed it seems more than probable that 'Fargate of the Laestrygons' is, or originally was, a picture coloured, if not drawn, from the report of some terrified mariners, who, trading from lands of pasture and agriculture, saw for the first time some place, on the Euxine, may be, where metal-work was practised on a large scale; a sort of black country, where 'the smoke went up from the land,' where the trolly, on paths of incredible facility, rolled down from the hills the wood for the furnace (κ 103), where shifts so extended the hours of labour that 'night and day near met in one[1],' and whence the visitor, roughly handled by the hard workmen and appalled by the signs of their skill and power, fled away to report that their figures were gigantic, and that they lived, like the Martians of Mr Wells' romance, on the flesh of men. Such at all events is in fact the Laestrygonian type; and it illustrates excellently the true Homeric sense of κλυτός, *grand*, *great*, a word for us not really translatable, but approximating in effect to *powerful* or rather *craftful*, implying awe rather than mere admiration, and from all such terms as *beauteous* or *goodly* to be sharply sundered and distinguished. The gracious life of Aeolus, and the hideous life of Antiphates, are passed alike in κλυτὰ δώματα (κ 60, 112), for this praise belongs to the

[1] κ 86. There is nothing inconsistent with this in the current suggestion, that the 'meeting of night and day' refers to the brief summer nights of the far north. It would be on the Euxine that a Greek would probably first hear a rumour of this phenomenon.

'brazen bulwark' and the 'sheer stone,' though it does not belong to the fairy's paradise nor to the witch's bower.

But against a general background of this shade, ascertained, as we must remember, by scores and scores of examples, three examples stand out in conspicuous disagreement, both with the general rule and with one another. Each offends against Homeric usage, and offends in a different way. They have long been observed for their peculiarity, and all receive special notice, for instance, from Liddell and Scott.

(1) Once, and once only, is broken the rule that natural things, products of nature, cannot be κλυτά. The *herds* of the Cyclops seem to be such (ι 308): καὶ τότε πῦρ ἀνέκαιε καὶ ἤμελγε κλυτὰ μῆλα.

(2) Once, and strangely, *mankind* as a whole seems to be a κλυτόν. When Sleep has done his errand for Hera, he departs ἐπὶ κλυτὰ φῦλ' ἀνθρώπων (Ξ 361).

(3) Once, most strangely of all, *the dead*, universally, seem to be κλυτοί or κλυτά. Odysseus, at the entrance of the lower world, must address his prayers to κλυτὰ ἔθνεα νεκρῶν (κ 526).

Now we have no right, until the severest scrutiny has shown that no other explanation is open, to assume, in the circumstances, that these three exceptions are genuine. The presumption against them is enormous. Take the first. The epic poets mention hundreds and hundreds of times domestic animals such as βόες, αἶγες, ἵπποι, κύνες, ὄϊες, μῆλα, αἰπόλια, etc., etc., and with many admiring epithets. The adjective κλυτός, expressing as it does a peculiarly characteristic feeling, is one of their favourite words. If such phrases as κλυτοὶ βόες, κλυτὰ μῆλα, had really been possible to their ears, what likelihood is there that we should be left with one single example? Why should the flocks of the Cyclops be selected for this praise, and what does it mean? To all the notions normally suggested by κλυτός, the life and manners of the Cyclops, a rude, easeful, sluttish simplicity without culture of any kind, present the extreme opposite. 'Celebrated' they were not, neither they nor anything of theirs, for they were cut off from the world and unknown; and as for their flocks, it does not appear that they differed from flocks in general. They are 'fat,' they are 'fleecy'; but how should they exhibit the greatness of *power* and *craft*? Expositors have felt this so strongly as even to suggest that κλυτά here should mean *noisy*, *loud*; but that is a counsel of desperation.

To call *mankind* or the *tribes of men* κλυτά is so far at least more intelligible, as the quality so predicated is proper to beings who are men or manlike. But it does not belong to the type of man. It is essentially a trait of superiority and dominion. We are told that here it indicates the superiority of mankind to the brutes. But why should this conception, than which surely none could be more alien from the general tone of the Epos, suddenly force itself upon the poet's mind, when contemplating mankind in a relation *essentially animal and common to the brutes*? In relation to *Sleep*, man is but a brute. Why, then, because visited by Sleep, should men excite, for this once, the peculiar admiration expressed by κλυτός, or indeed any admiration at all?

And *the dead*? The fame, lordliness, power, craft of the dead! They are the silent, strengthless, forgotten, the—all which κλυτοί are not. For though *Lexica* may say that this κλυτὰ ἔθνεα νεκρῶν refers to 'illustrious' dead, it does not refer to illustrious dead, but distinctly and expressly to 'all the dead' (κ 518), the dead in general, 'brides and grooms, long-laboured age and tender virginity' (λ 38). Perhaps nothing is more characteristic of the Epos than the absence and repudiation of all ideas attributing power and ability to the dead. They are essentially helpless and craftless, and, if they may ever recover activity for a time, can do so only by aid and gift of the living; and their intercourse with Odysseus on this occasion is especially impressed with that conception. Why then should they here for once be κλυτά, and in what sense?

In short, these passages are not explicable, and the presumption is that they are erroneous; a presumption hard indeed to prove, but not incapable of proof. Suppose that the error were the same in all three. Suppose there were a word which, while scarcely distinguishable from κλυτός, fitted each of the three unconnected contexts, and supplied in each a fresh point. Could it be reasonably doubted, that this word, and not κλυτός, was the word employed? Such a word is κλῐτός, *couched, lying down,* the participial adjective from κλῐ- *to couch,* related to κεκλῐμένος *couched* as χῠτός, φθῐτός, and many other words of this poetic and archaic type, to κεχῠμένος, ἐφθῐμένος and the rest. The flocks of the Cyclops, though not otherwise miraculous or marvellous, are remarkable in this, that *they share at night the home of their master.* It is the first thing that we hear of them; 'we saw a cave...near to the sea, and there many flocks and herds were used to sleep. And about it a high outer court was built with stones...... And a man was wont to sleep therein, of monstrous size, who shepherded his flocks alone and afar,' and so on (ι 182). The males lay usually in the yard, but the females, 'all that he milked,' actually within the cave (*ib.* 237), the filthiness of which is noted with epic simplicity (*ib.* 329); and the Cyclops lay among them, κεῖτ' ἔντοσθ' ἄντροιο τανυσσάμενος διὰ μήλων (*ib.* 298); and these arrangements, it will be remembered, are of the first importance, not only to the colour of the tale, but to the incidents. It is therefore natural and to the purpose, that the narrator, his mind full of this picture, should describe how at morning, after Odysseus' first night there, the giant 'kindled the fire and milked his *couchéd* flocks' (πῦρ ἀνέκαιε καὶ ἤμελγε κλιτὰ μῆλα, *ib.* 308), those, that is, who shared his bed, the word, more man-like than beast-like, glancing aptly at his beast-like habits. And it may be observed, that in the evenings, when the beasts have not been 'couched,' it is not the κλιτὰ μῆλα who are milked, but 'the ewes and bleating she-goats' (*ib.* 244, 341).

So, again, very properly Sleep, when he has finished the special employment for which he was summoned to Olympus by Hera, departs 'to the couches of mankind' (ᾤχετ' ἐπὶ κλιτὰ φῦλ' ἀνθρώπων); returns, that is to say, to his ordinary sphere and business. Where else should his visits be paid but to 'them that lie down'?

And among those that sleep, couch, and lie down, one class in particular receive the name, in Homeric language as in all others, specially and distinctively, those that have lain down for ever, κλιτὰ ἔθνεα νεκρῶν, the 'tribes of the couchèd dead.'

Now one of two things: either the exact and varied applicability of the word κλιτός to these three occasions, selected upon other grounds and without reference to such applicability, is accidental, or it proves that κλιτός was indeed the word there used. For myself, I hold the first alternative to be fantastically impossible, and therefore embrace the second, taking it as certain that the epic poets had a word κλιτός *couched*, which was liable (this is obviously true) to be confused with the homophonous κλυτός, and being archaic in type and replaced in later language by other equivalents, has actually given way to κλυτός and disappeared. It was still alive and known when these parts of the *Iliad* and *Odyssey* were composed; and we shall do well to consider whether we can trace it later.

As to the phrase from the *Iliad*, κλυτὰ φῦλ' ἀνθρώπων, we have some interesting evidence in the 'Pythian' part of the *Hymn to Apollo*, an imitative composition dating probably from the sixth century, later at any rate than the Epos in general, and bearing many marks of its lateness. Here we read, when Pytho is being recommended to Apollo for the site of his future oracle (270), 'There no fair chariots shall go the round, nor shall there be noise of swift-foot steeds about the fair-built altar; yet to that privacy (καὶ ὣς) *the great peoples of men* (ἀνθρώπων κλυτὰ φῦλα) may bring gifts to Ié-paion, and thou with glad heart mayst receive the fair victims of men that dwell around (περικτιόνων ἀνθρώπων).' And again, the monster snake of Pytho 'did many a mischief among *the great peoples of men*' who came to the place as builders and worshippers (355). 'Whoever met her, became the prey of his fate.' And again, 'All sacrifices,' says Apollo (537), 'that *the great peoples of men* (περικλυτὰ φῦλ' ἀνθρώπων) shall bring to me.' It is clear that the ear of this author had been caught, as well it might be, by the expression in this form, with κλυτά; and he treats it exactly as traditional phrases from our own archaic and consecrated literature, sometimes no better founded or more significant, are dealt with by our own poets and preachers. He does his best, that is, to accommodate it with a proper context and meaning. With this purpose, he has changed the sense of φῦλ' ἀνθρώπων. In the *Iliad* this means of course simply *mankind*, the human *species*, as φῦλα θεῶν means *gods*, and φῦλα γυναικῶν *the female sex*. But in the *Hymn*, conformably to later use, φῦλα means *peoples*, *nations*, the inhabitants of that earth of which Pytho was supposed the centre. And further, since it is for the glory of the god that these *tribes* are brought into view, the epithet κλυτά *great*, *grand*, *mighty*, has at least so much reflected propriety as is sufficient for a consecrated formula. It is plain therefore that into this phrase, by the sixth century, κλυτά had already obtruded itself, though whether this was the form in which the phrase first attached itself to the worship of Delphi (or rather Pytho), is not so clear. There is reason to think (see Euripides, *Iph. Taur.* 1262) that there, as at other sanctuaries of oracular and medicinal deities, prescriptions were once sought by the method of *sleeping* in the sacred precinct, and communicated by dreams. The appearance, in connexion with the gifts which the ἀνθρώπων φῦλα were to bring, of the name *Paion*, of the *snake*, and of the need for *quiet*, bears a strong suggestion of this Asclepian usage, and of κλιτὰ φῦλ' ἀνθρώπων, *couched* or *sleeping men*, as the primitive form belonging to it.

However in the sixth century κλυτὰ φῦλ' ἀνθρώπων somewhere certainly, and perhaps therefore in the *Iliad*, had established itself. But in the *Odyssey* κλιτὰ μῆλα not κλυτὰ (and probably therefore also κλιτὰ ἔθνεα νεκρῶν) might still be read a century later. For Sophocles read it, and copied it in this passage of the *Aias* (372):—

ὢ δύσμορος, ὃς χερὶ μὲν
μεθῆκα τοὺς ἀλάστορας, ἐν δ' ἑλίκεσσι
βουσὶ καὶ κλιτοῖς πεσὼν αἰπολίοις
ἐρεμνὸν αἷμ' ἔδευσα.

'Wretch that I am, who suffered the accursed men to slip through my hands, but fell on coilèd kine and couchèd flocks, and made their dark blood flow!' That he has here in mind the Homeric phrase, there can be little doubt, but that he read and wrote **κλυτὰ, κλυτοῖς**, is not easily credible. Even if such expressions as **κλυτὰ αἰπόλια**, 'fine herds,' had been familiar to the Epos (where in fact nothing of the sort ever occurs), they would still not have been suitable for transplanting into the style of Sophocles. Largely as the Attic dramatists use the Epic vocabulary, especially of course in lyrics, it is not their habit (unless I am mistaken) to adopt from the Epos the conventional simplicity of its 'fixed epithets'; nor do they use Epic words without regard to the changes and restrictions of meaning, which they had since undergone. As an example of the first point we may note, that this seems to be the sole appearance in Attic drama, perhaps in any poetry not professedly imitating the Epic, of ἕλικες βόες. And the second point is well illustrated by the Sophoclean use of κλυτός itself. The use of it in Homer, as we have seen, is strongly affected and limited by a special association which, so far as we can trace, has little to do with the etymology. In Sophocles, on the other hand, the special, archaic feeling and significance are naturally lost; the etymology recovers its hold; and κλυτός means simply *glorious, famous* in the strict sense. Thus in *Oed. Tyr.* 172 the fruits of the earth (κλυτᾶς χθονός) are her *glory*, and spoils are *glorious* in *Ai.* 177. It is the same, generally speaking, in Pindar, with whom, as might be expected, the word *famous* is a favourite[1]. It seems, then, strange that Sophocles should introduce κλυτός here in some vague sense which, even if it were Homeric, would still not be Sophoclean, inasmuch as it is irrelevant to the context and the thing described. There seems not to be, either in the nature of the beasts which the Greek army had collected for food, or in the situation of Ajax, any reason why he should speak of them with admiration. But there is much reason why he should speak of them as *couched* or *sleeping*, for he had massacred them *in the night*, an addition to their helplessness and his disgrace.

It will be noticed that ἑλίκεσσι βουσί is translated above by 'coiléd kine,' as if parallel to '*couchéd* flocks.' I believe that it is, or at least that Sophocles so intended; but this supposition is not necessary to a preference for κλιτοῖς over κλυτοῖς. In Homer ἕλικες βόες, whatever the first word signified or had

[1] Pind. *Pyth.* 9. 39 ὁσία κλυτὰν χέρα οἱ προσενεγκεῖν, ἦ ῥα; καὶ ἐκ λεχέων κεῖραι μελιαδέα ποίαν; is hardly explicable by this sense of κλυτός, or indeed by any other. That Apollo should speak, in this connexion, of his κλυτὰν χέρα, *glorious* or *famous* hand, has not been proved intelligible; and I believe that Pindar said κλιτὰν χέρα (from κλιτής, and equivalent to κλίνουσαν) with a meaning natural and obvious. Aeschylus and Euripides scarcely use κλυτός at all, and throw no light upon it.

signified, practically means no more than *kine*, and Sophocles might have borrowed it bodily in this sense. What was the true, original sense is a question so remotely connected with our subject, that it cannot be treated here otherwise than summarily. It is clear (see for example Ebeling *s.v.*) that the Graeco-Roman scholars had no information on the point, and were justly dissatisfied with their guesses. The conditions apparently are (1) that the word should describe some bovine characteristic, universal and obvious; and (2) that it should be deducible from the notion *curling*, *curled*, *curled up*, *coiled*, for ἕλιξ exhibits this sense, and no other, with peculiar distinctness in all Greek from Homer downwards. Indeed it is scarcely too much to say, upon the facts, that to a Greek ear ἕλιξ cannot have conveyed anything else, and the question really is, Why did the Epos speak of *kine* as *curled* or *coiled*? The bovine *horn* (one interpretation) is *not* universally and specifically ἕλιξ, nor, if it were, would it make the beast such; its *hair* is not more ἕλιξ than that of many other animals, nor so much; and its 'rolling' or rather swinging *gait*, due mainly to the great bulk of the body in proportion to the supports, is not ἕλιξ at all, for the word describes *shape*, not movement, and the equivocal 'rolling' is an illegitimate bridge. The alleged rolling or turning of the feet might explain εἰλίποδες, but not ἕλικες: nor can I think it likely, whatever may be the scientific truth, that herdsmen and poets would have chosen a mark which, as anyone may prove by watching, is, in the common, slow motions of the creature, to say the least, not conspicuous. It remains however very probable that the two standing epithets εἰλίποδες and ἕλικες are in some way connected. Is it possible —I put it only as a suggestion, which in any case, I believe, was favoured by Sophocles—that both were derived from the *couchant* posture, and pointed to the beast's manner and inveterate habit of *lying down*? Certainly nothing is more obviously characteristic, both the thing and the way of it. Whether a cow 'tucks up its feet,' when it lies, more completely than a sheep or goat, I cannot say, but from the bulk of its body it seems to do so. It will often look, from a little distance, as if it had no legs at all. In stepping also, the curl of its lifted fore-leg is, for some reason, very conspicuous. And, as every one knows, it is always 'tucking up' and remaining 'tucked up' for hours together. Now the prefix εἰλι- points to a *curling up* as well as to a *rolling along*, perhaps more naturally. It seems therefore not impossible that εἰλίποδες originally meant this, and that ἕλικες βόες, *coiled kine*, described the same thing from a slightly different point of view. Probably the epic poets scarcely felt in ἕλικες any separate significance at all; but we can less easily suppose this of Sophocles and his Athenian audience, who, if they took the view here propounded, had a case for it as students of Homer, and an excellent defence for the combination of ἕλικες βόες with κλιτὰ αἰπόλια.

Returning now to our theme, we have it, as the

result of this long excursion, that the Epic vocabulary contained the word κλιτός, overlaid in script, as might be expected, by the familiar κλυτός, which indeed may be called a mis-spelling of it. Like hundreds of other words, like most words of its class, it disappeared from the fully developed language, leaving relics in the grammarians' ἑτερόκλιτος, ἐγκλιτικός, in ἔκκλιτος *avoidable* (Photius), and perhaps elsewhere. A traditional κλυτόπωλος is therefore ambiguous between these letters and κλιτόπωλος. Now we have seen already that κλιτός *couched* was a description proper to *sleepers* and to *the dead*, and further that it was applied to sleepers as receiving the visits of the personified Sleep. But further it can be shown that πωλο- (πωλέομαι) was a proper term for the *haunts* or *visits* of such personages as *Sleep* and *Death*; for it is applied by Aeschylus to those of their kinsman the *Dream*. 'Visions of the night, coming ever to my maiden chamber' (αἰεὶ γὰρ ὄψεις ἔννυχοι πωλεύμεναι ἐς παρθενῶνας τοὺς ἐμούς...) says the Aeschylean Io (*P. V.* 672), adopting, as the archaic form shows, the language of some more ancient poet. Combining these elements, we have, in Hades κλιτόπωλος (*quasi* ὁ παρὰ κλιτοὺς πωλούμενος), Death *who frequenteth the fallen, who visiteth them that lie down*, whose *haunt* is among such. For the form of the compound we may compare ἄγραυλος (ὁ ἐν ἀγροῖς αὐλιζόμενος), ἀνδρόστροφος (ὁ ἐπ' ἄνδρας στρεφόμενος), Ἁιδοφοίτης (ὁ φοιτῶν παρὰ τὸν Ἅιδην), δικασπόλος (ὁ πολούμενος εἰς δίκας), etc. And since, when Death visits a person living, it is for the soul that he comes, it is natural that he should never appear as κλιτόπωλος except in the act of receiving it.

As for κλυτόπωλος, it may have existed in the Epos in the only sense there possible[1], *famous for foals*, but there is no proof of it. It might perhaps have been an epithet for *Dardania*, and it appears as such in one of the 'Lives of Homer,' but with ἐύπωλον (already discussed) as a variant. But in truth it was not with such things as *foals* (or *horses*) that κλυτός was associated by genuinely Homeric minds, and the balance of likelihood is against their having known κλυτόπωλος at all. To later poets it was perfectly natural, and in the sense *famous for horses*. Pindar (fr. 289) applies it in this sense to Poseidon, but whether he got it from his own invention, from Homer, or elsewhere there is nothing to show.

With the disappearance from Homer of Hades κλυτόπωλος disappears all reason (see Dr Leaf on E 654, 2nd edn) for thinking that by the Greeks, or at any rate by Homeric Greeks, Death and the Horse were associated. That Hades the god, like any other great personage, might use horses upon a suitable

[1] The only sense, that is, in which the word could have been originally and deliberately invented. The reading Ἄιδι κλυτοπώλῳ, with the explanation 'Death the ranger,' must, I should think, go back, as an alternative, to the fifth century at least, and may even, as an alternative, be 'Homeric.' But invention does not account wholly for its origin, which requires the co-operation of accident.

occasion, as for example to carry off Persephoné, goes without saying; but he was not thought, so far as appears, to use them much; and at all events between them and his function as Death, the Homeric imagination had not established any connexion. It is doubtful (but that is beyond our scope) whether the Greek imagination ever did.

THE PAEANS OF PINDAR AND OTHER NEW LITERATURE

(*Oxyrhynchus Papyri*, Part V[1].)

In the latest gift from Oxyrhynchus, lovers of great literature, and especially of poetry, have no contemptible portion. The recovered MS. of Pindar, comprising poems to be classed more or less certainly as paeans, has indeed sustained such damage that, in what the editors have made legible, much must be regarded as material for the student rather than as food for the reader. But there remain several passages which display the author (whose identity is established beyond question) in an aspect both characteristic and novel.

The impression we receive is that in this class of poem, composed for public ceremonies and upon public commission, Pindar must have been at least as successful as in the *Epinicia*, where (it is possible to think) the magnificence and the enthusiasm are sometimes imperfectly supported by the importance of the occasion, as it would be estimated by the

[1] Edited, with translations and notes, by Bernard P. Grenfell, D.Litt., etc., and Arthur S. Hunt, D.Litt., etc. London: Egyptian Exploration Fund, 1908.

average standards of human sentiment. No such objection, at all events, can be laid against a hymn composed for the citizens of Abdera, to celebrate their gratitude for the successful labour of past generations, which had carved out a home of Hellenic life in the rich but inhospitable barbarism of Thrace, their loyalty to the federal bond which, under the mighty direction of Athens, had given new security and opened new prospects to their enterprise, and their common resolve to be worthy of such a tradition and such opportunities.

The remains of this Ode, the second in orde among the seven of which comprehensible portions have been recovered, exhibit at least one passage which is a notable addition to our store of Greek poetry, and not less interesting as a document of Greek religion. A careful examination of this will perhaps be more profitable to students of literature than a description of the papyrus at large. It happens also that the finders and editors, whose work in both capacities we cordially appreciate, have here, unless we mistake, left an opening larger than usual, not merely for correction or supplement of details, but for general exposition of the theme and the purpose.

'Whatsoever is planted in prudence and respect (αἰδώς) grows ever happily in a gentle calm.

'And this gift may Heaven give us.

'Yet, for those that are long since dead, envy and the malice thereof are past and gone; and to his fathers a man should in duty bring an ample share of praise.

'They, having won by war a country of wealthy dower, planted prosperity firm, beyond the wild Paeonians and the land of Strymon, strong breeder of warriors.

'Yet upon their haste descended a sudden fate (?), which when they had borne, the gods thereafter aided accomplishment.

'Bright in the blaze of eulogy stands he by whom a glorious thing is achieved; but upon *those*, our fathers, fell—the light supreme, in front of Melamphyllon, facing the foe;

'(Ho, Paean, ho, for the Healer, and may he never cease from us!)

'Yet, when they came to the River, and close thereby, that host, so few in arms, were to meet with a numerous host. It was the first of the month when this befell; and these were messengers from kind Hecate, Maid of the red foot, showing the tale of the folk, who were fain to come to birth[1].'

τὸ δ' εὐβου-
λίᾳ τε καὶ αἰδοῖ
ἐγκείμενον αἰεὶ θάλλει μαλακαῖς εὐδίαις.
καὶ τὸ μὲν διδότω
θεός· ὁ δ' ἐχθρὰ νοήσαις
ἤδη φθόνος οἴχεται
τῶν πάλαι προθανόντων,
χρὴ δ' ἄνδρα τοκεῦσιν φέρειν
βαθύδοξον αἶσαν.

ἐπ. τοὶ σὺν πολέμῳ κτησάμενοι
χθόνα πολύδωρον, ὄλβον
ἐγκατέθηκαν πέραν ἀ[γρίων Παιόνων]

[1] *Oxyrh. Pap.* v, p. 29; Poem II (*For the citizens of Abdera*), *vv.* 50 ff.

αἰχματᾶν [τε Στρυμονίας γᾶ]ς
ζαθέας τροφοῦ· ἀλλὰ [θοὰ θοοῖς]
ἐπέπεσε μοῖρα· τλάντων δ'
ἔπειτα θεοὶ συνετέλεσσαν.
ὁ δὲ καλόν τι πονήσαις
εὐαγορίαισιν φλέγει·
κείνοις δ' ὑπέρτατον ἦλθε φέγγος
ἄντα δυσμενέων Μελαμ-
φύλλου προπάροιθεν·—
ἰήϊε παιάν, ἰήϊε· παιὰν
δὲ μήποτε λείποι—

στρ. ἀλλά μιν ποταμῷ σχεδὸν μολόντα φύρσει
βαιοῖς σὺν ἔντεσιν
ποτὶ πολὺν στρατόν· ἒν[1] δὲ μηνὸς
πρῶτον τύχεν ἆμαρ·
ἄγγελλε δὲ φοινικόπεζα λόγον παρθένος
εὐμενὴς Ἑκάτα
τὸν ἐθέλοντα γενέσθαι.

The text here, as generally wherever the MS. is legible, seems to be good and indeed almost faultless. Except in the places indicated, the supplements of the editors are minute and obvious, and I have adopted their readings, all but one. In the fifth verse of the epode (63) they give *ἆλλα* [*δ' ἄγοισά τοι*], which is possible, but in the word *τοι* perhaps not very satisfactory. However, the doubt is insignificant: whatever we should read, the sense of this clause is plain. What is not so plain is the connexion of the whole, and that we are now to consider.

The singers are praising their progenitors or predecessors, the founders of the colony, whose flourishing state they themselves enjoy. The topic,

[1] For ἐόν, ὄν: see Editors' note.

as possibly invidious and provoking to the Powers, is approached with the habitual wariness of the Greek. Even prudence (they say) may, and should, be liberal in praise of those whom death has removed from jealousy[1]. And in pursuance of the same precaution, as well as from a sense of justice, those especially are chosen for praise whose contribution to the work was not a triumph but a sacrifice, the loss of their lives in a temporary disaster, bravely sustained and eventually, but by others, redeemed. Those who in some sense failed, deserve praise not less, and need it more, because, as the poet finely says, the successful man has the blaze of his success. Such a disaster had arrested, as we here learn, the establishment or development of Abdera. 'Before Melamphyllon'—name of sad sound yet beautiful, which Pindar uses with characteristic skill—there came upon the victims of the day no blaze indeed of triumph, but the light, both *last* and *highest*, of a patriot's death, ὑπέρτατον φέγγος, *summa lux*, as it is called with tender ambiguity.

So far all is clear. But in the sequel the connexion is less obvious, and the editors do not seem to have found it. The sentence—

> ἀλλά μιν ποταμῷ σχεδὸν μολόντα φύρσει
> βαιοῖς σὺν ἔντεσιν
> ποτὶ πολὺν στρατόν—

they translate thus: 'But they shall put him to

[1] βαθύδοξον αἶσαν (58) is equivalent to βαθεῖαν αἶσαν δόξης.—'The descendant should himself carry to [the ancestors] the praise of a nobly spent life,' Edd. Papyri, citing *Nem.* vi. 46 ἐπεί σφιν κ.τ.λ.; but this seems less simple and appropriate.

confusion when he has come near the river, matched with a small army against a great host'; and upon this version, which plainly cannot be a continuation of the preceding story, they remark: 'The future indicative in φύρσει seems unintelligible, except on the view that these three lines give the substance of an ancient oracle.' The fulfilment of this oracle, we are to understand, is indicated in the next words, ἐν δὲ μηνὸς πρῶτον τύχεν ἆμαρ, translated by, 'It fell out on the first day of the month[1].'

But is this explanation acceptable? Is it possible that the passage, if so meant, could ever have been understood? It is not suggested that the supposed quotation verbally follows the alleged oracle, which, as the editors say upon the suggestion of Prof. Blass, would naturally run in hexameters. Nothing in the context, or in the sentence itself, indicates that the story is dropped, and that we are suddenly carried to a new subject and a new speaker. The former subject, that of the fight at Melamphyllon, is by no means plainly finished; on the contrary we expect, after the parenthetic appeal to 'the Healer,' that the theme will be resumed and carried on to a happy or consolatory termination. In these circumstances, how could the quotation be apprehended as such? Nor is

[1] Rather, 'It was the first of the month (when this befell).' The difference, though small, is not quite immaterial. See hereafter.—The schol. to *v.* 77, προέλεγεν τ[ὴν] μέλλ[ουσαν μάχην] τοῖς ἡμετέροις, as given by the editors, points to a prophecy of the battle; but the essential words are a supplement, and rightly marked as doubtful. In any case the note could not be conclusive; the scholia are often plainly wrong.

it explained how the interpretation leads to the sequel, and to the mention of Hecate and her 'message.' Was this message the oracle? It seems hard to suppose so, or to make out, on these lines, any continuity of thought. We demur, therefore, to the hypothesis of a quotation, as neither warranted nor useful.

All must be the words of Pindar and part of the story, and must relate to the same subject as the preceding, the fight at Melamphyllon, and, in particular, those who fell there. Nor does the future (φύρσει) make any difficulty. The future is of that kind which may be called 'historical,' and is equally admissible in English, when a narrator desires that the hearer should approach a certain event with something of the feeling which it aroused in the actors at the time, and should view the event as a surprise. 'When the host comes to the river, certain things *will* occur' means (in a story) that they did occur, but that we are to approach them in imagination along with the host[1]. Nor need we make any mystery about the unexpressed subject of the verb φύρσει. It is ποταμός, supplied from ποταμῷ. No other can be supplied, and this presents itself naturally[2]. An ordinary writer, a prose-writer or a

[1] In English, under such circumstances, we generally use the 'past future,' and say that the things 'were to' happen; Greek, which habitually narrates in the present tense (historical), naturally uses (as we also can do) the simple future.

[2] It is conceivable that Pindar *wrote* ποταμὸς (not ποταμῷ) leaving the *dative* to be supplied, a more common arrangement, but this supposition is not at all necessary. The arrangement actually given is both correct and clear.

poet less bold than Pindar, would no doubt have made the 'host' the subject of the sentence, writing it somewhat thus: ἀλλὰ παρὰ ποταμῷ σχεδὸν μολὼν μίξεται στρατὸς βαιὸς πολλῷ στρατῷ (or πρὸς πολὺν στρατόν), 'near by the river, the small host, when it arrives, will meet with a great one.' This common form Pindar characteristically varies and embroiders. First he personifies the river, ποταμὸς μίξει στρατὸν πρὸς στρατόν, 'the river will bring one host to the other'—thereby lifting the style, and at the same time indicating that the juncture or meeting will occur 'close to' the river indeed, but after the coming host shall have passed it. Next, for the familiar μίγνυσθαι (μιγνύναι), so freely used for *meet*, *encounter*, even in prose, that it had lost colour and force as a figure, he substitutes the synonymous, but not familiar, φύρειν: the river will *interfuse* (instead of 'join') one host with the other. Such freshening and strengthening of a metaphor is among the chief and most frequent marks of his manner. Lastly, to avoid the commonplace antithesis στρατὸν βαιὸν πρὸς πολὺν στρατόν, he develops στρατὸν βαιόν into στρατὸν μολόντα βαιοῖς σὺν ἔντεσι, and for στρατόν puts an anticipatory pronoun, μιν, which is afterwards interpreted by relation to the antithetic πρὸς πολὺν στρατόν. This last point, the use of the pronoun, is the only point in which the structure of the sentence presents obscurity; and even this is smoothed in Greek by a peculiarity of the language, which in English cannot be reproduced,—the ambiguous number of μιν, representing both singular and plural. As placed here, it must naturally be taken first as plural (*them*), referring to the plural (κείνοις *v.* 68) of the preceding sentence. Thus, when heard, it explains itself, and in the sense intended. The effect could be represented in prose by ἀλλ' αὐτούς, βαιὸν στρατὸν μολόντα, μίξει ὁ ποταμὸς πρὸς πολὺν στρατόν. But the fact that the actual form, μιν, can also in meaning be singular, makes easy to the ear the transition to μολόντα, the case of which is determined by στρατόν, afterwards supplied. English, being incapable of this phonetic accommodation, cannot with convenience reproduce the sentence verbally. The sense we may represent thus: 'But close by the river, when they arrive, this host so few in arms will, at the passing, meet a numerous host.' *They* means, as shown by the context, the dead of Melamphyllon; the description of them as 'few in arms' suggests that in that disaster the small force of the nascent Abdera was wholly or nearly destroyed. *Them* therefore, the dead, we follow, as directed by the future tense, to see what further befell them after their death.

Where then, we are next to ask, did this 'meeting' take place, and whom did the warriors meet? The story answers both questions. It was 'by the River,'—by *the* River, which in such a connexion needs neither name nor description, and indeed has no universally accepted name, though it is known without name in the religious poetry of all times and peoples, not least in our own:

> "Part of the host have crossed the flood,
> And part are crossing now."

It is the River of Death[1], the boundary between the seen world and the unseen, and the passage into that other. By this water the fallen warriors were carried to their meeting, on the further shore, with a multitude far exceeding their little number. And this multitude were not, as we might for a moment suppose, their ancestors and predecessors, but, as we are immediately told, their successors and descendants, those who 'were fain to be born.' The conception assumes and depends upon the doctrine which is used, with the same consolatory purpose, in the Sixth *Aeneid.* In the other world, the world of the dead, dwell and may be seen not only the souls that have lived, but also those which are to be born and live hereafter. Indeed the distinction of the two classes is rather one of stage and condition than of personal identity, if as Virgil declares and Pindar may here imply[2], the same soul passes through successive births. At all events, there they are and may be seen, the souls that are destined and desire to be born. And as Anchises saw and showed to Aeneas with delight the many and mighty forms of the future Romans, so did the warriors who had given their lives for Abdera, see with joy and consolation the 'many' that were to be,—the host of

[1] Anonymous, as here, and with great advantage to the effect, in Homer, *Il.* 23. 72: the ghost of Patroclus says τῆλέ με εἴργουσι ψυχαί, εἴδωλα καμόντων, | οὐδέ μέ πω μίσγεσθαι ὑπὲρ ποταμοῖο ἐῶσιν—a passage which, by μίσγεσθαι, may have suggested Pindar's φύρσει.

[2] There is perhaps a suggestion of this in the phrase τὸν ἐθέλοντα γενέσθαι, which may refer to the preparation by which, according to Virgil, the soul is led to desire the renewal of life.

future Abderites, among them doubtless the singers of Pindar's paean, for whose happy lives their sacrifice had prepared the way.

Nor had they to wait for this consolation until, like Aeneas, they had reached some secret Elysium, some inner place in the spectral territory, where the future souls habitually dwelt. 'Close by the River' it was, and 'at their arrival,' that the great host met them—a special favour this from Hecate, Queen of that Realm. For it happened that the new-comers had a special claim to the favour of Hecate, the *diva triformis*, Lady of Birth and of Death, and Lady of the Moon, *Proserpina*, *Luna*, *Diana*. The day of Melamphyllon chanced to be 'the first of the month,' the day sacred to Hecate in her lunar aspect. Therefore the Queen, in honour of the day, graciously sent[1] the future souls to meet them, as her messengers, and to show 'the number that were fain to be born,' the great and prosperous population by which their own small number was to be happily replaced.

Here again, in the words *ἄγγελλε λόγον τὸν ἐθέλοντα γενέσθαι*, we have a characteristic specimen of Pindar's pregnant phrase. In λόγος there is the same ambiguity as in the English *tale*. It means both *number* and *story*, as λέγω is either *count* or *relate*. Here, by reference to πολὺν *many*, *numerous*, it means primarily *number*, and is a poetical synonym

[1] Note the imperfect tense of ἄγγελλε, marking that the message is coincident with the coming of the 'great host,' and is another aspect of it,—'Hecate *was thereby sending* a message.'

for ἀριθμός. But the connexion with ἄγγελλε also imports the more common meaning, *story*. The future souls were not only to show their number, but also to tell their destinies, as the destinies of Rome and of the Roman souls are told by Anchises to Aeneas. And to suit the latter sense, λόγον τὸν ἐθέλοντα γενέσθαι is written boldly for λόγον (ἀριθμόν) τὸν τῶν ἐθελόντων γενέσθαι, 'the number of those that would be born.' The word ἐθέλοντα, *fain, wishing*, applies literally to the multitude, the souls, who were eager for the life they were to enjoy, but to the 'story' applies in figure only, as a poetical equivalent for μέλλοντα.

The allusion to the date of Melamphyllon, 'the first of the month,' might suggest that the ode was intended for performance on the anniversary of the battle. But the inference would be doubtful. More probably that day was black in the calendar of Abdera, and celebrated, if at all, by offices of mourning. But in a paean, this and all topics are to be turned to the purpose of joy, comfort, and gratitude, as Pindar very happily does. The fallen heroes, *because of the day*, received instant assurance of the prospect since realized, by which their heroism was repaid. And to signify this transition, the cheering refrain, 'Oh Healer, oh the Healer! Never may He cease from us!' is introduced between the sorrow and the consolation.

To Hecate is given the epithet φοινικόπεζα, which the editors render by 'rosy-footed.' They remark that it is applied to Demeter in *Ol.* vi 94, where the epithet has been supposed...to refer to the red colours of harvest; but no such allusion can be claimed in the case of Hecate, and no doubt in both passages the adjective is used, like ῥοδόπηχυς, of personal charms only.

That 'harvest' is irrelevant we must agree, and indeed it is scarcely admissible in the place cited, where 'red-footed Demeter' is associated with Hecate 'her daughter of the white steeds.' But neither there nor here is it apparent why the 'personal charms' of the goddesses should be noticed, nor is φοινικο- (*red, crimson*) quite the same thing as ῥοδο- (*rosy*), nor is it certain that the foot itself has the colour; it may be a sandal or foot-gear of some kind with which both the Mother and the Maid, in certain aspects, were represented or invested. As to the meaning of the symbol, nothing precise seems provable either from *Ol.* vi 94 or from the paean; but a happy significance would suit that place, and in the paean seems to be required.

This passage, on the meeting of the spectral hosts, is, I think, the most interesting, from a poetical point of view, in the new Pindar. It is one of the longest fragments intact, and appears to include everything necessary to comprehension. Earlier in the same poem (p. 27, ii 24), we have a piece which exhibits the poet in a vein perhaps without example in the *Epinicia*. The City of Abdera speaks for itself, and with the joyful gaiety befitting a 'youthful' town. 'My home is the land of Thrace, rich in vines and in corn. May my increasing age hereafter not fail to stand secure! Young as I am, I have been a mother to her from whom my own mother came, when the fire of the foe had smitten her.'

> νεόπολίς εἰμι· ματρὸς
> δὲ ματέρ' ἐμᾶς ἔτεκον ἔμπαν
> πολεμίῳ πυρὶ πλαγεῖσαν.

The allusion, explained by a marginal note and sufficiently obvious, is to the burning of Athens by the Persians: from Athens came the colonizers of Teos, and from Teos was founded Abdera. The restoration of Athens is claimed by Abdera as her work, a boast which may have had some special explanation unknown to us, but does not seem to require it. In a political sense, the elevation of the new Athens, the Athens of the hegemony and the empire, was in fact the work of the Ionian cities, and of Abdera therefore as one of them. If the grandchild exaggerates her part, that is not surprising on a festal occasion. The form of expression, ματρὸς ματέρ' ἔτεκον, though quaint, is simple and passable as a jest[1],—not perhaps a particularly admirable jest, but we should hardly expect Pindar to be very dexterous in this line. It is amusing to see that at the call of the people, and inspired by the frank rejoicing of a popular holiday, he could condescend to such a caper. The same subject, the restoration of Athens, and the material rebuilding and refortification of the city, as a type of the political construction, seems to be pursued in the sequel (*v.* 37),

[1] The editors would substitute ἔπιδον for ἔτεκον, but upon consideration of the purpose, ἔτεκον seems to be necessary.

where, combining the remains of the text with the indications of the marginal notes, we should read apparently something like this:

ἦ μὲν οὐκ ἀπάταις ἀλκᾷ δὲ τεῖχος ἀνδρῶν
ὕψιστον ἵσταται·
. . . . μάρναμαι μὰν
ἀντίστροφα δᾴοις.

'Truly not by deceit, but by valour of men, is a wall builded highest; ...but I fight an enemy with weapons answering to his own.' If this was the substance, we can hardly be wrong in supposing a reference to the famous craft and diplomacy of Themistocles by which the refortification of Athens was secured against Spartan interference, and to the animated controversy, on the merits of fortifications as compared with braver defences, which, as we know already from Plato[1], arose out of the occurrence. The Abderites, loyal to 'the mother of our mother,' defend the use of guile where guile was so plainly intended, and the barrier of a rampart against those who could best be so met. At all events, the plain allusion to Athens which precedes, is an interesting testimony to the enthusiasm of the confederates, while the great liberation was still fresh, for the capital and protectress of the Ionian race.

Even more remarkable, as material for history in some of its most instructive aspects as well as in poetic quality, is, or must have been, the Paean written 'for the Delphians' and addressed 'to Pytho' (p. 41, *Poem* vi). It is deplorably injured, and the

[1] *Laws*, 778 D.

gaps leave obscure, in connexion or meaning, much of what is solid. But the title and the opening passage afford a glimpse, in some ways rather surprising, of the conditions still subsisting, so late as the decade 470–460 B.C.[1], between the sanctuary of Pytho, perhaps on the whole the most fascinating to our curiosity of all Greek foundations, and the township or people which eventually so absorbed the ancient oracle, that *Pythian* and *Delphian* are for us, and were for later Hellas, convertible and synonymous terms. Evidently this was by no means the case when 'Delphians,' or Pindar speaking for 'Delphians,' could apply, 'in the name of Olympian Zeus,' to be permitted to assist 'Pytho' in the choric worship of Castalia, on the ground that the rites 'lack men,' whom Pytho, it would seem, is not able effectively to supply. Such is the purport of the opening address, spoken, as we should rather suppose, by the Delphian performers of the Paean in their public and representative capacity[2]. They distinguish

[1] Date fixed by reference to *Nemean* vii; see below, and the editors' Introduction, p. 20.

[2] The practice of Pindar in the *Epinicia* would admit, quite naturally, the supposition that it is the poet who speaks, identifying himself with his poem and requesting acceptance; nor would this much affect our point. But it does not yet appear, so far as I have observed, that in Paeans he used (or used so freely) this personal manner, less appropriate, if admissible, when his employers were not persons or families, but cities, public bodies, or their deputies appointed for an official performance. An article on this volume in the *Berliner Philologische Wochenschrift* (Otto Schroeder) cites as examples ἐραταί μοι γλῶσσα (*Paean* vi 58) and ἐκράνθην (ix 34), but in both it seems that the *choreutes* may be the speaker.

themselves from 'Pytho' completely, and speak of 'hearing about' the circumstances of the sacred foundation, precisely as they might if they resided elsewhere. Something of this kind, some distance and delicacy of relation between town and sanctuary, might be inferred from the cautious and scrupulous way in which their respective names are used, or rather avoided, by Aeschylus in the (almost contemporary) *Choephori* and prologue to the *Eumenides*. But the new paean is plainer and more definite. Totally different, we may remark, is the Delphi of forty or fifty years later, as depicted by Euripides in the *Andromache* and the *Ion*. Indeed, in the circumstances of the paean, the town of those plays can hardly be conceived to exist; it had probably been much developed during half a century by consultants, dedicators, and celebrants of the Pythian Games.

Of this paean, *For the Delphians*, and of another[1] out of the six or seven now partially legible, the existence was already signalized by references in the *Epinicia*,—a remarkable illustration of Pindar's copiousness in personal allusion. In the Seventh *Nemean*, written for an Aeginetan, he relates the death of the Aeacid hero Neoptolemus, killed at Delphi, and adopts the version of the story which was approved at Aegina. According to this, the quarrel in which Neoptolemus lost his life arose out of the exactions and insolence of the Delphians who

[1] *Poem* IV. *For the Ceans, to Delos.* See the editors' Introduction.

served the temple. To obtain their alleged dues, they fell upon the sacrifice which Neoptolemus was offering (one is reminded of Hophni and Phinehas), and for resisting this outrage he was assassinated. The Delphians, as might be supposed, had quite another story. According to them, the provocation came from Neoptolemus himself, who insolently and impiously claimed to be paid by Apollo, out of the Delphian treasures, for the slaying of his father Achilles. The scholia to the Seventh *Nemean* inform us that the explicit adoption there of the Aeacid story—that the quarrel was 'for meats' (περὶ κρεῶν) —has an apologetic purpose, inasmuch as Pindar had given offence by the way in which the incident was related in his paean for the Delphians. This offending narrative, that of the paean, described the quarrel, according to the scholia, as arising μυρίαν περὶ τιμάν. Boeckh, upon the suggestion of a scholium which speaks of νομιζόμεναι τιμαί (*accustomed payments*), changed the text of the quotation to μοιριᾶν περὶ τιμᾶν, where μοίριος, a dubious word, was supposed equivalent to νομιζόμενος, *customary*. We have now the original passage (p. 47, vi 118), where the disputed phrase appears as . υρ . . ῀ν περὶ τιμᾶν, pointing *prima facie*, when compared with the pre-existing citation, to μυριᾶν περὶ τιμᾶν. Professor Housman[1], following the lead of Boeckh but greatly improving it, proposes κυριᾶν περὶ τιμᾶν, which would undoubtedly bear the sense sought,

[1] *Classical Review*, vol. XXII, p. 11.

authorized payments, or payments demanded according to custom.

The point is of little importance; but in view of the interest bestowed on this legend by the *Andromache* of Euripides, which principally rests upon it, we may suggest a doubt whether *authorized payments* or *customary payments*, however expressed, is a phrase quite suitable to the paean. The mention of *νομιζόμεναι τιμαί* in the scholium does not prove that a corresponding epithet stood in the text; and if it was in the text, how can we account for the offence which the paean appears to have given at Aegina? With this epithet, the phrase seems to point clearly and exclusively to the Aeginetan version,—that the quarrel turned upon the exactions of the Delphian ministers[1]. It does not apparently even admit the Delphian version, the alleged claim for blood-money brought by Neoptolemus against Apollo, a claim assuredly not 'authorized' or customary? Why then was Aegina displeased?

Is it after all quite certain that Pindar did not write, as we are told, *μυρίαν περὶ τιμάν*, or *μυριᾶν περὶ τιμᾶν*, *about an enormous payment*? The phrase is vague and scarcely intelligible; but in the circumstances this may rather confirm than impeach it. Writing for Delphians, Pindar, if he would touch on this delicate matter at all, could hardly fail to

[1] That the exactions were 'authorized,' that is to say, authorized by Delphi, must have been assumed by the Aeginetans themselves, and their displeasure can hardly therefore have rested on the mere epithet.

allow for the view of his employers. Yet his personal and professional connexions with Aegina would dictate caution on the other side. Is it not conceivable, that in this dilemma, he deliberately tried to cover both the alleged causes of quarrel,—the Delphian exactions and the claim of Neoptolemus, and wrote *enormous payment* in the hope that each party would be content to take it as they preferred? If his hope was disappointed, and he was forced to explain himself afterwards, at Aegina, in the Aeginetan sense, that is no unlikely result of such a prevarication. Indeed the phrase *enormous payment* points at least equally, and rather, to the claim of Neoptolemus against Apollo, and his intention, as alleged by the Delphians, to satisfy his demand by plundering the temple-treasure. It would be so interpreted by the Delphians, and the Aeginetans might well apprehend that it was so intended by the poet[1], whom they blamed accordingly. We may observe that a marginal note to the papyrus (vi 118) gives both the Aeginetan story and the Delphian as alternative explanations of the text, which implies that the text was ambiguous, and may possibly mean that the author of the note recognized this ambiguity as intentional[2].

[1] The more easily because the slaying of Achilles is previously mentioned in the paean, *vv.* 81—86.

[2] *ἤτοι τῶν κρεῶν, ἃ διαρπαζόντων συνήθως τῶν α...ων (?) ἐδυσχέραινε καὶ ἐκώλυε, διὸ καὶ ἀνῄρηται· ἢ τῶν χρημάτων, ἃ διαρπάζων εἰς ἐκδικίαν τοῦ πατρὸς ἀνηρέθη.* Prof. Housman, whose reading and punctuation I follow, adopts *ἄλλων*, with the editors, for the

But we are travelling beyond our purpose, and must not pursue the many questions of history and legend raised by the new 'find.' We are concerned rather to exemplify the accessions to poetry as such; these, notwithstanding the ruin of the MS., are considerable, and a subject for much congratulation to the finders.

Less attractive, and indeed to the mere reader hardly commendable at all, is the other chief novelty of the volume, a large piece from a historian, apparently of the fourth century B.C., who wrote a continuation of Thucydides. The recovered portion belongs to the middle of the decade 400—390 B.C., the commencement of hostilities between Thebes and Sparta, Agesilaus in Asia, etc. The authorship is disputed. If Theopompus was the man, certainly he was once, as the editors say, 'a worse stylist than has generally been supposed.' The sole merit of the new writer, in this respect, seems to be that he is easy and clear. Whether we should add, with the editors, that the fragment would make Theopompus 'a greater historian,' depends upon the definition of such greatness. To me it seems rather that the new annalist, with his desultory summers and winters, and his persistent silence as to any reasons why the

imperfect word. If it was so written, one may suspect it to be an error for some contraction of ἀμφιπόλων, *e.g.* αμφλων. As the full word occurs in the text (ἀμφιπόλοις), it could bear abbreviation. The meaning seems to be that *the temple-ministers*, in pursuance of a bad custom (συνήθως), tried to seize the sacrifice of Neoptolemus in satisfaction of alleged dues.

facts which he details should excite an intelligent interest by their bearing upon large and permanent issues, illustrates very instructively what the Thucydidean theory of history would have produced, if Thucydides had not been greater than his theory. A rival claimant for authorship is the misty figure of Cratippus, to whom the editors incline, though they find some difficulty in supposing that so authentic a writer could be so little celebrated, as Cratippus was. After conscientiously perusing the remains, I cannot feel that this objection is invincible. Nevertheless here is a fine field for the investigation of sources.

On the other hand, we would gladly read more, if more there were, of the ' Uncanonical Gospel':

λέγει (ὁ Φαρισαῖος τῷ Σωτῆρι)· Καθαρεύω· ἐλουσάμην γὰρ ἐν τῇ λίμνῃ τοῦ Δαυείδ, καὶ δι' ἑτέρας κλίμακος κατελθὼν δι' ἑτέρας ἀνῆλθον, καὶ λευκὰ ἐνδύματα ἐνεδυσάμην καὶ καθαρά, καὶ τότε ἦλθον καὶ προσέβλεψα τούτοις τοῖς ἁγίοις σκεύεσιν. ὁ Σωτὴρ πρὸς αὐτὸν ἀποκριθεὶς εἶπεν· Οὐαί, τυφλοὶ μὴ ὁρῶντες. σὺ ἐλούσω τούτοις τοῖς χεομένοις ὕδασιν, ἐν οἷς κύνες καὶ χοῖροι βέβληνται νυκτὸς καὶ ἡμέρας, καὶ νιψάμενος τὸ ἐκτὸς δέρμα ἐσμήξω, ὅπερ καὶ αἱ πόρναι καὶ αἱ αὐλητρίδες μυρίζουσιν καὶ λούουσιν καὶ σμήχουσι καὶ καλλωπίζουσι πρὸς ἐπιθυμίαν τῶν ἀνθρώπων· ἔνδοθεν δὲ ἐκεῖναι πεπλήρωνται σκορπίων καὶ πάσης κακίας. ἐγὼ δὲ καὶ οἱ μαθηταί μου, οὓς λέγεις μὴ βεβαπτίσθαι, βεβάμμεθα ἐν ὕδασι ζωῆς αἰωνίου κ.τ.λ.

Here we are at least in contact with the warm mind of somebody with beliefs and purposes. Nor need one be a specialist in the matter to perceive the deeply interesting comparisons which both style and substance by likeness and by unlikeness invite.

But we must make an end, and quit an interesting volume with gratitude all the greater that it includes the hope of favours to come.

THE BELL AND THE TRUMPET

(κώδων, σάλπιγξ.)

The bell, as is well known, plays in Hellenic life a very limited part. From prose authors, describing the actual facts of life, οἷς χρώμεθ', οἷς ξύνεσμεν—to use a phrase of Aristophanes closely connected with this topic—we hear of *κώδωνες* or *bells* in two functions only, I think. They are the attribute of the crier, and of the sentinel on the wall. The first use of them was familiar enough to create a proverb διαπράσσεσθαί τι ὡς κώδωνα ἐξαψάμενος, 'to do a thing like a crier with a bell tied to him,' *i.e.* ostentatiously, a proverb roughly corresponding to our 'be one's own trumpeter,' which the lexicon cites with it. Of the second use, which, we may observe, was confined, for anything that appears to the contrary, to times of special apprehension, we have a well-known example in the last chapter of the fourth book of Thucydides. Brasidas, in the course of his brilliant campaign ἐπὶ Θρᾴκης, made a daring though unsuccessful attempt to convert the instrument of precaution into an occasion of surprise, by scaling part of the wall of Potidaea at the very moment when a sentinel watching it had gone to the end of his beat, 'to pass the bell' to the next man. The object of the round was of course to give a noisy proof to the authorities and the inhabitants that at the fixed hour the sentinels were all at their posts. Sometimes, as we see from Aristophanes, *Birds* 842, a different way was used —a tour of inspection being made by one bellman: *κωδωνοφορῶν περίτρεχε καὶ κάθευδ' ἐκεῖ* is one of the glib commands which Peithetairos pours out upon the long-suffering Euelpides. The ironical hint that he should take a nap on the way suggests the dangers of trusting so much to one functionary. The tour of Euelpides is properly speaking an inspection of the works in course of building, not of sentries; and it is very probable that 'the bell' was then, as it is still, a familiar voice where large parties of workmen are employed over a considerable area, whether in civil or military constructions. Later in the same play (1160) the carrying of the bell is duly mentioned among the protections of the new-built Nephelococcygia against surprise on the part of the hostile gods.

Such was the bell in daily Greek life. But the poets give us glimpses of a different 'bell,' not carried but worn as a military decoration and instrument of terror, whether on the personal armour, the shield or the helmet, or on the chariot and gear of the horses. It is with this smaller decorative *κώδων* that we are now concerned. As I have already said, the most noticeable thing about it is that it is not a truly Greek decoration—or at least not, if one may so say, classical. In the *Frogs* of Aristophanes, 'Euripides,' it will be remembered, takes credit to himself and his type of tragedy, in comparison with the manner of Aeschylus, for having made poetry of the real facts of life, οἷς χρώμεθ', οἷς ξύνεσμεν, and contrasts the bearded, scowling, mock-Titanic militaires, formed by the old teaching, with the supple and dexterous politicians of his own school (*Frogs*, 964).

γνώσει δὲ τοὺς τούτου τε κἀμοὺς ἑκατέρου μαθητάς·
τουτουμενὶ Φορμίσιος Μεγαίνετός θ' ὁ Μανῆς,
σαλπιγγολογχυπηνάδαι, σαρκασμοπιτυοκάμπται·
οὑμοὶ δὲ Κλειτοφῶν τε καὶ Θηραμένης ὁ κομψός.

It is interesting to note that the thing selected by Euripides as the type of the poetry which sought dignity and impressiveness in the unfamiliar, is the *armour-bell.* 'I did not,' says the poet of culture (σοφία), 'I did not tear my audience from thought to bombastic noise, I did not startle them with representations of a Cycnos or a Memnon with bells upon the harness of their steeds.'

ἀλλ' οὐκ ἐκομπολάκουν
ἀπὸ τοῦ φρονεῖν ἀποσπάσας, οὐδ' ἐξέπληττον αὐτοὺς
Κύκνους ποιῶν καὶ Μέμνονας κωδωνοφαλαροπώλους.

'No,' he says, 'I invited reflexion, sober judgement, by keeping to objects which my hearers knew well enough to criticise.'

ξυνειδότες γὰρ οὗτοι
ἤλεγχον ἄν μου τὴν τέχνην.

If we refer to the extant specimens of tragedy, this position is fully justified. The κώδων is not apparently mentioned in Euripides. Whether Sophocles actually introduced it upon the stage we cannot say. It is not upon the stage in the fragment (738) cited by Plutarch, where the κωδωνόκροτον σάκος, the shield with clashing bells, is *mentioned* as an accoutrement *of the Trojans*, φίλιπποι καὶ κερουλκοὶ σὺν σάκει δὲ κωδωνοκρότῳ παλαισταί. It is impossible to mistake the depreciatory tone of these words, which bring the empty terrors of a barbarian chivalry, the τοξόδαμνον Ἄρη of men who drew the bow-tip, into comparison with the grim earnest of the Greek spearman on foot. Once in the extant tragedies of Sophocles we find a κώδων. To the voice of the brazen-mouthed Italian κώδων is compared the clear voice of Athena, caught by the ready ear and mind of her faithful Odysseus (*Aias* 14):

> ὦ φθέγμ' Ἀθάνας, φιλτάτης ἐμοὶ θεῶν,
> ὡς εὐμαθές σου, κἂν ἄποπτος ᾖς, ὅμως
> φώνημ' ἀκούω καὶ ξυναρπάζω φρενὶ
> χαλκοστόμου κώδωνος ὡς Τυρσηνικῆς.

The traditional interpretation of this passage, descending from the scholia, would exclude it from our theme, by giving to κώδων the unusual sense τὸ πλατὺ τῆς σάλπιγγος, 'the broad end of the trumpet.' This explanation seems however somewhat doubtful. A 'special meaning' is a common device of careless commentators, and the epithets χαλκόστομος and Τυρσηνική, both proper to the trumpet, would be quite sufficient to provoke the note. Really they prove nothing. The bell was as certainly a foreign thing by origin as the trumpet, and may well have been also Italian, or so supposed; and when we see that the armour-bell was to Sophocles a characteristic of Troy, we are reminded that a legend of unknown antiquity, which derived from later history an unforeseen importance, did connect Asia with Italy, the Lydian allies of Troy with the 'Tyrrhenian' Tiber. Going back to Aeschylus, we see from Aristophanes that the actual bell, as a part of theatrical costume, was employed by the poet to add the effect of a strange terror to such heroic and imaginary figures as Cycnos the son of Ares, and Memnon the son of the Dawn—with the advantage, as 'Euripides' kindly suggests, that the unwonted noise saved the accompanying words from the animadversions of a reflecting spectator. The author of the *Rhesus*, who imitates all the triad in turn, has imitated Aeschylus in the entry of the Thracian monarch, the ally and kinsman, by the way, of the Trojans. When a messenger announces his approach, we are told that bound on the foreheads of his horses, as on the goddess' aegis, is a brazen Gorgon, 'ringing terror with many a bell' (*Rhes.* 308); and when he arrives, the soldiers shout in admiration of his armour bound with gold, and the proud rattle of his bells (*Rhes.* 383):

ἴδε χρυσόδετον σώματος ἀλκήν,
κλύε καὶ κόμπους κωδωνοκρότους
παρὰ πορπάκων κελαδοῦντας.

Here we are given another 'special meaning';

for the lexicon will have it that *πόρπαξ* is not *πόρπαξ* here but *πόρπη*, though why or how a bell should be attached to a buckle-pin rather than to the handle-bar which crossed the interior of the shield is a question to be asked. Wherever they were fixed, these bells of Rhesus are the expression of that feeling so peculiarly detestable to the Hellenic mind, the noisy and unsober pride which goes before a fall. It is again in this aspect that the bell is presented in the *Seven against Thebes.* If this were a proper place, it might be shown that the whole colouring of the military descriptions in that play is archaic, while those of the proud invaders, doomed to the punishment of pride, are designedly offensive and, it may be said, non-Hellenic. For the present we are concerned only with the wild and wicked Tydeus, whose taunts against his too unworthy associate in arms, the calm and pious Amphiaraus, are significantly followed by the description of his umbrageous triple crest and his intimidating bells.

λόφοι δὲ κώδων τ' οὐ δάκνουσ' ἄνευ δορός,

is the comment of Eteocles. A question of some interest arises upon the details of the description, which runs as follows (*Theb.* 384)—

τοιαῦτ' ἀυτῶν τρεῖς κατασκίους λόφους
σείει, κράνους χαίτωμ', ὑπ' ἀσπίδος δὲ τῷ
χαλκήλατοι κλάζουσι κώδωνες φόβον·
ἔχει δ' ὑπέρφρον σῆμ' ἐπ' ἀσπίδος τόδε, κ.τ.λ.

and so follows his arrogant device of a nocturnal sky, moon, and stars. It would thus appear that the bells are fixed in some way *under* the shield, to the handle (πόρπαξ) perhaps, where Rhesus wore some of his. But on a closer examination there is reason for a different view. The replies of Eteocles to the successive descriptions given by his scouts are throughout close commentaries upon those descriptions. Now, in his remark, above quoted, on the harmless gauds of Tydeus, it will be noticed that the bell is associated not with the shield but with the crest. I add the context:

> κόσμον μὲν ἀνδρὸς οὔτιν' ἂν τρέσαιμ' ἐγώ,
> οὐδ' ἑλκοποιὰ γίγνεται τὰ σήματα·
> λόφοι δὲ κώδων τ' οὐ δάκνουσ' ἄνευ δορός.
> καὶ νύκτα ταύτην ἣν λέγεις ἐπ' ἀσπίδος, κ.τ.λ.

and so follows the refutation of the emblematic boast. The first two lines point to the whole description; the fourth, with those that follow it, refer specially to the shield. It would certainly be natural to refer the third to the helmet; more especially as the phrase οὐ δάκνουσι, *do not sting*, is plainly aimed at the comparison of Tydeus to the δράκων—

> μεσημβριναῖς κλαγγαῖσιν ὡς δράκων βοᾷ—

the serpent whose 'hairy mane terrific' is celebrated by Milton, following ancient fable with his usual preference of literary colouring to natural fact, and is represented in the armour of Tydeus by the λόφος or κράνους χαίτωμα. If the harsh sound of the κώδων is not to be associated with this comparison, half the point of Eteocles' retort is lost. Noticing this, if we go back to the description, we see that it has a flaw. After the words ὑπ' ἀσπίδος in 385, the occurrence of ἐπ' ἀσπίδος in 387 is not only poor in sound, but pointless in sense; for ἔχει δ' ὑπέρφρον σῆμα τόδε requires no explanation, and to give any emphasis to the difference between ἐπὶ and ὑπὸ is rhythmically impossible. To which it may be added, that if τῷ in 385 stands for Τυδεῖ, as it must, the pronoun, despite its prominent place, is wholly superfluous: the sentence would have the same meaning without it. I draw the conclusion that in the true text τῷ stood not for Τυδεῖ, but for κράνει or λόφῳ, and that ὑπ' ἀσπίδος is a patch to supply the place of some word signifying 'attached to,' and governing the dative pronoun, which in that case could not conveniently be omitted. Thus the bells and the crest are alike decorations of the helmet, and the joint reference of Eteocles is justified. If a word has been lost, the presumption is that it was lost through a repetition of letters. Can we find a word which satisfies this condition for the present case? The passage just cited from the *Rhesus*, which exhibits a minute imitation of the phrase κλάζουσι κώδωνες φόβον in the passage of Aeschylus before us, will furnish the unique word which we want,

> Γοργὼ δ' ὡς ἀπ' αἰγίδος θεᾶς
> χαλκῆ μετώποις ἱππικοῖσι πρόσδετος
> πολλοῖσι σὺν κώδωσιν ἐκτύπει φόβον.

Write in Aeschylus

> πρόσδετοι δὲ τῷ
> χαλκήλατοι κλάζουσι κώδωνες φόβον—

and the origin of the MS. text is clear. The

somewhat strange looking πρόσδετοι was robbed of its two last syllables ΔΕΤΟΙ by the repetition ΔΕΤΟΙ or ΔΕΤΩΙ, and the impossible remnant was conjecturally replaced by ὑπ' ἀσπίδος. We may compare the precisely similar corruption of another passage in the play (Aesch. *Theb.* 122) where the syllables required by the metre after διάδετοι have been properly replaced by the repetition of δέ τοι.

Upon the facts respecting the κώδων as above stated a question arises which others may perhaps assist me to answer. The dramatists represent the κώδων as a savage and generally as a non-Hellenic decoration. That it was not used by Athenians of the fifth century is clear. Is there any evidence that it was used by Greeks of an earlier period, or by less civilized Greeks? Are the bells of Tydeus a piece of genuine Greek antiquity, or an imaginary decoration attributed to Greeks whose behaviour is barbarous?

It has been already noticed that in its traditionally foreign and Italian-Asiatic character the κώδων is allied to the σάλπιγξ, and it is significant that though the 'Euripides' of the *Frogs* does not, of course, make the blunder of separating from 'the familiar things we use' the instrument whose note invited the families of Athens to the dearest feast of the year—

> ἀκούετε λεῴ· κατὰ τὰ πάτρια τοὺς χοὰς
> πίνειν ὑπὸ τῆς σάλπιγγος (Ar. *Ach.* 1001),

and whose solemn and 'Chthonian' sound preceded the reverend meeting of the Areopagus, nevertheless we find he is not afraid to sneer at the trumpet and the σαλπιγγολογχυπηνάδαι who admired it; and it seems certain that the trumpet, as a military instrument, was at Athens at all events not popular. Nowhere, I think, is there a trace of that enthusiasm for the trumpet-call which breaks out so often in modern poetry. Tydeus is indeed likened to 'a horse that waits panting for the sound of the trump,' but then we have already seen how far we are meant to sympathize with the feelings of Tydeus; moreover the trumpet of the simile is probably not the trumpet of battle, but that which started both horses and chariots in the national games. Aeschylus, in his immortal picture of the nation's victory at Salamis, is careful to note that *the trumpet* inflamed the ardour of '*the other side.*'—(*Pers.* 395).

σάλπιγξ δ' αὐτῇ πάντ' ἐκεῖν' ἐπέφλεγεν.

In Sophocles, the anxious Tecmessa reminds Aias, as he goes out upon his fatal errand, that this time it is not the trumpet which calls him from her side (*Ai.* 291). Euripides in the *Phoenissae* (1377), following the *Seven against Thebes* in treatment as in theme, places the trumpet among the proud emblems of an unholy war; it is the trumpet which in the *Troades* (1267) is to apprise the Trojan captives that the final moment of expatriation has arrived; and twice in the *Rhesus* (144, 989) the Trojan Hector names the trumpet as the signal of his attempt, so nearly successful, to burn the Greek ships and destroy their hope of return, emphatically warning his men not to neglect it. In the *Heracleidae* (381) the 'Tyrrhene trumpet' is the prelude to a scene so horrible that the narrator declines the task of describing it and appeals to the imagination of his hearer. Certainly it is not without significance that the dramatists of Athens direct the attention of their audience so frequently to the birthplace of this barbarous instrument; nor are these traces of popular sentiment to be neglected, if we would read the Athenian poets in their own spirit[1].

[1] The κώδων is not mentioned in Homer. The σάλπιγξ is mentioned twice. This evidence, in the uncertainty which rests upon the date and origin of any particular passage in Homer, is scarcely sufficient for a conclusion. Among the earliest references to the war-trumpet of which the date is certain, must be Bacchylides *Paean* 9, pointed out to me by Mr J. A. Platt.

[In connexion with the reference to Soph. *Ai.* 17 χαλκοστόμου κώδωνος on p. 139 f. above, the editors think it proper to state that the traditional explanation is confirmed by Bacchylides 17. 3 χαλκοκώδων σάλπιγξ. This essay was written several years before the discovery of the Bacchylides MS.]

THE CALENDAR IN THE *TRACHINIAE* OF SOPHOCLES

In submitting some observations upon the chronological framework of the story adopted by Sophocles in the *Trachiniae*, I desire to guard at once against a misunderstanding which is obvious and possibly prejudicial. In the present state of mythological controversy it may be difficult to advance the proposition that a certain Heraclean legend is closely connected with a certain development of the Calendar, without being suspected of a desire to fortify the theory which makes the hero himself a symbol and representative of the sun. Be it said therefore emphatically, that with this theory, or with any Heracles other than the human combatant familiar to Greek legend as we actually know it, we have for the present not the smallest concern. Our proposition is simply that, in respect of the chronological framework, the story presented in the *Trachiniae* exhibits and is founded upon a certain calendar, and certain institutions relating to the calendar, which existed when the story was first thrown into this shape; and that this fact, interesting in itself as a piece of historical evidence, is not without significance even for the reader of Sophocles, as accounting for some peculiarities of structure and expression which were naturally accepted by the poet from his traditional authority, but would not be justifiable if we supposed them invented by him for the purpose of his play. Manifestly all this may be true, whether the hero was or was not by remote origin symbolic of the sun, or symbolic at all. That has nothing to do with the matter.

The story of the *Trachiniae*, as compared with other legends of the Attic stage, presents a chronology uncommonly copious and precise. The event of the play is the death of the hero, agreeing in date with the terms of an oracle, received by himself at Dodona, which with oracular ambiguity fixed 'the end of his labours' at the completion of the twelfth year from the date of the prophecy. With the exception of visits to his home 'rare as those of the husbandman at seed-time and harvest to a distant farm,' his wanderings occupied the whole of his time, and from the last of these absences he returns only to die. At his last departure he solemnly delivered to his wife the tablet containing the oracle, explaining to her that there wanted then 'a year and three months' to the date fixed, so that if by that time he were not heard of, she must presume his death, for which case he made disposition. At the opening of the play the prescribed period has elapsed, that is to say, 'fifteen months' according to the wife, though another speaker marks the duration as 'twelve months' (*Trach.* 44 f., 155 ff., 647 ff., 821 ff., 1164 ff.).

Now, as compared with the habits of ancient Greek legend, this chronology is, as we have said, uncommonly full and exact, especially with regard to the duration of the last absence. We do not usually find in the tales adopted by the tragedians dates precise to the month, or dates unnecessary for the comprehension of the facts, or indeed any dates at all. If we had been simply informed that at the opening of the play the time had arrived which was fixed by the oracle for the end of Heracles' labours, we should have had all that we needed and as much as we usually get. It is already something extra, when we are told that this time is twelve years from the giving of the oracle; and still more remarkable is the superfluous specification of fifteen months (or twelve months) as the distance of this same time from that of the last departure. Terms of months are very rarely mentioned in Attic drama; never, I think, except in connexion with natural processes regularly so limited, such as the 'six months' of the herdsman's summer in the hills (*Oed. Tyr.*), or the 'ten months' of the woman's gestation (*Ion*). As being an artificial term, limited only by the events of the story, this 'fifteen months' is perhaps unique. Odd therefore also, in the circumstances, is the variation already noticed in the number, from fifteen months (*v.* 44) to twelve (*v.* 648). A period of fifteen months might no doubt be described loosely as 'a year,' but why it should be called 'twelve months' is not obvious. If the exact length of the period was not important (and in the existing play there is nothing to show that it was), why number the months? And if it was important, why number them wrong?

Passing by for the moment other questions which will emerge when we come to explanation, we may remark that chronology is not the only matter in which we find here a numerical precision beyond the apparent need. Concerning the sacrifice with which Heracles celebrated his final victory, and which became the occasion of his death, we are told (*v.* 760) that 'he began his offering with twelve bulls, free from blemish, the first of the spoil; but altogether he brought a hundred victims, great or small, to the altar.' To Sophocles, so far as appears, these figures signified nothing, except generally the magnificence of the ceremony; but that they were once significant remains clear even in his version, which presents not only the specific combination of 12 and 100, but also a sharp and unexplained opposition between the two figures, the one apparently correcting something which might have been wrong or defective in the other:—

> ταυροκτονεῖ μὲν δώδεκ' ἐντελεῖς ἔχων
> λείας ἀπαρχὴν βοῦς· ἀτὰρ τὰ πάνθ' ὁμοῦ
> ἑκατὸν προσῆγε συμμιγῆ βοσκήματα.

It is now to be shown that all these facts, with others, hang together, and have one common origin in a certain calendric practice to which the story was originally adjusted. It will be simplest first to state this practice continuously, and then to justify the statement by reference to the Sophoclean expressions which it serves to account for and elucidate.

The calendar in question, like all ancient calendars, presupposes a time, of very remote antiquity, when infant agriculture was content with empirical notes of the seasons, and the course of the sun had not yet been measured or divided. Time was then reckoned, on a decimal system, by days, and by 'moons' counted, as the nearest decimal approximation, at 30 days. The next denomination (the year, so far as there was then any year) was the ten moons, and the next the hundred moons, probably the largest unit by which in those times it was ever found necessary to reckon. Each period, moon, ten-moon, and hundred-moon, was marked by an appropriate ritual, and the largest, the hundred-moon, by a great calendric feast with a corresponding sacrifice of one hundred victims. This institution offered, besides its symmetry, the incidental advantage of a simple and symmetrical rectification of the inevitable error in days. With thirty days to a moon, the end of the hundredth moon would so fall, in relation to the end of a true moon, that by allowing ten days for the feast itself it might be celebrated with a quite respectable appearance of accuracy. Next, with the increasing importance of agriculture, came the observation of the solar year, and the connected practice of counting moons not by tens but by twelves. The minor period or common year was now a *twelve-month*, 360 days, and the major period, or 'great year,' by analogy twelve twelve-months. Accordingly at the calendric feast which marked the period, the supremacy of the number 12, and also the fact that each twelve-month made up (as was at first supposed) a perfect solar course, was recognized by a principal sacrifice of 'twelve perfect' animals; while, to propitiate antique usage, the number 100 was nevertheless retained as the total of indiscriminate victims. And if sacrifice could have persuaded the heavenly bodies to be reasonable, all would now have been well. But of course it could not escape notice that in fact, though the single year seemed correct to the sun, the 'great year' was much too short, the end of the twelve twelve-months preceding the expected solar epoch by a very considerable space. In this discrepancy itself, however, the depositaries of religious learning supposed themselves to have detected, upon further observation, an element of rationality; for the defect was estimated to amount exactly, as in fact it did amount very nearly, to sixty days or two months. The discordance thus revealed, adjusted since by innumerable and highly complicated devices, was adjusted then by a method which had at least the advantage of an irreducible simplicity. The whole complement of sixty days, or two months, was added to the last year of the twelve; but as it seemed irrational and improper that there should not be in every 'twelve-month' twelve months and no more, the increase was made, in a fashion of which the history of the calendar presents frequent examples, by means of an artificial or pretended 'month.' In the last 'twelve-month' the first eleven months were ordinary months of thirty days, but the last 'month' consisted of an ordinary month *plus* the complement; that is to say, it had ninety days and was, vulgarly speaking, not a month but three months. The residual error (for of course there was still a residue) would accumulate so slowly that a primitive society would be content to rectify it by arbitrary and occasional expedients, and the feast could be celebrated without suspicion of impiety.

It is to this condition of the calendar that the story of Heracles was adapted by the narrator whose version descended to Sophocles. Probably (though this supposition is not necessary) it was held that the system had originated with Heracles or with his adventures, and that he actually founded the calendric feast in the form which corresponded to the improved system, as he was believed to have founded the feast at Olympia, itself calendric, and others of the same character. At all events the chronological scheme of the story is calculated by this system, and designed to exhibit it. Heracles, like other heroes in legend and like the offending gods in Hesiod, is condemned to a period of expiatory labour, measuring the length of a *μέγας ἐνιαυτός*, *magnus annus*, or 'great year.' The length and divisions of this period are set forth to him in a tablet which he receives at Dodona, containing a symbolic representation of the calendric cycle. With the beginning of each year he is to go forth from his home to a fresh adventure or course of adventures, and with the end of each year he is to return. Accordingly, upon his departure for the twelfth course, he delivers the tablet to his wife, explaining to her that according to its significance this 'year' is the last, and that it differs in length from the other eleven; that is to say, that for the last 'month' is to be reckoned not an ordinary month, but a term of three ordinary months. Finally, having worked out the sentence, he returns and celebrates the great feast with the symbolic offerings since customary. Of course this chronological scheme did not make the story, of which the main interest lay from the first where it lies now, in the adventures and destiny of the hero; though for the primitive audience, by whom the adjustment of the cycle, rude as it seems to us, must have been regarded as a work of mysterious and superhuman wisdom, profoundly important to life and religion, the chronological scheme itself had probably more interest than we can easily appreciate.

We are now to see how much there is in the play of Sophocles which from his altered point of view is not meaningless indeed nor offensive, but nevertheless not accounted for and not perfectly intelligible, until we refer his expressions to that historical authority, the lines and language of which he inevitably followed, even where they were no longer of much significance. We can justify for instance the strangely mysterious terms in which Deianira describes the tablet delivered to her by

Heracles at his last departure, 'an ancient tablet, inscribed with tokens, which he had never brought himself to explain to me before, many as were the ordeals to which he had gone forth....And he fixed the time; saying that when a year and three months should have passed since he had left the country, then he was fated to die; or, if he should have survived that term, to live thenceforth an untroubled life[1].' Now what the tablet contained, according to the account which we receive long afterwards from Heracles, was simply the words or substance of the oracle, taken down in writing by the hero himself, to the effect that his labours should end at the expiration of twelve years from that time[2]. If this were so, there really seems to be little reason for calling it 'ancient,' and still less reason why Heracles should have spoken to his wife of his own note as if it were something abstruse and required explanation. Indeed we might even ask why the tablet should be so prominent in the story, or should figure there at all, since it adds nothing either in substance or weight to the all-sufficient evidence of Heracles. But when, as was the original conception, this tablet contained the 'tokens' or symbols of a calendric cycle, when it was actually in existence as a venerable relic, and was supposed to have existed from a dateless antiquity in the divine archives, until the day came when through Heracles it was revealed to mankind,

[1] 157 ff. Prof. Jebb's version, from which I cite generally, unless the context shows otherwise.

[2] 1164 ff.

the language applied to it by Deianira was perfectly natural, and the thing itself an essential feature in the story. We are reminded of the bronze tablet, recording a far more scientific improvement of the same kind, which was dedicated at Olympia in the fifth century by the mathematician Oenopides of Chios.

But above all, it is in the calendric import of the legend that we are to find the reason for its chronological details, and not only for the existence of these details (which, as was said above, is itself remarkable), but still more for the striking peculiarities of the language in which they are given by Sophocles. We see, for example, that there is, or at least there once was, something more than a graceful verbiage in 'the divine word of the old prophecy which said that when the twelfth year should have run through its full tale of months, it should end the series of toils for the true-born son of Zeus.'

> ὁπότε τελεόμηνος ἐκφέροι
> δωδέκατος ἄροτος, ἀναδοχὰν τελεῖν πόνων
> τῷ Διὸς αὐτόπαιδι[1].

Those who first used this language, or language closely resembling it, meant by each word exactly what it implies. It was 'the *twelfth* year,' or rather 'the twelfth *tillage*,' which 'came to its end by completion of months,' because this twelve-month, the last of the cycle, and not any other, received the supplementary months required to bring the period of twelve 'twelve-months' into agreement with the

[1] 824.

tillages, that is to say with the facts of nature and the necessities of agriculture. The twelfth year, by means of the supplement, coincided in its termination with the 'tillages,' whereas throughout the cycle up to this year there was a progressive discordance.

But if here the language of Sophocles receives, by relation to its origin, a more full significance, there are elsewhere places where, apart from this relation, it is hardly to be understood or justified at all. 'He fixed the time; saying that, when a year and three months should have passed since he had left the country, then he was fated' &c. Undoubtedly this is what Sophocles meant his Deianira to say. And this is the fashion in which he words it:—

> χρόνον προτάξας, ὡς τρίμηνον ἡνίκα
> χώρας ἀπείη κἀνιαύσιος βεβώς,
> τότ' ἢ θανεῖν χρείη σφε κ.τ.λ.[1]

That the poet wrote ἐνιαύσιος (and not ἐνιαύσιον, as expositors naturally wish that he had) must be taken as certain, the substitution and preservation of the nominative being on the contrary hypothesis incredible. And Professor Jebb, who duly retains the nominative, seems also to indicate justly what may be said for the construction as an equivalent for the meaning of Sophocles. It is just 'conceivable' that τρίμηνον (χρόνον) κἀνιαύσιος βεβώς should mean 'gone for a year and three months,' the nominative being mentally explained as adapted to βεβώς, upon the analogy of χρόνιος ἦλθε, χθιζὸς ἔβη and the like. But it is a question to be asked,

[1] 164 ff.

what possible advantage there could be in such a contortion, and what put the obnoxious nominative into the poet's mind. And the answer is that he is repeating, as all men do when they write or speak upon consecrated themes, the language of tradition, although, as he would interpret it, it has altogether ceased to be natural. If the 'three months' and the 'year' are to be added together, to express them in different cases is to verge on absurdity. But the equal correctness of either case offered a natural device to those who meant, and were known to mean, that the two terms were *not* to be added together, but counted *separately* to the same termination. The tablet, as explained by Heracles to Deianira, showed that this twelfth of twelve 'years,' the 'year' of his last absence, was to be more than an ordinary year, that it was to conclude with a period of three months, a χρόνος τρίμηνος, substituted for the last of its twelve months, and counting as the last month of it. And therefore he fixed the time when he was to be expected home or assumed to be dead, as the time 'when his absence should have covered the three-month, and (*thereby*) have covered the (extended) year.' When Sophocles elsewhere designates the same period as 'ten months and then five more[1],' he is translating the archaic formula, as he understood it, into language of his own, and translates it, as we see from his citation, not exactly. 'Fourteen months,' not 'fifteen months,' would have been the correct equivalent in common parlance,

[1] 44.

and neither expression would have been truly archaic; for according to the primitive reformers of the calendar, the last 'year' of their cycle was a *twelve-month* just as truly as the rest. This also Sophocles, faithful as a poet loves to be to sacred tradition, whether comprehended or not comprehended, allows us to see when, notwithstanding his 'ten months and five months more,' he permits his Chorus to designate this self-same period of expectation as δυοκαιδεκάμηνον χρόνον or 'long months *twelve*[1].' That the last of these months must be a χρόνος τρίμηνος was no reason for disallowing the designation 'twelve-month' to the final year. On the contrary it was a principal merit of the scheme that it achieved a reconciliation with the heavenly bodies without distressing piety and sense by a departure from the accustomed names of things. Such is, and in all times has been, the regular way of progress in this department of life: change the thing, if you must, but for that very reason do not change the words.

Again, in the verses which immediately succeed this reference to 'the three months' and 'the year,' we have other language confessed to be obscure, but explicable, as I think, by the same hypothesis. It follows ancient form, that is to say, without much regard to change in the signification.

τοιαῦτ' ἔφραζε πρὸς θεῶν εἱμαρμένα
τῶν Ἡρακλείων ἐκτελευτᾶσθαι πόνων,
ὡς τὴν παλαιὰν φηγὸν αὐδῆσαί ποτε
Δωδῶνι δισσῶν ἐκ Πελειάδων ἔφη.

[1] 648.

'Such, he said, was the doom ordained by the gods to be accomplished in the toils of Heracles; as the ancient oak at Dodona had spoken of yore, by the mouth of the two Peleiades.' How the ancient oak proposed to construe the genitive τῶν Ἡρακλείων πόνων, or how Sophocles construed it, are questions which, as will be seen by a reference to Professor Jebb, have exercised commentators and emendators not a little. As to Sophocles, we may well agree with Professor Jebb, that for him it was a 'genitive of connexion,' equivalent to the genitive with περί, and going with the whole phrase εἱμαρμένα ἐκτελευτᾶσθαι rather than with either word alone. "'He said that such things were destined to be accomplished *in regard to* the toils of Heracles.'" But it remains none the less clear that, to common apprehension, the genitive ought to depend strictly on ἐκτελευτᾶσθαι, and the translation ought to be 'Such, he said, was the *result* ordained by the gods to be accomplished *by* the toils of Heracles'; and if no one propounds this version, that is only because, from the position of Sophocles, such a statement would be scarcely explicable. Nevertheless it is likely that this, or something near it, was actually said and meant by 'the ancient oak,' that is to say by the traditional authority which Sophocles follows as closely as he can. The thing that was to 'result as an accomplishment from the toils of Heracles,' was the very thing which Sophocles has just before described; that is to say, the perfection and achievement of the cycle, the inestimable boon which, through and by means of the labours of Heracles, was to be realized and presented to the world. The dramatist, resolved, like Burke, when building with antique materials at all events 'not to be guilty of tampering,' repeats or paraphrases the prophetic *dictum* as he found it, and understands it in his own mind presumably as Professor Jebb did.

Further again, from this point of view we may perhaps get some light on the puzzling state in which we find the conclusion of the Second Stasimon. We are justified in looking for it, because that ode contains, as we have seen, at least one borrowed phrase (δυοκαιδεκάμηνον χρόνον), which is natural and significant only in reference to the primitive purport of the story, and not to the story as interpreted and partly remodelled by Sophocles. The situation is this. It has been announced that Heracles is about to celebrate his sacrifice in Euboea, the anointed robe has been sent to him there, and the Chorus now pray for the speedy completion of his return to his home in Trachis.

> ἀφίκοιτ' ἀφίκοιτο· μὴ σταίη
> πολύκωπον ὄχημα ναὸς αὐτῷ,
> πρὶν τάνδε πρὸς πόλιν ἀνύσειε,
> νασιῶτιν ἑστίαν
> ἀμείψας ἔνθα κλῄζεται θυτήρ·
> ὅθεν μόλοι πανάμερος
> τᾶς πειθοῦς παγχρίστῳ
> συγκραθεὶς ἐπὶ προφάσει θηρός[1].

The last three lines were plainly meant to express the hope that by Deianira's philtre, the ointment

[1] 655 ff.

upon the robe, the heart of Heracles may be turned to his wife; but as they are given, they do not signify this, nor indeed anything. To this extent there is a general agreement. Jebb, accepting πανίμερος (from Mudge) and φάρους (from M. Haupt and after Whitelaw's φάρει) gives the text and translation thus:

ὅθεν μόλοι πανίμερος
τᾶς πειθοῦς παγχρίστῳ
συγκραθεὶς ἐπὶ προφάσει φάρους[1].

'Thence may he come, full of desire, steeped in love by the specious device of the robe, on which Persuasion hath spread her sovereign charm.' On every point, so far as he carries the matter, he seems to me perfectly right: πανάμερος 'admits of no satisfactory explanation,' while πανίμερος gives what is wanted to fill up and determine the force of συγκραθείς: φάρους, *of the robe*, or something equivalent, is indispensable to complete the sense of παγχρίστῳ ἐπὶ προφάσει, words of which the integrity is certified by every sort of evidence that affects a textual problem. But there remains, before we can be contented, the question how then the MS. version was produced. That mere carelessness should make πανάμερος out of πανίμερος is possible,

[1] We need not here consider the doubt left by Prof. Jebb between συγκραθείς and the conjecture συντακείς. It rests entirely upon the assumption of syllabic correspondence with v. 654, ἐξέλυσ' ἐπίπονον ἁμέραν. The sense of συγκραθείς (see Jebb) is unexceptionable, and the metre, as I think, also. The metrical objection to θηρός is graver, but this also may be neglected, as θηρός is otherwise condemned.

though, in this place and all things considered, we shall hesitate to call it probable. But whence and how came θηρός? The resemblance to φάρους (even when we have gone back, with Prof. Jebb, to the Sophoclean spelling φάρος) is but slight; nor could it well explain, were it stronger, why one familiar word which makes a plain sense, should have been altered to another which makes none. Here is the point upon which our present discussion may bear. Let us remember that when our MSS. of Sophocles give θηρός, they do not prove or even go to prove that contemporaries of the poet read that very word; we can infer only that they read *either* θηρός, *or* θέρος, *or* θέρους, the script then still representing all three by θερος. The copyist who in this place first converted θερος to θηρός did so doubtless because, while θηρός, *of the Centaur*, seemed at least to have some possibility of connexion with the subject, the other interpretations, θέρος and θέρους, appeared to him inconceivable. But was he right? He was not right. His predecessor, who wrote θερος, did not mean θηρός but θέρους, which he gave, as he gave πανάμερος (or perhaps πανήμερος), not carelessly but intentionally, presenting Sophocles absurdly indeed but nevertheless exactly as he was commonly read and sung. We will explain why.

According to Sophocles, as we have just seen, the final sacrifice of Heracles was offered upon Mount Cenaeum, the N.W. promontory of Euboea. But this was not the only form of the legend, and there is every reason to think that it was not the oldest. In the tale of Ovid[1], though the deity is *Cenaean Jove*, the place is not Cenaeum, but the immediate neighbourhood of Mount Oeta, in the entrance, that is to say, of Thermopylae, where as a historical fact the memory of Heracles prevailed. When we consider how closely the catastrophe of the sacrifice is connected with the removal of the dying hero to Oeta itself, we cannot but see that the scene of Ovid is natural, the scene of Sophocles unnatural to the verge of impossibility. And when we add that the top of Cenaeum never was, so far as appears, the scene of a great festival, and never was likely to be, whereas the gate of Thermopylae was a famous place of assembly, associated (as Sophocles himself notices in this very ode[2]) with just such gatherings as at Pytho, at Olympia, and elsewhere became the occasion of similar periodic celebrations, we are confirmed in the conclusion that the transference of scene was from Thermopylae to Cenaeum, and not the other way. Nevertheless the change must have been made for grave reason, and the later version must have taken firm hold, or we should not find Sophocles adhering to it, as he does, notwithstanding its particular inconvenience as a theme for the Attic stage. By simply putting the sacrifice, as does Ovid, in the proper place, the dramatist would have freed his story at a stroke from embarrassments which he ignores, but must have seen. Now the passage before us indicates what was the religious necessity which enforced this

[1] *Metam.* 9. 135 ff. [2] 638.

cumbersome alteration. The legend had to be changed, because it was the base and sanction of the calendric cycle, *and the cycle proved to be wrong.* The error was indeed not great, a defect of three days in the cycle of twelve years. But to correct it, by removing the anticipated feast to the true season, would with lapse of time become imperative, if the plan was to be saved at all. The terminus of the cycle, according to the legend, was the end of the labours of Heracles, comprising in one event his return home, sacrifice, and death on Oeta. It was now discovered (it had to be discovered) that these terminal events had not been so nearly simultaneous, that the sacrifice had really preceded the death by a short interval—perhaps a day or two; and to give plausibility to this, the scene of the sacrifice to *Cenaean Zeus* was relegated to the opposite coast and the promontory of *Cenaeum.* In celebrating the festival according to the date of the sacrifice, whereas it should have been determined by the true 'end,' that is the death, men had constantly anticipated the intention of the heavenly powers. And so, in the usual fashion, the credit of the gods was saved, and a place made for practical correction. We need not indeed suppose that the sacrifice on Cenaeum was then for the first time invented. That Heracles offered there a part of his spoil had probably always been an incident in the tale. What was new was to identify this as the final sacrifice, the occasion on which he received the fatal robe.

To this amendment of the story and the practice

refer both the traditional phrases presented by the MS. version of our passage. When it was said that from 'the island altar' Heracles ἔμολε πανήμερος, *came home with all his days*, the point to be made was that only after this last journey from Euboea to Oeta, and not before, had he absolutely and exactly completed the period fixed by the gods for the instructive cycle of his toils. And the πρόφασις θέρους, the *pretence*, or more strictly *pre-appearance, of summer*, signified the error itself which had been committed, first in a manner by Heracles and since by mankind, in celebrating 'the close of his labours' by a festival some days too soon. What was the exact solar epoch of the calendric feast does not appear in Sophocles; but it was certainly θέρος, as appears not only from the incidental description of the meadows as *summer haunt of oxen* (βουθερής v. 188), but plainly from the important part in the catastrophe which is played by the heat of the sun (vv. 685 ff., 765 f.). The variety of range in which the word θέρος was applied, forbids any nearer definition than that the epoch fell somewhere in the warm half of the year; if we should connect it, as the allusion in Sophocles might suggest (v. 637), with the Amphictyonic assembly of historic ages, θέρος would be the *harvest*, and the time autumn, which is one of its many possible meanings. However, this question is of no importance: it was at any rate θέρος, and so called.

Now, it is a familiar literary phenomenon that traditional or consecrated phrases haunt the mind, and produce, especially when the theme in hand is itself sacred, all sorts of imitations and echoes. Under such influences Sophocles was composing when he wrote, as it is justly inferred that he did,

> ὅθεν μόλοι πανίμερος
> τᾶς πειθοῦς παγχρίστῳ
> συγκραθεὶς ἐπὶ προφάσει φάρους.

His terms are not precisely those of the legend, but they are very like them, and pleased his ear the better for that likeness. But for common ears this delicacy was too much. Being led by the poet so near to the accustomed language, scribes, singers, and reciters took, as was to be expected, the last step for themselves, and repeated their nonsense

> ὅθεν μόλοι πανήμερος
> τᾶς πειθοῦς παγχρίστῳ
> συγκραθεὶς ἐπὶ προφάσει θέρους

with no more qualms about the meaning than are felt by those who now chant with fervour 'Or ever your pots be made hot with thorns, so let indignation vex him, even as a thing that is raw.'

Lastly, the existence of this archaic cycle, of which the memory and even the practice may well have survived in backward parts for a long time, will explain a tradition which has been a stumbling-block to historians of the calendar. The *Octaeteris* or *Enneateris*, the calendric cycle chiefly used by the Greeks in historic times, had three complementary or intercalary months. Ancient authorities report[1] that originally all these three months were

[1] See Smith's *Dict. Ant.* s.v. Calendarium.

inserted in the last year of the cycle. As applied to the Octaeteris, this is justly rejected as incredible. This cycle was a scheme of considerable complication, presuming as its basis a system of *unequal months.* We cannot believe that a society, settled and instructed enough to devise and work such a plan as this, would be contented with an error accumulating within eight years up to three months. It will at once be seen that, as an imperfect reminiscence of our rude archaic cycle, the statement becomes intelligible. Our primitive intercalation was actually made in the last year of the then prevailing cycle; and though it did not really amount to three months, but to two, the fact that it was made by means of a *χρόνος τρίμηνος*, offered a ready opportunity for confusion with the three separate months intercalated under the common system. Indeed this confusion, or some such, seems to have been already made by Sophocles or before him, and probably helped to produce the interpretation 'fifteen months,' which we have already cited as erroneous.

In this account no pretence is made to have exhausted the subject. Probably there is much more in the play which, with closer examination or more knowledge, might be proved to betray the influence of the primitive legend and its purpose. Enough has been said perhaps to show that the legend deserves attention, both for historical curiosity and for the sake of the literary flower to which it has served for a subsoil.

APHRODITE PANDEMOS AND THE *HIPPOLYTUS* OF EURIPIDES

Euripides, in the prologue to the *Hippolytus*, connects the story of his hero and of Phaedra with the erection of a certain statue of Aphrodite at Athens, and with the title or titles which this statue commonly bore. The statue was evidently the Aphrodite ἐπὶ Ἱππολύτῳ, a title known to us from other evidence. It has generally been supposed, and in my opinion rightly, to be identical with the Aphrodite Pandemos, so that Πάνδημος and ἐπὶ Ἱππολύτῳ would be alternative names, or parts of a single name. Such, for example, is the view adopted by Miss Harrison in the *Mythology and Monuments of Ancient Athens*. Recently however a distinction has been attempted, and it has been maintained that the sanctuary and cult of *the* Aphrodite Pandemos, properly and officially so called, were different from the sanctuary and cult of the Aphrodite ἐπὶ Ἱππολύτῳ. Materials for considering this question are given by Dr Frazer in his commentary on Pausanias (I. 22. 1—3). I do not propose to discuss it here, and will assume for the present purpose no more than this, that between the Aphrodite ἐπὶ Ἱππολύτῳ and the title

Pandemos there was for some reason a close association. This much at least the passage of Pausanias (which, in my opinion, presumes the identity) must be held to presume and prove; nor indeed am I aware that it has been disputed. What I propose to show is that the story told by Euripides is based upon this association; that he assumes his Aphrodite ἐπὶ Ἱππολύτῳ to be at least *an* Aphrodite Pandemos, representing the goddess in that aspect, and commonly connected with that appellation; and that in this connexion of thought is to be found the solution of a certain difficulty which the story presents.

Hippolytus, says Aphrodite, is destined to expiate his defiance of her, and the way is prepared:

ἐλθόντα γάρ νιν Πιτθέως ποτ' ἐκ δόμων
σεμνῶν ἐς ὄψιν καὶ τέλη μυστηρίων
Πανδίονος γῆν πατρὸς εὐγενὴς δάμαρ
ἰδοῦσα Φαίδρα καρδίαν κατείχετο
ἔρωτι δεινῷ τοῖς ἐμοῖς βουλεύμασι.
καὶ πρὶν μὲν ἐλθεῖν τήνδε γῆν Τροζηνίαν,
πέτραν παρ' αὐτὴν Παλλάδος, κατόψιον
γῆς τῆσδε, ναὸν Κύπριδος ἐγκαθίσατο,
ἐρῶσ' ἔρωτ' ἔκδημον· Ἱππολύτῳ δ' ἔπι
τὸ λοιπὸν ὠνόμαζεν ἱδρῦσθαι θεάν.
ἐπεὶ δὲ Θησεὺς Κεκροπίαν λείπει χθόνα,
μίασμα φεύγων αἵματος Παλλαντιδῶν,
καὶ τήνδε σὺν δάμαρτι ναυστολεῖ χθόνα,
ἐνιαυσίαν ἔκδημον αἰνέσας φυγήν,
ἐνταῦθα δὴ στένουσα κἀκπεπληγμένη
κέντροις ἔρωτος ἡ τάλαιν' ἀπόλλυται
σιγῇ. (24 ff.)

Phaedra gave her Aphrodite a name, ὠνόμαζε θεάν. But what name? Not ἐπὶ Ἱππολύτῳ. It cannot be meant that she published, by her own act and declaration, the very passion which she desired to conquer, suppress, and conceal. Not *Pandemos*; for that title, however it be interpreted, has in this application no meaning and cannot be found in the words. Such is the difficulty.

It has been proposed to get rid of it by so changing the text that the title meant (which is assumed to be ἐπὶ Ἱππολύτῳ) shall not be bestowed by Phaedra, but by some one else. Such is the principle of Jortin's emendation,

Ἱππολύτῳ δ' ἔπι
τὸ λοιπὸν ὀνομάσουσιν ἱδρῦσθαι θεάν,

'*men* hereafter *shall name* the statue the Aphrodite ἐπὶ Ἱππολύτῳ.' And on the same lines, though with more discretion and better taste, proceeds that of Meineke, ὠνόμαζον, 'I, Aphrodite, gave the name.' But not even this will pass. At the time when Aphrodite speaks, at the dramatic time of the prologue, the name ἐπὶ Ἱππολύτῳ has manifestly not yet been attached to the statue; the goddess may intend that it shall be attached; but this is not expressed by ὠνόμαζον. Moreover the matter in hand is the feeling and purpose of Phaedra, when the dedication was made; if the name in question was not then given by her, this is no place to mention it; both ὀνομάσουσιν and ὠνόμαζον convert the sentence into a mere parenthesis, offensive in such a story and at such a point. In fact this road leads nowhere; the conferring of the name ἐπὶ Ἱππολύτῳ, as a name, cannot, from the nature of the case, be that which the poet has here directly in view. If any way is to be found, we must start afresh.

The difficulty arises, as I think, from the fact that Euripides, repeating a legend which, whatever it was, must have been familiar to his audience, has told it, as a poet in such circumstances would, allusively; so that a certain point in it, though necessary and central, is not so much stated as implied. The legend did actually explain how the statue came by the description ἐπὶ Ἱππολύτῳ, and how the goddess came by the title *Pandemos*; it derived both the description and the title from a name conferred on the statue by Phaedra in dedicating it. But this name was neither ἐπὶ Ἱππολύτῳ nor *Pandemos*. The name which Phaedra gave, but which, with only too much reason, was afterwards changed to another, was *Aphrodite Endemos* or 'Love at Home.' When Hippolytus had returned from Athens to Trozen, Phaedra, finding that her heart had gone after him, and virtuously desiring to be rid of the passion with which Aphrodite had afflicted her, endeavoured to propitiate, and perhaps to control, the goddess by a symbolic offering and ceremony, signifying that she called back her errant affection, and bade it thenceforward abide and dwell in its own place. Because 'she was in love with one *not of her home*' (ἐρῶσα ἔρωτα ἔκδημον) 'she set up *in* her home' (ἐγκαθίσατο) a shrine and figure of the representative goddess, 'and gave the figure a name (*Endemos*) importing and intending that henceforth for ever the goddess was *there fixed'* or '*there established'* (ἐν-ιδρῦσθαι). This name in itself, *Love at Home*, sounded of nothing but innocence and happiness. That she gave it ἐπὶ Ἱππολύτῳ 'in reference to Hippolytus,' and in the hope to cure herself of an ἔρως ἔκδημος already kindled in her heart, was her own secret. Thus it was that

> πέτραν παρ' αὐτὴν Παλλάδος, κατόψιον
> γῆς τῆσδε, ναὸν Κυπρίδος ἐγκαθίσατο,
> ἐρῶσ' ἔρωτ' ἔκδημον· Ἱππολύτῳ δ' ἔπι
> τὸ λοιπὸν ὠνόμαζ' ἐνιδρῦσθαι θεάν.

The change, if such it is to be called, of ὠνόμαζεν ἱδρῦσθαι to ὠνόμαζ' ἐνιδρῦσθαι is preferable, though perhaps not necessary. However Aphrodite was not to be so appeased or so confined, as soon appeared when, in the course of fate, Theseus himself removed to Trozen, and Phaedra was compelled to share the city and home of Hippolytus, so that her 'Love at Home' in Athens became an idle figure, and its title a miserable irony—a connexion of thought which Euripides, with skilful touch, indicates by contriving, naturally and as if casually, to repeat and echo the significant word ἔκδημος:

> καὶ τήνδε σὺν δάμαρτι ναυστολεῖ χθόνα
> ἐνιαυσίαν ἔκδημον αἰνέσας φυγήν.

At Trozen the plan of Aphrodite went victoriously forward and her victims perished as the tragedy sets forth. Now when all this came to be known, men drew from it the lesson which Aphrodite meant to teach, that She is not of this place or of that place, not by any title or any figure to be fixed here or there, in Athens or in Trozen; She is *of all peoples*, *of all places* and *everywhere at home*, and Her power is everywhere under heaven (*vv.* 1—6):

πολλὴ μὲν ἐν βροτοῖσι κοὐκ ἀνώνυμος
θεὰ κέκλημαι Κύπρις οὐρανοῦ τ' ἔσω·
ὅσοι τε Πόντου τερμόνων τ' Ἀτλαντικῶν
ναίουσιν εἴσω φῶς ὁρῶντες ἡλίου,
τοὺς μὲν σέβοντας τἀμὰ πρεσβεύω κράτη,
σφάλλω δ' ὅσοι φρονοῦσιν εἰς ἡμᾶς μέγα.

And that Her name might remind men of this, and warn them to bear themselves humbly towards Her, they called Her thenceforward *Pandemos*; and of the statue which Phaedra had dedicated in the hope to confine the goddess, and had so ineffectually named *Endemos* ὡς μελλούσης δὴ τῆς θεᾶς ἐνδημεῖν, they said that it was the Aphrodite ἐπὶ Ἱππολύτῳ, the image of One who was not *Endemos* but *Pandemos*.

Such was the Athenian legend in the fifth century B.C., and not an ill one. It has at all events more religion in it, and not less morality, than the philosophic allegory made famous by Plato, and more interest than the curiously frigid piece of fictitious history attached to *Pandemos* in Pausanias: to wit, that Theseus established the name and cult, in conjunction with that of *Peitho*, to commemorate his success in wooing and *persuading all the townships* (δῆμοι) of Attica to unite in one common city. A marriage of united parishes indeed! When paganism was vivid, men had a notion of Aphrodite which certainly was not that.

It may not be superfluous to add, since the Euripidean version, equally with those of Plato, Pausanias and Harpocration[1], in explaining the name *Pandemos* puts a strain upon the word, that none of these stories, nor whatsoever others the ancients may have related, are relevant to the question, what, if anything, that title, or the description ἐπὶ Ἱππολύτῳ, really meant or properly was. It would be unsafe even to assume that the very dialect in which these appellations were first formed, was what we know as Greek, still more unsafe to assume, that their origin was such as the Greeks or we should consider appropriate, or are able to divine. They were merely names. Of their beginning the Athenians, it is safe to suppose, knew nothing, and we are not likely to know.

[1] Connecting *Pandemos* locally with the agora.

EURIPIDES, *ANDROMACHE* 655–6

(The Death of Achilles—Medial Pauses in the Tragic Senarius.)

'Why should one say that old men are wise men, those even whom the world once thought sensible, when you, Peleus, *you* disgrace yourself in rebuking me for the sake of a foreign woman? Rather should you have hunted her to the ends of the earth, and bidden me help in the chase! A woman of that Asia where Greek warriors, in numbers never equalled, lost their lives! A woman part-guilty of your son's blood! You dwell with her under one roof, you admit her to your table, you suffer her in your house to bear children of her detestable race!'

In such terms Menelaus, in the *Andromache* of Euripides, reproaches the father of Achilles for his domestic relations with the widow of Hector. To the natural suggestion[1] that the Trojan woman, as such, is associated with the death of Achilles,

τοῦ σοῦ δὲ παιδὸς αἵματος κοινουμένην,

the traditional text appends an explanation which,

[1] Cf. *Andr.* 247 μισοῦν γε πατρίδα σὴν Ἀχιλλέως φόνῳ.

if the reader does not happen to remember it, will surprise him: 'For Paris, who slew your son Achilles, was brother to Hector, and Andromache was Hector's wife.'

> Πάρις γάρ, ὃς σὸν παῖδ' ἔπεφν' Ἀχιλλέα,
> Ἕκτορος ἀδελφὸς ἦν, δάμαρ δ' ἥδ' Ἕκτορος.

This unacceptable interpretation was expelled from the text by Nauck, who gives no reasons, but doubtless held the aesthetic objection to be sufficient, as perhaps it is. The purpose of this paper is to show that Nauck's surmise can be strictly proved. The verses impugned would be astonishing in Euripides anywhere, and in the *Andromache* are impossible. The failure of the imitation, though only two lines are attempted, is grotesque, and the divergences instructive. The second verse,

> Ἕκτορος ἀδελφὸς ἦν, δάμαρ δ' ἥδ' Ἕκτορος,

judged by the standard of Euripides, is hardly a verse. It is as bad as, without breach of absolute rule, it could be made—weak in beginning, middle and end; and it might conveniently be given to a tiro in composition as a *memoria technica* of things undesirable. It combines three distinct and extreme licences.

I. *The first foot*[1] *should not consist of a single dactylic word.*

This variation, perhaps the least eligible of all

[1] This use of 'foot' is, I am aware, not scientific, but it saves some cumbrousness of expression, and seems to me harmless.

which the practice of the tragedians does not prohibit, is here something like an anachronism. It appears, very rarely, in Euripidean plays of the middle period: the *Troades* (about 415 B.C.), for example, has one or two specimens of it[1]. Later still, when most licences increase in frequency and the initial *foot* is often a dactyl, a *dactylic word* so placed becomes naturally more common, though it remains to the last exceptional. In the early period, on the other hand, in plays of Euripides which certainly or probably were acted before (say) 423 B.C., the licence is hardly, perhaps never, to be found[2]. Now the versification of the *Andromache* is 'early,' resembling in regularity that of the *Medea* or the *Hippolytus*. The dactylic first *foot* is itself a rarity in the play[3], and a dactylic *word* in this foot, as might be expected, does not occur at all. Yet the interpolator not only uses it, but actually signalizes it by repeating the same word with the normal scansion (– ⏑ –) at the end of the verse. Such a treatment would be surprising, perhaps even suspicious, in itself.

[1] *Tro.* 415, 653 (648). Here and elsewhere I naturally do not reckon phrases such as μηδένα (*Tro.* 510), which contain not one word, but two, and when emphatic, as in this position they almost necessarily are, would be better so printed.

[2] A proper name, such as Ἕκτορος, would be the most likely occasion for the licence; but in fact, down to the *Hecuba* (inclusive), it does not occur, so far as I have observed. It might, no doubt, have occurred in the *Andromache* or anywhere; but that is not the point.

[3] *Andr.* 169 (οὐ Πρίαμος), 387, 1157, 1214, 1266.

II. ***A punctuation, a pause necessary to the sense, should not (without special reason) occur at the centre of the verse,*** i.e. ***between the third foot and the fourth.***

This is the most important of all general rules for the tragic senarius, more important even than the rule of the *caesura*, which is indeed only another and a subordinate application of the same principle. Euripides observes it carefully, and departs from it, generally speaking, only under special conditions, which the imitator does not fulfil.

The reason for the rule is obvious. A verse of six feet is liable, from the nature of the human ear, to break up into symmetrical sections; above all, it is liable to break into a distich, two verses of three feet each. To prevent this is the purpose, and the sole purpose, of the general rule that a *caesura*, a separation of word from word, must occur either in the third foot (where it is most efficient for the purpose and therefore commonest) or in the fourth. But it is manifest that, if a much stronger break, such as the division of clause from clause, is made at the centre, the effect of the *caesura* is overpowered and the unity of the verse is destroyed. Such a sentence as

Ἕκτορος ἀδελφὸς ἦν, δάμαρ δ' ἥδ' Ἕκτορος

will and must be naturally recited as a distich.

Now Euripides, in his departures from this rule[1],

[1] Such verses as

σιγῇ δόμους εἰσβᾶσ', ἵν' ἔστρωται λέχος,

with an *elision* between the third foot and the fourth, do not fall observes a distinction, delicate indeed but approved by common sense. The vice of the medial punctuation is that it gives to the first half of the line the semblance of a completed verse; therefore the less this resemblance, the less is the objection; and therefore there is difference of degree according to *the nature of the third foot*, the foot preceding the pause. There are three possibilities:

(1) a trisyllabic foot, dactyl or tribrach, as *Bacch.* 841

ὁδοὺς ἐρήμους ἴμεν· ἐγὼ δ' ἡγήσομαι.

(2) a spondee, as *Ion* 1019

τούτῳ θανεῖται παῖς· σὺ δ' ὁ κτείνων ἔσει.

(3) an iambus, as *Bacch.* 922

ἀλλ' ἦ ποτ' ἦσθα θήρ; τεταύρωσαι γὰρ οὖν.

It is plain to the ear that the separate unity of the first half, regarded as a verse in the iambic measure, is greatest by far in the third example, less in the second, and much less again in the first. And the practice of Euripides differs accordingly.

(1) *Medial punctuation after a trisyllabic foot (resolved thesis)*.

This appears in all parts of Euripides as an artifice, employed with intention and for some special effect, as for instance in *Supplices* 1060: Iphitus is

within the scope of our consideration, the pause not being strictly medial. They have, 'virtually,' as the phrase is, a caesura in the fourth foot. They are more common than those without elision; the use of them I believe to be similar though distinguishable. However they do not concern us at present.

expostulating with his daughter Evadne, who stands over the pyre of her husband and has resolved (though the father does not know this) to throw herself into it:

> ΙΦ. κἄπειτα τύμβῳ καὶ πυρᾷ φαίνει πέλας;
> ΕΥ. ἐνταῦθα γὰρ δὴ καλλίνικος ἔρχομαι.
> ΙΦ. νικῶσα νίκην τίνα; μαθεῖν χρῄζω σέθεν.

The broken verse marks the rising anxiety (cf. *Orestes* 401), and has therefore a rhetorical justification. With different and subtle purpose the pause is used in *Troades* 1177, the lament of Hecuba over the mangled corpse of the babe Astyanax:

> δύστηνε, κρατὸς ὥς σ' ἔκειρεν ἀθλίως
> τείχη πατρῷα, Λοξίου πυργώματα·
> ὃν πόλλ' ἐκήπευσ' ἡ τεκοῦσα βόστρυχον
> φιλήμασίν τ' ἔδωκεν, ἔνθεν ἐκγελᾷ
> ὀστέων ῥαγέντων...φόνος,—ἵν' αἰσχρὰ μὴ λέγω.

The punctuation accents the euphemism substituted for the more horrible expression (*μύσος*?) which rises in the mind. Similar in principle is *Helen* 1399

> ὦ καινὸς ἡμῖν...πόσις, ἀναγκαίως ἔχει,
> τὰ πρῶτα λέκτρα νυμφικάς θ' ὁμιλίας
> τιμᾶν.

Helen, just widowed, as she pretends, of Menelaus, and falsely plighted to her wooer Theoclymenus, modestly hesitates in addressing him for the first time as her 'husband.' The punctuation emphasizes this. Other examples, where the irregular break seems to have an obvious rhetorical justification, are *Andr.* 47, *Heracles* 593 (the sharp note of warning), *Helen* 1043, 1520, etc.

But in the later plays, from the *Heracles* onwards, other examples are found, where there seems to be no special emphasis or other such justification. There is visible a tendency, corresponding to other changes in the style, to treat medial punctuation, *when preceded by a trisyllabic foot*, as a mere licence, admissible, though not common, for mere variation of rhythm ; so for example in

Heracles 978 :

ὁ δ' ἐξελίσσων παῖδα κίονος κύκλῳ,
τόρνευμα δεινὸν ποδός, ἐναντίον σταθεὶς
βάλλει πρὸς ἧπαρ.

Ion 1030 :

οἶσθ' οὖν ὃ δρᾶσον; χειρὸς ἐξ ἐμῆς λαβὼν
χρύσωμ' Ἀθάνας τόδε, παλαιὸν ὄργανον,
ἐλθὼν κ.τ.λ.

See also[1] *El.* 43, *Iph. T.* 484, 1040 ; *Helen* 290, 449, 1236, 1241, 1449 ; *Phoen.* 46, 449, 846 ; *Or.* 549, 1585 ; *Bacchae* 298, 353, 841, 975 ; *Iph. A.* 468, 747, etc. The specimens cited will show the effect which, though strange to an ear trained on the *Medea* or the *Hippolytus*, must be taken as in itself unobjectionable. In the *Andromache*, as in

[1] I ignore here and elsewhere cases (such as *Heracles* 8, *Hecuba* 398) where, though we may put a comma, we cannot say that there is any break of sense, and *a fortiori*, cases such as *Andr.* 698, where not even a *comma* is required. My lists are fairly full, but completeness is not necessary for the present purpose, and it is probable that some instances have been overlooked. Indeed completeness is scarcely possible where in delicate cases there must be room for difference of judgement and estimate.

the early plays generally, I find no example of this pause treated merely as a licence.

(2) *Medial punctuation after a spondee.*

As a rhetorical device, to mark a sharp emphasis or specially significant pause, this is extremely effective, and is found in Euripidean work of all periods, *e.g.*:

Alc. 789:

εὔφραινε σαυτόν, πῖνε, τὸν καθ' ἡμέραν
βίον λογίζου σόν,—τὰ δ' ἄλλα τῆς τύχης.

with which, for the emphasis given to the word σόν compare *Hecuba* 253, *Hipp.* 888, *Phoen.* 521, 524, *Helen* 987, *Orestes* 1053. See also *Med.* 701:

δίδωσι δ' αὐτῷ τίς; πέραινέ μοι λόγον.

Hec. 879:

τίς σοι σύνεσται χείρ; πόθεν κτήσει φίλους;

Heracles 1256:

ἄκουε δή νυν, ὡς ἁμιλληθῶ λόγοις
πρὸς νουθετήσεις σάς, ἀναπτύξω δέ σοι
ἀβίωτον ἡμῖν νῦν τε καὶ πάροιθεν ὄν.

where the gravity of the opening is produced mainly by the unaccustomed pause.

Helen 585:

τίνος πλάσαντος θεῶν; ἄελπτα γὰρ λέγεις,

with which compare *Phoen.* 738.

Phoen. 1005, where the whole passage from *v.* 991 should be read, in order to appreciate the value of the break in

ἐγὼ δὲ πατέρα καὶ κασίγνητον προδοὺς

πόλιν τ' ἐμαυτοῦ, δειλὸς ὥς, ἔξω χθονὸς
ἄπειμ'; ὅπου δ' ἂν ζῶ,—κακὸς φανήσομαι;
μὰ τὸν μετ' ἄστρων Ζῆνα κ.τ.λ.

Different in kind, but equally satisfactory, is the unusual rhythm of *Heraclidae* 837:

τὸ δεύτερον δὲ ποὺς ἐπαλλαχθεὶς ποδί,
ἀνὴρ δ' ἐπ' ἀνδρὶ στάς, ἐκαρτέρει μάχῃ.

To these add *Alc.* 939, *Andr.* 412, *Heraclidae* 238, *Hipp.* 1319, *Hec.* 232, *El.* 248, 1042, *Heracles* 1301, *Ion* 1019, *Iph. A.* 667, 1461 (in all of which a rhetorical purpose is obvious), and also *Andr.* 973, where the purpose should not be overlooked. Orestes speaks to Hermione:

ἐπεὶ δ' Ἀχιλλέως δεῦρ' ἐνόστησεν γόνος,
σῷ μὲν συνέγνων πατρί, τὸν δ' ἐλισσόμην
γάμους ἀφεῖναι σούς, ἐμὰς λέγων τύχας
καὶ τὸν παρόντα δαίμον', ὡς φίλων μὲν ἂν
γήμαιμ' ἀπ' ἀνδρῶν, ἔκτοθεν δ' οὐ ῥᾳδίως,
φεύγων ἀπ' οἴκων ἃς ἐγὼ φεύγω φυγάς.

The point of the emphasis on σούς is that *Hermione*, and only Hermione, being in the circumstances a possible bride for Orestes, Neoptolemus, to whom the world was open, should in fairness have resigned his pretensions to *her*.

That medial punctuation after a spondee is never admitted by Euripides without special purpose, would be too much to say, but examples of such treatment will be found very rare[1]. Three I find in the *Supplices*,—a play distinguished from all extant

[1] In *Tro.* 386 I do not find any pause. In *Hecuba* 979 I should prefer to punctuate before, not after, σούς, though if the

works of the poet by other and more important peculiarities:

Suppl. 268:

ἔχει γὰρ καταφυγὴν θὴρ μὲν πέτραν,
δοῦλος δὲ βωμοὺς θεῶν, πόλις δὲ πρὸς πόλιν
ἔπτηξε χειμασθεῖσα.

ib. 704:

λέχος δ' ὀδόντων ὄφεος ἐξηνδρωμένος
δεινὸς παλαιστὴς ἦν· ἔκλινε γὰρ κέρας
τὸ λαιὸν ἡμῶν.

ib. 754:

ὧν οὕνεκ' ἀγὼν ἦν, νεκροὺς κομίζετε;

Nothing so lax as these two last[1] is to be found, I believe, anywhere else; but *Hec.* 1133, *Electra* 382 (if we make any stop), *Hel.* 1410, and *Orestes* 1220 may be noted as perhaps less careful than usual. Little reliance should be placed on the prosaic and (as I think) rather clumsy verses in *Bacchae* 680:

ὁρῶ δὲ θιάσους τρεῖς γυναικείων χορῶν.
[ὧν ἦρχ' ἑνὸς μὲν Αὐτονόη, τοῦ δευτέρου
μήτηρ 'Αγαύη σή, τρίτου δ' 'Ινὼ χοροῦ][2]
ηὗδον δὲ πᾶσαι κ.τ.λ.

other punctuation be preferred, the emphasis thus put on σούς can be justified. In *Hecuba* 321 it is possible that the comma should follow, not precede, τάδε.

[1] Contrast the calculated and excellent effect of a similar flatness, followed by change of tone, in Sophocles *Phil.* 435. For the general practice of Sophocles, which is similar to that of Euripides, but I think rather less strict, see *Phil.* 57, 297, 366, 389, 503, 589, 907, 1009, 1021, 1049, 1237, 1302.

[2] τοῦ δὲ δευτέρου and τρίτη δ' 'Ινώ MSS.

The names of Agave's sisters are of no importance to the play, and on the other hand an erudite commentator would like to supply them. This couplet (and *Bacch.* 229–230) may well be spurious[1].

The *Andromache* itself has an example of medial punctuation after a spondee (*v.* 1268), where the unwonted pause has a singularly delicate and pathetic significance. Thetis, having promised immortality to Peleus, continues thus:

ἀλλ' ἕρπε Δελφῶν ἐς θεόδμητον πόλιν,
νεκρὸν κομίζων τόνδε, καὶ κρύψας χθονί,
ἐλθὼν παλαιᾶς χοιράδος κοῖλον μυχὸν
Σηπιάδος ἵζου· μίμνε δ', ἔς τ' ἂν ἐξ ἁλὸς
λαβοῦσα πεντήκοντα Νηρῄδων χορὸν
ἔλθω κομιστήν σου·—τὸ γὰρ πεπρωμένον
δεῖ σ' ἐκκομίζειν· Ζηνὶ γὰρ δοκεῖ τάδε.
παῦσαι δὲ λύπης κ.τ.λ.

The best commentary on this is furnished by Euripides himself, who does the same thing, with a difference, in the similar address of Artemis to the dying Hippolytus (*Hipp.* 1426):

σοὶ δ', ὦ ταλαίπωρ', ἀντὶ τῶνδε τῶν κακῶν
τιμὰς μεγίστας ἐν πόλει Τροζηνίᾳ
δώσω· κόραι γὰρ ἄζυγες γάμων πάρος
κόμας κεροῦνταί σοι,—δι' αἰῶνος μακροῦ
πένθη μέγιστα δακρύων καρπουμένῳ. κ.τ.λ.

[1] In *Andr.* 929 πῶς οὖν τάδ', ὡς εἴποι τις, ἐξημάρτανες; a medial punctuation, very strange and peculiar, is produced by the conjecture πῶς οὖν, ἂν εἴποι τις, τάδ' ἐξημάρτανες; which for this and other reasons is to be rejected. As I have said elsewhere (note *ad loc.* in Appendix to my essay on this play, in *Four Essays* etc.), I believe the archaic optative without ἂν to be, in such a traditional formula as ὡς εἴποι τις, admissible and natural.

(3) *Medial punctuation after an iambus.*

This division, which, as we have already remarked, breaks up the verse completely, may of course be used, like any other irregularity whatever, if there is sufficient reason, but without grave reason ought manifestly not to be admitted. Such a verse as that cited above, *Bacchae* 922

ἀλλ' ἦ ποτ' ἦσθα θήρ; τεταύρωσαι γὰρ οὖν

violently arrests the ear accustomed to tragic rhythm, and is of course here intended to do so. It is the exclamation of Pentheus, when he first sees in the 'Lydian stranger' the signs of his divinity. For other examples, differing in kind, but all appropriated to great agitation, see *Hipp.* 313, *Heraclidae* 424, *Helen* 86, *ib.* 575, *Phoen.* 761, *ib.* 1317. In two places the break serves to mark hesitation before the suggestion of something extremely painful: *Ion* 1527

ὅρα σύ, μῆτερ, μὴ σφαλεῖσ' ἃ παρθένοις
ἐγγίγνεται νοσήματ' ἐς κρυπτοὺς γάμους
ἔπειτα τῷ θεῷ προστίθῃς τὴν αἰτίαν,
καὶ τοὐμὸν αἰσχρὸν ἀποφυγεῖν πειρωμένη
Φοίβῳ τεκεῖν με φῄς,—τεκοῦσ' οὐκ ἐκ θεοῦ.

See also, with the context, *Troades* 619 (615). The peculiar and in some respects unique verse, *Ion* 1041,

ἄγ', ὦ γεραιὲ πούς, νεανίας γενοῦ,

a pure iambic with medial punctuation, is excellently adapted to the meaning, as is the similar, but delicately differentiated, *Troades* 1275

ἀλλ', ὦ γεραιὲ πούς, ἐπίσπευσον μόλις,

where the 'aged foot' makes an effort, but instantly flags. Such examples are no rule for anything beyond themselves.

To find a single example of this pause (medial punctuation after an iambus) treated by Euripides as a mere licence and without regard to the effect, is harder than might be supposed. It occurs naturally, among all imaginable blunders of prosody and rhythm, in the spurious part of the *Iphigenia at Aulis* (1593). Another instance, much less objectionable,

Λήδας μὲν εἰμὶ παῖς, Κλυταιμνήστρα δέ μοι | ὄνομα, κ.τ.λ.

occurs in the same play 827, where it may be genuine, but considering the history of the play, one cannot be sure. *Ion* 1580 is doubtful in reading[1]. *Iph. T.* 87

λαβεῖν τ' ἄγαλμα θεᾶς, ὅ φασιν ἐνθάδε
ἐς τούσδε ναοὺς οὐρανοῦ πεσεῖν ἄπο

will be a case of negligence (though a very mild one) if we admit the punctuation; but since the genitive θεᾶς belongs to ναούς as much as to ἄγαλμα, the comma is better away. In *Bacch.* 49 we may suppose an intentional emphasis on εὖ, and so elsewhere. The plain truth is that the thing ought not to be done without reason, and Euripides hardly ever, if ever, so did it. Nor, by the way, does that extraordinary imitator (if imitator he is), the author of the *Rhesus,* whose practice in this matter (see *vv.* 161,

[1] Ὅπλητες Ἀργαδῆς τ', ἐμῆς δ' ἀπ' αἰγίδος κ.τ.λ. (Dindorf), which modifies the medial punctuation by an elision. The whole passage (1575–1594) is poor and of doubtful authority.

388, 579) is as good as, and rather better than, that of the *Supplices*. But the author of

Ἕκτορος ἀδελφὸς ἦν, δάμαρ δ' ᾗδ' Ἕκτορος

does it without scruple or palliation. And he treats in the same way a third rule.

III. *The rule against a 'cretic pause' (or cretic caesura).*

The author thinks, as mechanical composers commonly do, that he satisfies this rule because in ᾗδ' Ἕκτορος the cretic word is preceded by a monosyllable. He does not perceive that, to make this remedy effective to the ear, the monosyllable should be linked in sense to the cretic, joined to it more closely than to what precedes, as in *Andr.* 680

Ἑλένη δ' ἐμόχθησ' οὐχ ἑκοῦσ', ἀλλ' ἐκ θεῶν,

and generally throughout the play[1] and in the practice of the tragedians. It is hardly worth while to discuss here the exact limits of the rule, and the shades of possible infringement with or without special reason. The interpolator's treatment is slovenly, and is made peculiarly offensive (to my ear) by the ugly sound of the peccant monosyllable (δ' ᾗδ') in δάμαρ δ' ᾗδ' Ἕκτορος.

To sum up then, this imitator of Euripides' *Andromache* unites in a single verse three licences,

[1] See *Andr.* 367, 378, 460, 640, 680, 750, 905, 975, 979, 1081. In *ib.* 875 there is no 'cretic pause': the scansion intended is δωμάτων τῶνδ' ἐκ-πεσεῖν, the preposition being treated as separable. In *ib.* 230 τῶν κακῶν γὰρ μητέρων | φεύγειν τρόπους χρὴ τέκνα, the rule is violently broken, and we must either correct (δὲ Pierson) or suppose an intention, a sharp and intentionally disagreeable emphasis on τῶν κακῶν. I prefer the second alternative.

the dactylic word in the first foot, the medial punctuation after an iambus, and the cretic caesura, of which not one is justified by the model. Nor is his first line flawless:

Πάρις γάρ, ὃς σὸν παῖδ' ἔπεφν' Ἀχιλλέα.

It is by no means certain that Euripides, in the pure, simple, and normal language of this speech and scene, would have admitted such an archaism as ἔπεφνε for ἔκτεινε, though he might doubtless have used the word in a proper place. The couplet is a monster, and should be expiated without hesitation.

To establish this point is of more than merely technical interest; for the interpolator is as little acquainted with the facts of the play as with its metre, and misrepresents an important part of the story. He imports into the *Andromache* the common legend, made familiar to us by the Latin poets, that the slayer of Achilles was Paris. But that is not the version of the *Andromache*; for we read there that Neoptolemus, Achilles' son, fell 'by the hand of the same Delphian who slew Achilles himself' (*vv.* 1149 foll.)

Ἀχιλλέως πίτνει
παῖς, ὀξυθήκτῳ πλευρὰ φασγάνῳ τυπεὶς
Δελφοῦ πρὸς ἀνδρός (ὅσπερ αὐτὸν ὤλεσεν)[1],
πολλῶν μετ' ἄλλων κ.τ.λ.

This version of the death of Achilles, that he was slain, either accidentally or (as we should rather

[1] That this means αὐτὸν Ἀχιλλέα, opposed to Ἀχιλλέως παῖς, is in my opinion certain. The words cannot be otherwise translated. The attempts to improve the passage (by omitting ὅσπερ ...ἄλλων and otherwise) proceed upon the mistaken assumption that αὐτόν must mean Neoptolemus.

suppose) treacherously, by a Greek soldier from Delphi, is not mentioned, so far as I know, else where; but this is by no means the only point in which the *Andromache* diverges from common tradition. Indeed the whole story is peculiar, and was invented in all probability by the dramatist. That Delphi was directly responsible for the death of Achilles, as well as for that of his son, is an assumption harmonious with the story, and almost necessary to it. For the very basis of it is the demand of Neoptolemus (*v.* 52) that the god of Delphi should 'pay' for the death of Achilles. The Delphians clearly understood this demand as a literal demand for blood-money, made upon Apollo *and themselves* as proprietors of the Delphic treasure; for they conceived, in consequence of it, a suspicion that the demander intended to compel payment by pillage (*vv.* 1085–1099); and I see no reason to doubt that, according to the story of this drama, the demand of Neoptolemus was really preferred against Delphi, and not only against an inaccessible deity. Now such a demand, impious of course according to orthodoxy in any case, would be scarcely intelligible, and certainly impudent, if Delphi had no nearer connexion with the death of Achilles than that Paris, who slew him, was alleged to have done it by the aid of the Trojan Apollo. But the demand was natural enough and, though retracted by Neoptolemus under pressure of adversity, was not unreasonable, if the responsibility of Delphi at any rate, according to the facts as conceived at Phthia, was certain. A reader familiar with the play will feel that such a conception suits it in all respects better than the common version, which brings in Paris. This therefore, notwithstanding the interpolator of our couplet, we should here exclude and reject.

A starting-point or hint for the story that Achilles as well as his son was the victim of Pythian hatred and fanaticism, is furnished by the *Iliad.* That the treasures of the Phocian sanctuary were envied and coveted by the fierce cavaliers of Thessaly, was already a tradition when the 'Embassy' (*Iliad* IX) was composed, and Achilles himself was made to say (*v.* 404) that, *as the price of his life*, he would not accept all the wealth contained in the Pythian precinct, since 'oxen and sheep may be won by plundering, and tripods and horses may be gotten,' but life is irrecoverable. This language may be innocent, but it would not sound very well in Pythian ears. And when we consider the enmity of Thessaly and Phocis in the fifth century, and the natural disposition of Achilles to offend everybody, there is all the material required for that version of his death which Euripides invented or used. The Delphian traitor and assassin would of course be an anachronism in Homer, but is a proper figure in the *Andromache.*

To account for the allusive reference to the Delphian in this play, we must of course suppose that somewhere the story of Achilles' death was so related. There is no difficulty in supposing this, nor is it perhaps difficult to guess where it was told. But to discuss that, would take us beyond the present subject.

EURIPIDES, *HELENA* 962—974

The situation is this. Helen has been committed to the protection of the good Proteus, king of Egypt. By the death of Proteus, his obligations have devolved upon his daughter Theonoe. A claim for the restoration of Helen is now made by her husband Menelaus, who in the course of his plea speaks as follows:

969 ὦ νέρτερ' Ἅιδη, καὶ σὲ σύμμαχον καλῶ,
ὃς πόλλ' ἐδέξω τῆσδ' ἕκατι σώματα
πεσόντα τὠμῷ φασγάνῳ, μισθὸν δ' ἔχεις·
ἢ νῦν ἐκείνους ἀπόδος ἐμψύχους πάλιν,
ἢ τήνδ' ἀνάγκασόν γε † εὐσεβοῦς πατρὸς
κρείσσω φανεῖσαν τἄμ' ἀποδοῦναι λέχη †.

The god of the nether world, who has profited (such is the argument) by the many dead whom Menelaus has sent to him for the sake of Helen, is called upon either to give back these dead as a payment not earned, or else now to make repayment by compelling Theonoe to restore Helen to her husband.

The last two verses have no metre. But the attempts to mend them by repairing the metre only, are useless. The sense is equally defective. Hades is to *compel* Theonoe to restore Helen. But how is he to do this? What power or function in the matter has the god of the nether world? This is what the concluding verses, in their genuine form, must explain. And upon consideration, it seems that between Hades and the office proposed to him there is but one possible link. To control and compel Theonoe, *he must release, for the moment, her father Proteus.* Proteus, if he could return and appear, would of course be master of the situation. His authority would displace that of his heiress (ἡ νῦν κυρία, *v.* 968), and he could deal as he pleased with the deposit (Helen) entrusted to himself. But Proteus cannot appear except by permission of Hades, and this it is which Menelaus demands:

> ἢ τήνδ' ἀνάγκασόν γε, πατρὸς εὐσεβοῦς
> κρείσσω γ' ἀνεὶς φαντάσματ', ἀποδοῦναι λέχη.

'Or else *compel* Theonoe to restore my wife, by sending up, to *control* her, the apparition of her pious father.' For the use of ἀνιέναι in this connexion, see Liddell and Scott *s.v.* The important words ἀνάγκασον and κρείσσω (*superior*, to the daughter) are thus each enforced by γε. Other arrangements, with the same sense, are possible, *e.g.*

> ἢ τήνδ' ἀνάγκασόν γ' ἔμ' ἀποδοῦναι λέχη,
> κρείσσω γ' ἀνιεὶς φάσματ' εὐσεβοῦς πατρός.

But the first seems on the whole the most probable, and, as will be seen, a slight confusion in the letters γανεισφαν would account for the actual tradition.

Thus explained, the passage continues naturally the sense of the preceding (962 ff.), in which Menelaus appeals directly to the deceased Proteus, but adds that, being dead, he *can now act only through his daughter* and representative. The connexion of thought thus indicated may perhaps throw light upon the defective verse 965,

οἶδ' οὕνεχ' ἡμῖν οὔποτ' †ἀπολέσεις† θανών.

Here ἀπολέσεις is nonsense, and nothing satisfactory has been suggested. Possibly the lost word signified, not 'you will restore (Helen)' or the like, but 'you will *return*.' 'I know that, being dead, you cannot come back to us,' would be appropriate to the context, and would be given by ἀπονίσσῃ (or -ει), whether taken as a present or as a future—a point upon which the ancients differed. Or ἀπονοστεῖς would give the same sense. This would afford a natural, though not necessary, lead for the subsequent appeal to Hades and the request that he will, for this occasion, make possible the impossible, and permit the return of the deceased.

THE THREE ACTORS[1]

THIS well-reasoned pamphlet raises a question which any one, familiar with the present state of inquiry, might have seen to be coming before long. What evidence is there for the common assumption that at the dramatic festivals of Athens in the fifth and fourth centuries B.C., the number of actors performing in a tragedy (or a comedy) was normally limited to three, or limited at all?

It is of course notorious, and is proved both by extant plays and unimpeachable testimony, that *as a general rule with occasional exceptions*, three was in tragedy the greatest number of *characters* permitted to take part *in the same scene and dialogue.* Even tripartite dialogue tended to fall into a series of duos, and beyond the tripartite form complication was not extended. Aristotle notes the limit as matter of fact, and Horace presents it as a precept. It was not a law; it was not absolute or universal as a practice; but it was a general practice and, so understood, is unquestionable.

[1] A review of *The Rule of Three Actors in the Classical Greek Drama; a Dissertation...for the Degree of Doctor of Philosophy.* By Kelley Rees. University of Chicago Press, 1908.

The practice has certain obvious advantages (in securing clearness of situation and relation, and otherwise) from the Greek point of view. If it had not, Aristotle would not have treated it as he does, —as a limit natural to the type of tragedy which he knew, and as completing finally the normal development of that type. But having such cause and sanction, the limit of practice does not prove, by its existence, the existence of any mechanical compulsion or necessity for it. The general preference of dialogue in parts not exceeding three does not, in itself, throw any light on the question how many *actors* the dramatists had at their disposal.

But for plays so constructed, performance by three actors only (with a little help occasionally to turn a difficulty) would be possible, however many the characters, provided that there was no limit to 'doubling,' that is, to the multiplication of characters played by a single actor. And with the use of masks for all parts, any amount of doubling, however unsatisfactory or inartistic, becomes possible.

Now there is full evidence that, from the fourth century B.C. onwards, when acting in Greece had become a common profession, practised for profit by private persons and private associations, this possible economy of players was freely used, and plays, including those of classical tragedy (or more probably, acting-editions of them, cut and garbled for the purpose), were habitually, and perhaps regularly, performed by parties of three.

But the use of this economy by those for whom

economy was an essential object, affords in itself no presumption whatever that such thrift was even permitted, much less that it was imposed as a regulation, in the public festivals of imperial Athens. And on the other hand, the economic practice of centuries does afford some reason for discounting the testimony of scholars, named or anonymous, who, in times near or posterior to the Christian era, say or imply that Sophocles and Euripides were restricted from the first to that allowance of performers which had subsequently been established by commercial custom. That these antiquarians could make mistakes is certain; and here is a mistake which they were likely to make, a pit prepared for their feet.

By the texts of the extant plays their statement is (to say the least) not fortified. It may conceivably be true, it is not strictly impossible, that, as the 'three-actor rule' would require us to suppose, Aeschylus in the *Choephori* meant a 'Servant' to be transformed into 'Pylades' within a few minutes or seconds; that in the *Oedipus at Colonus* Sophocles expected to have the part of Theseus divided, for different scenes, between three distinct performers; that in the *Ion* (for example), and in the tragedies of Euripides and Sophocles generally, a whole series of important and incongruous personations was, by the design of the authors, to be accumulated upon the least accomplished member of a company consisting of three. These things are conceivable, but they would certainly not suggest themselves to a reader of the poets; nor, as a fact, do readers really and effectively imagine them.

And further, of what passed as testimony for the rule, part at all events, a considerable part, has been long seen to admit and even require a different interpretation[1].

It was high time then to raise, as Mr Rees does raise, the question, what precisely is the weight of such evidence for the rule as may be supposed to remain. His conclusion is that the evidence is insufficient, indeed almost nothing, and that, for anything we know to the contrary, Euripides (and *a fortiori* Aristophanes) may have commanded at the Dionysia or the Lenaea as many performers as there were characters in the play. And for myself I have only to say, provisionally and subject to what may be alleged on the other side, that I agree with him. The investigation, however slight may be its bearing upon the enjoyment of the plays in a book, is historically important, and interesting in itself as a specimen of development in opinion.

But it will be observed—any critic may observe it in himself—that the impugner of a tradition is apt to be emphatic in confirmation of any commonly accepted belief which he is not for the moment concerned to deny. A heretic likes to show incidentally that he is at all events no reckless iconoclast. We see therefore without surprise that Mr Rees, whose business is to deny, so far as concerns the

[1] νεμήσεις ὑποκριτῶν in Hesychius and Photius.—Rees, p. 18.

original performances, the limitation of classical drama to three *actors*, affirms strongly, and even with a certain solemnity, his adherence to another modern doctrine, which he touches incidentally but does not discuss. He assumes that the limitation of the *scene or dialogue* to a tripartite form, a limitation which, as he truly says, has no inherent connexion whatever with the supposed rule of 'three performers,' was not only a general and typical practice (as it was) but almost universal; and he repeats the common statement, that the extant tragedies of the fifth century exhibit no departure from it, that there is no instance in our three tragedians[1] of a scene demanding a fourth speaker.

This is not the fact, and is not even commended, like the three-actor rule, by the testimony of ancient, if insufficient, witnesses. Our principal witness (Pollux IV 109) asserts the contrary, specifying two different kinds of exception to the general practice, and adding expressly that one of these exceptions is illustrated by the *Agamemnon* of Aeschylus. So it is. The *Agamemnon*, rightly understood and properly cast, could not be played by three speakers only in addition to the principal chorus. I have discussed the case in my editions of the play, particularly in an appendix to the second edition.

Nor is there any reason to think that this exception is unique. The limitation to tripartite dialogue,

[1] Excluding the *Rhesus*, according to the now common but dubious opinion, as a work of the fourth century, and possibly not meant for performance.

as a *normal* form, has aesthetic and artistic justification; but if it had been applied rigidly, it would have been irrational, inartistic, and absurd. Whatever the number of the principal group in a scene, whether two, three, or what else, there will be situations in which a composer will desire and need an incidental remark from a by-stander; and a by-stander appropriate to the occasion could not always be supplied from such a body as the Chorus of Greek tragedy. There never was any reason to doubt (and there is less than none, so to say, if we are to accept the views of Mr Rees respecting the number of performers) the ancient doctrine that in such cases the tragic poets of Athens in the great age obeyed common sense, and without thereby infringing their general principle, introduced, and provided with words, extraneous and subordinate personages when the situation could not otherwise be well expressed.

In our MSS., where the cast and distribution is everywhere slovenly and incorrect, we could not expect that these exceptional discriminations would be preserved. They have disappeared in one case (the *Agamemnon*) where we have positive testimony that they once existed. And they have probably disappeared elsewhere. The little parts of the necessary 'citizen,' 'guard,' 'servant' or the like, have naturally lost their designations and lapsed to the Chorus, or to any one whom the copyist had in mind. Thus in the *Bacchae*, a speech of three verses (775 ff.) is assigned, in despite of sense, to the Chorus. It appears to be spoken by a bystander, a subject or servant of Pentheus[1]; and this personage with the others present (the Messenger from Cithaeron, Pentheus, and Dionysus) makes a fourth. Other like instances may be suspected, as I have myself suggested, in the final scenes of the *Choephori* and of the *Eumenides*. Every such case is a matter for judgement, of more or less probability upon the evidence. But such did occur; and they should be supposed wherever the sense, upon a fair construction, so indicates.

Distinct, though not unconnected with the subject, is the question of the mask, upon which also Mr Rees touches, but prudently gives no opinion. If, as he thinks and I think, the original performers of Sophocles and Euripides were not limited in number, the universal use of the mask is not, for those times, a supposition necessary to make the performances possible. But we must not, merely for that reason, deny it.

[1] To the same speaker belongs apparently *v.* 847, for which no speaker can be found in the ordinary cast.

NOTES ON ARISTOPHANES' *KNIGHTS*

The following notes have been suggested by the posthumous commentary of the lamented R. A. Neil[1]. All are upon passages which he marks, more or less distinctly, as still awaiting explanation, and I publish them as a tribute to his memory. His book, in fulness of knowledge, in distaste for nonsense (even ancient nonsense), and in genial spirit, is so like himself, that a friend cannot read it without an impulse to do something, if possible, in the same cause.

531 *νυνὶ δ' ὑμεῖς αὐτὸν ὁρῶντες παραληροῦντ' οὐκ ἐλεεῖτε,*
ἐκπιπτουσῶν τῶν ἠλέκτρων, καὶ τοῦ τόνου οὐκ ἔτ' ἐνόντος,
τῶν θ' ἁρμονιῶν διαχασκουσῶν· ἀλλὰ γέρων ὢν περιέρρει κ.τ.λ.

I take first this problematic passage from the famous lament over the supposed decadence of the poet Cratinus, because of its interest as illustrating the tendency of discussion to run in a rut, and the difficulty of a logical 'fresh start.' At first sight one may easily suppose that *ἠλέκτρων*, *τόνου* and *ἁρμονιῶν* are items in the same metaphor, parts of

[1] *The Knights* of Aristophanes, edited by R. A. Neil, M.A., LL.D. (Aberdeen), Late Fellow and Tutor of Pembroke College, Cambridge, University Lecturer in Sanskrit. Camb. Univ. Press, 1901.

something to which Cratinus is compared. A *scholium* so supposes, and suggests, not happily, that the object is a bed or bedstead. The moderns, improving the lead, suggest a lyre, and there to this day the matter stands. But upon ἐκπιπτουσῶν τῶν ἠλέκτρων they encounter, with this theory, the objections that (1) ἤλεκτρος (ἤλεκτρον) is not feminine; (2) no such word as ἠλέκτρα (if we prefer the accentuation ἠλεκτρῶν) is discoverable; (3) if ἤλεκτρος, or a cognate, denoted any part of a lyre (or something else), that part would naturally, from the known history of the word, be an ornament or ornamental part, whereas the supposed metaphor manifestly requires an essential part, something necessary to the efficiency of the instrument. Now, these objections, long ago noted, and duly exhibited by Mr Neil, are *prima facie* fatal to the whole supposition upon which the *scholium* proceeds. But the commentaries have continued to move within the lines of the discredited *scholium*, and to debate very peaceably the question, what part of what thing an ἤλεκτρος (feminine) or ἠλέκτρα may be supposed to be, if we first suppose the said ἤλεκτρος or ἠλέκτρα to exist. And we are thus left at this date to submit the remark that such speculations are premature, because the term in debate is a familiar word with a known meaning. 'Ηλεκτρῶν (feminine) is the genitive plural of the proper name *Electra*; it is this and, so far as we know, nothing else; and therefore until we have ascertained that the name does not fit, no other conjecture is legitimate.

But hereupon we immediately perceive that the proper name not only may be intended but must, because Ἀρμονιῶν (*sic*), another of the connected terms, is also such a proper name, and one closely associated with Ἠλεκτρῶν. Electra, the Theban Electra, who gave her name to the gate Electrae, was the sister of Cadmus (Pausanias 9. 8. 4), and Harmonia was his wife. That these two names, thus coupled by legend, should have come into our passage by accident, the words representing them not being really names at all, would be incredible, even if both words were capable, which one is not, of another interpretation. Therefore they certainly are names, and it remains only to translate the sentence accordingly: *now that his Electras fail, and the old vigour is not in them, and his Harmonias do not hang together.* 'Electra' and 'Harmonia' are of course personages of Cratinus, presumably characters in the same play and scene, parody-characters borrowed from legend or tragedy, like many in Aristophanes. This we learn from the passage itself, and particularly from ἐκπιπτουσῶν, which is no metaphor but bears its ordinary sense as applied to theatrical works, persons, and figures, *disapproved, rejected, hissed off.* Nor is τόνου, as first used, metaphorical; it means (see Mr Neil's note) literally *energy, vigour, force.* But following on τόνου, Ἀρμονιῶν naturally recalls, by relation to *tone*, the meaning *harmony, joining* or *fitting together*, and hence the play upon this meaning, διαχασκουσῶν, *gaping, parting, going to pieces*, that is to say, without metaphor, missing the intended effect.

One ambiguity appears to remain and cannot perhaps be determined. Are *Harmonia* and *Electra* personages in a recent work of Cratinus which failed, or are they on the contrary former successes, typical and famous examples of his vigour,—as it might have been said of Scott in his latest years that 'his Boisguilberts and Ivanhoes are not what they were,' meaning that his recent figures of romance were inferior to Boisguilbert or Ivanhoe? This latter interpretation seems preferable, as explaining and requiring the plural, whereas the other would admit, and perhaps more naturally, the singular.

It should be noted that the allusion to Electra and Harmonia does not exclude a simultaneous reference by way of pun to the ἤλεκτρος (-τρον, -τρα) of a bed or a lyre, if the existence of such an object can be sufficiently established. Whether it can, we need not here discuss, being concerned only with the primary and certain meaning of the word.

But the 'Electra' of this passage had a further history, and throws light upon another place in Aristophanes. In the year after the triumph of the *Knights*, Cratinus turned the tables, and repaid the condolences of Aristophanes over his 'decay' by beating the *Clouds* out of the field. The play with which he won seems to have been actually suggested by a line in our passage (see Mr Neil on *Eq.* 526), and we may be sure at any rate that its back-handed compliments were not left without an answer. Some years later Aristophanes, we know, appealed against the condemnation of the *Clouds*, though without success, by presenting it in the revised and existing form. His play, he then said, looked for judges as discerning and favourable as those who had rewarded him formerly; 'like Electra' (of course the Argive) 'she will recognise, if she sees it, her brother's hair' (*Nub.* 534). Now this comparison, though explicable, is far from obvious; and we might well ask why the heroine should be brought in. This question we are now able at least in part to answer. To bring in the name *Electra* anyhow was worth while, and a happy stroke, as proving at all events that Aristophanes was not ashamed or afraid of it. To mention it, in connexion with an attempt to retrieve the defeat of the *Clouds* by Cratinus, was to show in the circumstances both boldness and good humour.

503 ὑμεῖς δ' ἡμῖν προσέχετε τὸν νοῦν
τοῖς ἀναπαίστοις,
ὦ παντοίας ἤδη μούσης
πειραθέντες, καθ' ἑαυτούς.

Punctuate so, with comma after πειραθέντες. The words καθ' ἑαυτούς belong to τοῖς ἀναπαίστοις, 'a parabasis (*i.e.*, a comedian) appearing in its proper name' (*i.e.*, the poet's own), as Aristophanes now with the *Knights* did for the first time (see Mr Neil's *Introduction*). The construction is τοῖς καθ' ἑαυτοὺς ἀναπαίστοις, but the qualifying words are purposely extruded and separated for emphasis. The expression καθ' ἑαυτούς is technical (note *ad loc.*): Mr Neil endeavours to construe it with ὦ...πειραθέντες, but is plainly not satisfied. The other way must, I think, have been suggested, though I find no notice of it.

526 εἶτα Κρατίνου μεμνημένος, ὅς, πολλῷ †ῥεύσας† ποτ' ἐπαινῷ, διὰ τῶν ἀφελῶν πεδίων ἔρρει κ.τ.λ.

The unsuccessful attempts to correct the soloecistic ῥεύσας (βρύσας, λάβρος, etc.) all apparently assume that we must have something equivalent to ῥεύσας in sense, connecting the phrase with the comparison, which follows, of Cratinus to a torrent in flood. But is this certain? The only condition seems to be that πολλῷ...ποτ' ἐπαινῷ should describe Cratinus as formerly victorious (τὰς προτέρας νίκας 535); the phrase need not be metaphorical at all, still less need it anticipate the figure of the torrent. On this wider view I suggest for consideration πόλλ' ἱρεύσας ποτ' Ἐπαινῷ (or ἱερεύσας), 'having formerly offered many thanksgivings to Applause,' that is to say, having celebrated with sacrifice many a dramatic success and dedication of the prize. To personify the applause, which led to the rite, in the figure of a deity 'to' or in honour of whom it was performed, appears not unsuitable to the abounding personification of the comedian's style. The tragic form ἱρεύσας would, I conceive, be as likely in such a word and connexion as the prosaic form ἱερεύσας, and it may be preferred as accounting for the error: πολλαιρευσας was first mis-divided, πολλαὶ ῥεύσας, and then mis-corrected in the obvious way, πολλῶι.

755 κέχηνεν ὥσπερ †ἐμποδίζων ἰσχάδας†

open-mouthed as [a person ?] hindering figs.' Neil

cites four interpretations of this, dryly distinguishing the one which 'seems the least possible.' The words are surely nonsense, if so much. The fondness of Aristophanes for birds and especially their beaks (*e.g.* λάρος κεχηνώς *Eq.* 956), together with the fact that -ᾶς is a characteristic ending of bird-names (Neil on 534), strongly suggest that a bird-name lies in the letters ισχαδας. What name, we cannot hope to say with certainty, but why not ἰσχαδᾶς itself? Such a name 'fig-bird' seems likely enough. Then for ἐμποδίζων we want the act in which it 'opens its mouth.' Probably ἐμπιδίζων, *gnatting*, *i.e.* gnat-hunting. The existence of such a word, available for Aristophanes, is as direct a corollary from the existence of the stem εμπιδ-, *gnat*, as any case of the noun ἐμπίς. In the Attic of the comedians verbs are formed in -ιζω with exactly the same freedom as we in colloquial English make a verb out of a substantive (see Neil on *Eq.* 825, 1189, etc.). In *Eq.* 523 we actually have in a group of such words ψηνίζων, *midging*; it happens there to mean 'exhibiting in the theatre *midges*,' but that is given by the context. The word means *per se* 'doing something connected with *midge*,' and similarly ἐμπιδίζων, *gnatting*.

774 ὅς πρῶτα μέν, ἡνίκ' ἐβούλευόν σοι, χρήματα πλεῖστ' ἀπέδειξα
ἐν τῷ κοινῷ, τοὺς μὲν στρεβλῶν, τοὺς δ' ἄγχων, τοὺς δὲ μεταιτῶν.

'μεταιτῶ,' says Mr Neil, 'a rare compound, generally means "blackmail, claim a share" as an accomplice or partner in some dubious transaction.... Does it mean more than "*dunning*" here?' Surely, yes: it means 'blackmail' as usual. The words τοὺς δὲ μεταιτῶν are an 'aside,' a *sotto voce* confession of the truth, escaping in the midst of Cleon's self-laudation.

> οὐ τοῦτό φησ᾽ ὁ χρησμός, ἀλλ᾽ ὁ κύων ὁδὶ
> ὥσπερ θύρας σου τῶν λογίων παρεσθίει.
> ἐμοὶ γάρ ἐστ᾽ ὀρθῶς περὶ τούτου τοῦ κυνός.

Cleon has produced an oracle (1015 ff.) promising Demos a faithful dog, and has applied it, though it contains no personal identification, to himself. The Sausage-man here denies this application; he himself has an oracle, which he proceeds to quote (1030 ff.), really applicable to Cleon the dog: he is a dog indeed, but a Cerberus. But what of *v.* 1026 *he eats as it were some of the door of your oracle*? 'It seems to mean that Cleon suppresses parts of oracles unfavourable to himself. But the reading is uncertain and the full meaning obscure' (Neil). Nothing in the context explains the supposed 'suppression of a part,' and the metaphor *eat the door* is surely absurd. Mr Neil, following Hermann (ἀθάρης), suspects the word θύρας. I think the error is in παρεσθίει and in the punctuation:

> οὐ τοῦτό φησ᾽ ὁ χρησμός, ἀλλ᾽ ὁ κύων ὁδί.
> ὥσπερ θύρας σου τῶν λογίων παρεισέθει·
> ἐμοὶ γάρ ἐστ᾽ ὀρθῶς περὶ τούτου τοῦ κυνός.

'That is not the meaning; the true dog is myself. He slipped in at the door (so to speak) of your oracle, did this dog; I have an oracle which really describes him.'

In claiming the benefit of the oracle about the

faithful dog, Cleon practised a theft and an intrusion, like *a stray-dog who should slip in at the house-door* in the hope of course to pick up something at the expense of the master and the true guardian. *θύρας* (*fores*) is acc. plur., not gen. sing. In *παρεισέθει* the imperfect tense is correct and necessary; the act of *running in surreptitiously* describes what Cleon 'was doing' when, in the preceding lines, he cited the complimentary oracle in his own favour. For the corruption to *παρεσθίει* (for which, by the way, we should in any case rather expect *παρατρώγει*) a ready occasion would be the common spelling *παρεσ-*: indeed in certain uncials the two words would be scarcely distinguishable.

THE VERSE-WEIGHING SCENE IN THE *FROGS* OF ARISTOPHANES

The contest between Aeschylus and Euripides in the *Frogs* concludes, as will be remembered, with a scene in which the comparative 'weight' of their poetry is tested by a singular experiment. Standing with a balance between them, they speak single verses, each into his own scale. The scale of Aeschylus proves the heavier every time, and the cause of this superiority is explained at each repetition by Dionysus. The scene is the last episode in the literary competition proper; when it is finished, Dionysus prepares to decide (*v.* 1411), and it is followed only by a dialogue about temporary politics which, whatever its intention, has no bearing upon the literary debate.

It is evident that for some reason Aristophanes was anxious about this verse-weighing business, and doubted whether, in the theatre, it was likely to take, or to be understood. He prepares us for it by no less than three explanations or apologies. First, in the dialogue between the slaves Aeacus and Xanthias, which foreshows the contest generally, the scales, which apparently are then placed upon the stage, are particularly noted, and a contemptuous remark is bestowed upon the application of such a machine to the criticism of tragedy (*vv.* 797–8). Again, when the machine is actually to be used, Dionysus protests in similar terms against the idea of treating poetry 'like cheese'; and the Chorus roundly declare that, if any one had reported such an invention to them, they would not have believed it, and would have thought 'that he was talking nonsense' (*vv.* 1368–77). And on the other hand, we must suppose that this scene, as well as the grammatical and musical disputes which precede it, is included in the warning (*vv.* 1109–18) that we are now to go into details of literary discussion, which cannot be appreciated without some erudition, though the author of course asserts that his auditors are learned enough.

It is easy to see the purpose of the repeated and emphatic declaration that the scene is nonsensical, and that the author, as a critic, is here not to be taken at his word. The principle upon which Dionysus accounts for the superior weight of the Aeschylean verses, is absurd. According to him, the weight of a verse depends on that of the things which are named in it. The word *chariot* preponderates over the word *mace* because a real chariot is heavier than a real mace (*v.* 1405). A verse with *water* in it is likely to turn the scale, because things wetted are heavier than when dry (*v.* 1386). Such a line as

The death of Mr A. is in the *Times*

will prove heavy, because 'death is a very heavy misfortune' (*v.* 1394); whereas

> To be or not to be, that is the question

will be not worth putting into the scale. Between

> O that this too too solid flesh would melt!

and

> I'll put a girdle round about the earth

the balance will be as much in favour of the latter as the terrestrial globe weighs more than the body of Hamlet. Considering that this stuff is propounded after a series of arguments which are all plainly meant to have some bearing, more or less grave, upon poetical merit, and of which a large portion is almost as serious as a debate in the Assembly, Aristophanes might well prefer to guard explicitly against the horrid possibility of being taken to mean what he says.

But his disclaimer adds stress and sharpness to a question which, in any case, we ought to have raised. The conception of the scene being so silly, where is the humour of it? And in particular, what does Aristophanes mean by saying, as he certainly seems to do, that he appeals here specially to the intelligent and the accomplished? Nonsense, merely as such, is not amusing; and if it were, no special sense or knowledge, nothing above the average faculty required by the *Frogs* as a whole, is wanted to perceive that this scene, on the face of it, is senseless,—especially when we are twice told so by the author himself. How then does it appeal to learning, and what point has it for anybody? Surely we must suppose that the point lies not in the nonsense professed, but in something beyond, something not explicitly stated, but visible to competent persons having notice to look for it.

Such a point in fact there is, the sole excuse and reason for the composition. The notion of comparing verses in respect of weight, though merely foolish if pursued upon the principles of Dionysus, is in itself rational, interesting, and important. At Athens, by the end of the fifth century, the fact that verses do really differ in weight must have been widely known in a society long accustomed to the discussion of literary art. And in particular the capacities of the *iambic senarius*, the verse of tragedy and comedy, in this as in other respects, would naturally be a theme familiar to criticism. The examples propounded by Aristophanes are in fact carefully chosen to illustrate the true conception of 'weight' as applied to rhythm and vocabulary. And the point and humour of the scene lies in the fact that, as competent persons would see, the judgements of Dionysus not only ignore the true criteria, but positively reverse and contradict them.

Three comparisons are made. In each case Euripides is the first speaker. This circumstance, we may observe, would in itself suffice to condemn the proceeding as preposterous and silly, if the outcome of it were to be decision in favour of Aeschylus upon the grounds alleged. If verses weigh according to the weight of things named in them, the first propounder of a verse can always be beaten—unless indeed he were to name *the universe*. Euripides is not allowed to do this; and there, if we seek no more, is the sum total of the stupid affair.

But in truth and sense the case is palpably otherwise. Upon the first trial Euripides puts in the opening verse of the *Medea*:

εἴθ' ὤφελ' Ἄργους μὴ διαπτάσθαι σκάφος,

and Aeschylus competes with

Σπερχειὲ ποταμὲ βουνόμοι τ' ἐπιστροφαί.

The silly scales incline for the latter, and Dionysus caps the absurdity by explaining that Aeschylus has got weight, like a wool-dealer, by 'wetting' his verse, and by 'putting in *river*,'—εἰσέθηκε ποταμόν. But, as any one may hear and feel, the Euripidean verse is the weightier, in the only applicable sense of weight. One could not easily find an iambic senarius more weighty. It has no resolved feet, the principal cause of lightness in this metre. It has all the three possible spondees, and they are heavy spondees. The syllable εἴθ', burdensome both in sound and (as a sigh) in sense, acts as a drag upon the whole movement; and there are other such traits, which any one may observe. The Aeschylean verse on the contrary is light and tripping, uncommonly light for Aeschylus, which shows that it has been sought for that quality. Many things contribute to make it light, but the chief and most obvious is the very word alleged by Dionysus as the cause of weight. It is just because Aeschylus 'has put in ποταμός,' and thus gives, what he very seldom gives, a tribrach in the second foot, that this verse is conspicuously the less weighty of the two.

The same point and intention appears in the second pair of examples:

> ΕΥΡ. οὐκ ἔστι Πειθοῦς ἱερὸν ἄλλο πλὴν λόγος.
> ΑΙΣΧ. μόνος θεῶν γὰρ θάνατος οὐ δώρων ἐρᾷ.

Here in point of true weight there is small difference, practically none, if ἱερὸν be pronounced as a full trisyllable. But in tragedy the pronunciation would rather be ἱρὸν (which Dindorf accordingly would write), whereas the dactyl γὰρ θάνατ- is incapable of such modification, and must make a 'resolution of the long syllable.' Euripides therefore is again the heavier, in spite of the scales, and in spite of the sage remark that Aeschylus has prevailed because εἰσέθηκε θάνατον, by putting into the verse a thing so heavy as θάνατος, *death*! The third and last comparison exhibits the same principle, but with more subtlety. Euripides, now alive to the peculiarity of the scales, searches his memory for a verse with something heavy in it, and chooses not injudiciously

> σιδηροβριθές τ' ἔλαβε δεξιᾷ ξύλον.

Aeschylus, notwithstanding σιδηροβριθές, has of course no difficulty in putting down the balance with

> ἐφ' ἅρματος γὰρ ἅρμα, καὶ νεκρῷ νεκρός

—'two chariots and two corpses' against a mere mace! The case however, apart from the foolery of Dionysus, is really remarkable and illuminating. The weight, of sound rather than sense, which really is given to the Euripidean verse by the word σιδηροβριθές, is lost again in the conclusion, chiefly by the 'resolution' in ἔλαβε and the character of the word. The verse of Aeschylus is a pure iambic, a type which would not generally tend to weight, but does achieve weight here by the special effect of the accumulations. Of all this Dionysus has no suspicion and the well-informed auditor is supposed to appreciate his ignorance. Nor does Dionysus know what he is about, when he ironically suggests to Euripides, as a verse likely to carry weight,

βέβληκ' Ἀχιλλεὺς δύο κύβω καὶ τέτταρα.

It *is* of course a light verse if weighed by true criteria, the rhythm and the impressiveness, or want of it, in the vocabulary. But the meaning of Dionysus is that there is not much (material) weight in dice,—a standard at which we may laugh.

Such is the point, and the only point, of this scene, which, like all the scenes which follow the warning of Aristophanes to that effect, does in fact demand more special and technical acquaintance with literary matters than the rest of the play and the works of Aristophanes generally. It is the furthest of his ventures in this line, and he risked it (in the theatre) with some trepidation. Of course the scene, under its humorous form, does really convey or suggest a truth pertinent to the comparison of Aeschylus and Euripides, namely that in every proper and relevant sense of 'weight,' Aeschylus, by rhythm and vocabulary, is on the average far the 'weightier'; and that a critic who held the general views which Aristophanes is pleased to adopt in the *Frogs*, would possibly or probably reckon the 'weight' of Aeschylus as a superiority. But a serious exposition of this topic could have had in it nothing comic or fit for the stage. To bring it in, the author has exaggerated a little the habitual foolishness of his Dionysus, and has got his effect out of a contrast between the judgements of the god and those of rational criticism.

The method and requirements of this weighing-scene should not be overlooked in considering what is or may be meant by the allusion to 'a book' (*βιβλίον*) in the remarkable notice or appeal which, as we have already more than once observed, Aristophanes, before approaching the stiffer parts of his subject, addresses to the better qualified of his auditors (*v.* 1114). It takes the form of an assurance, given to the contending poets by the Chorus, that they may, without fear, be as learned in discussion as they please, because *now-a-days* the spectators are 'no tiros,' but 'every man has a book in which he studies the matter of art (*τὰ δεξιά*).' Thus much seems here to be certain, that some definite literary or at all events written aid to understanding is meant, and that the use of this aid was of quite recent introduction, so that not only Aeschylus but even Euripides would be ignorant of it until he was informed. Nothing less than this will satisfy the words. It does not however seem necessary that the *βιβλίον*, the aid in question, should have been proper to the theatre or supplied there. It would be enough if any book, likely to be useful, had recently appeared and become notorious.

Now in the weighing-scene it is, I think, probable,

if not clear, that Aristophanes himself has in mind some genuine and serious discussion about the principles of poetic weight; and he would have been glad to think, whether or not he really thought, that acquaintance with these principles, and with the discussion, was common among the audience. The verses which he cites must certainly have been chosen in the first instance as illustrative of a true and reasonable criticism. It would be hard to select any better or more instructive cases. They are open to many pertinent remarks, besides those which present themselves obviously and have been made above. If they were taken from among the illustrations of some known treatise, manifestly this would be an immense advantage to the comedian, and would greatly increase his chance of finding in the theatre a sufficient proportion of understanding auditors to carry him without danger through the moderate length of the scene. Nor would there be any difficulty for Aristophanes in adopting examples chosen by another. For his own purpose, his ostensible purpose, any examples would serve. Any set of verses taken at random might be made the text of such arbitrary and absurd comments as he assigns to Dionysus. In the conditions of literature at this time, the appearance of a book or treatise, attempting to summarize and popularize the main principles of literary composition, is a conceivable and not improbable thing. It seems possible therefore (one must not say more) that the 'book in which people now study the matter of arts,' the book upon which the poets are told to rely, is some recent work of this kind, popular enough to be described rhetorically as in the hands of everybody.

However this may be, the scene of the verse-weighing does in fact require, to be appreciated, auditors acquainted with the rational standards of verse-weight, and able to contrast them with the absurd standard of the stage-critic. This it is which accounts for the anticipatory explanations and apologies of Aristophanes. The fact is of some moment in estimating the testimony of the *Frogs* to the state of culture in Athens at the close of the great century.

ON A CERTAIN DEFECT IN 'LONGINUS'

THE author of the treatise 'On the Sublime,' whatever was his name and date, is justly reputed one of the best representatives of ancient criticism. All the better does he illustrate a strange and characteristic defect of it, by repeatedly ignoring the possibility, or even the certainty, that a striking word, phrase, or sentence, which is not in keeping with the style of the context, was chosen by the writer for the sake of its literary associations, and owed its effect, the effect of a quotation, to the very fact of its peculiarity.

Let us illustrate this familiar principle by the first example that comes to hand.

'America, gentlemen say, is a noble object. It is an object well worth fighting for. Certainly it is, if fighting a people be the best way of gaining them. Gentlemen in this respect will be led to their choice of means by their complexions and their habits. Those who understand the military art will of course have some predilection for it. Those who *wield the thunder of the state* may have more confidence in the efficacy of arms. But I confess, possibly for want of this knowledge, my opinion is much more in favour of prudent management than of force,' etc.

The pompous phrase here italicized instantly catches the ear, as incongruous with the studied and ironical simplicity of the passage. And therefore in Burke we should suspect, even if we did not know, that it is a quotation, and that the source of it will be worth examining. It comes of course from the famous couplet of Pope,

> Argyle, the state's whole thunder born to wield,
> And shake alike the senate and the field;

and it depends upon this origin for its meaning. Not military men merely, but military orators, soldiers speaking in parliament, the opponents of conciliation with America, are 'those who wield the thunder of the state'; Burke is sneering at the violence of their declamations. But it is by Pope, by the context in Pope, and not by the context in Burke, that the innuendo is explained; and in the incongruity of style, as directing the memory to Pope, lies the principal merit of the passage. What would be said of a critic who, ignoring all this, were to tax the incongruity as a fault in the orator?

Yet this is what 'Longinus' does again and again. He ignores the possibility of quotation, not only where there is a presumption in favour of it, but where his own citations, if the idea had occurred to him, are sufficient to prove it. And in some cases perhaps in all, he is following precedent, an established error of criticism and common to the stock.

'A hazardous business...is periphrasis, unless it

be handled with discrimination; otherwise it speedily falls flat, with its odour of empty talk and its swelling amplitude. This is the reason why Plato (who is always strong in figurative language, and at times unseasonably so) is taunted, because in his *Laws* he says "that neither gold nor silver treasure should be allowed to establish itself and abide in the city." The critic says that if he had been forbidding the possession of sheep or oxen, he would obviously have said "ovine treasure" or "bovine[1]"'—*ἐν τοῖς νόμοις λέγοντα 'ὡς οὔτε ἀργυροῦν δεῖ πλοῦτον οὔτε χρυσοῦν ἐν πόλει ἱδρυμένον ἐᾶν οἰκεῖν.'*

It is assumed that the words criticized are simply Plato's, and that his negligence or want of taste is responsible for the dissonance between them and the proper simplicity of the conversation. Now *first*, such a writer as Plato might claim the contrary presumption: even without evidence we should assume that he is quoting, and meant the quotation to be recognized. *Secondly*, the context confirms this presumption: Plato is warning composers of public prayers to pray only for things beneficial; it has been shown, he says in the words cited, that gold and silver are not truly beneficial; and he adds that '*not all* composers' or 'poets' (*ποιηταί*) are capable of this distinction, indicating by 'not all' that some of them are, and that the warning against the precious metals, as here shaped, comes itself from a poet. And *finally*, Longinus, whose text of

[1] Long. XXIX. 1 (Plato, *Laws* 801 B): transl. of Prof. W. Rhys Roberts, slightly modified in the last clause.

the *Laws* was correct and better than some[1], could have proved the presumption; for his citation contains, to a syllable, the words of the iambic couplet to which Plato refers:

ὡς οὔτε Πλοῦτον ἀργυροῦν ἱδρυμένον
ἐᾶν ἐνοικεῖν οὔτε δεῖ χρυσοῦν πόλει.

What periphrasis is, and what it would be, if misapplied, the example may show; but the criticism of Plato is itself misapplied[2].

Similarly fare Xenophon and Timaeus, the historian of Sicily. In the chapter on frigidity, τὸ ψυχρόν[3], Xenophon is solemnly rebuked for punning upon κόρη (*maiden, pupil of the eye*) in αἰδημονεστέρους δ' ἂν αὐτοὺς ἡγήσαιο καὶ αὐτῶν τῶν ἐν τοῖς ὀφθαλμοῖς παρθένων[4], 'you would deem them more modest than the very maidens in their eyes'; and Timaeus is charged with stealing the pun from Xenophon, when he wrote ὃ τίς ἂν ἐποίησεν ἐν ὀφθαλμοῖς κόρας, μὴ πόρνας, ἔχων; As if the occurrence of the same quip in two writers, both of whom place it in such a context as to surprise us, and who yet frame it in words so different that the later is manifestly *not* borrowing from the earlier, were not in itself enough to prove that the thing belonged to neither of them, and was claimed by neither, but was a notorious

[1] Baiter-Orelli-Winckelmann give ἐνοικεῖν (for ἐᾶν οἰκεῖν): ἐνοικεῖν may be right, but the omission of ἐᾶν is demonstrably wrong.

[2] Aristoph. *Plutus* 1191, cited by Prof. Rhys Roberts, alludes doubtless to the same passage of tragedy, and proves it notorious.

[3] IV.

[4] *de Rep. Lac.* III 5.

commonplace, an old favourite of literary speech, introduced by each because of its interesting associations. And in fact each writer points to a prior use. Timaeus cites almost literally from tragedy or tragicomedy,

ὃ τίς ἐποίησεν ἂν
κόρας ἐν ὀφθαλμοῖσι, μὴ πόρνας, ἔχων;

Whether on grounds of merit he is entitled to the presumption that he is here quoting, we are not in a position to say, but the censures of 'Longinus' prove nothing to the contrary. Xenophon is so entitled, and also manifestly does quote, but less accurately, and from another passage of tragicomedy, something like this,

αἰδήμονας δὲ μᾶλλον ἡγήσαιτό τις
αὐτοὺς ἂν αὐτῶν τῶν ἐν ὀφθαλμοῖς κορῶν.

As for the equivocation itself, it was probably as old, and as sacred, as the hills, like the similar one upon κόρος (*pride*, *son*). Among authors known to us, the most likely to have stamped it for currency are Aeschylus and the oracle of Delphi. We might really as well censure a modern moralist or historian for compromising the dignity of his style, if he used *Tekel* in the sense of 'Thou art found wanting.'

'Yes, and Plato (usually so divine) when he means simply *tablets* says "They shall write and preserve *cypress memorials* in the temples[1].''

But for the other examples, it would be scarcely conceivable that the critic had seen this place with

[1] Long. IV 6 (Rhys Roberts), Plato, *Laws* 741 C.

his own eyes, and one would hope that he had not. Plato does *not* 'simply mean tablets,' and there is no more to be said. He is speaking, with great solemnity, of an official prayer, a commination akin to our 'Cursed is he that removeth his neighbour's landmark.' The passage is too long to quote; but let the reader turn to it, and say whether κυπαριττίνας μνήμας is not palpably borrowed from poetry, and designed to enhance the dignity of Plato's own language by the recognized majesty of the place (whatever that was) from which it comes. It is less obvious but, considering the author, fairly presumable that Herodotus, when he makes his Persian revellers, who otherwise talk pure prose, describe the Macedonian beauties, seated out of reach on the other side of the table (ἀντίας ἱζομένας), as 'paining their eyes' (ἀλγηδόνας σφι ὀφθαλμῶν)[1], is not using mere words of his own, but alluding, not in compliment, to some poem, contrary in sentiment but otherwise similar to the ὅστις ἐναντίος τοι ἰζάνει, the *qui sedens adversus identidem te spectat* of Sappho and Catullus. At all events to censure Herodotus for 'an unseemly exhibition,' without noticing the possibility of such an allusion, is blindness. Since the last speech of the Persian guest at the banquet of Attaginus[2] is palpable poetry, and in fact is almost entirely made up of poetical quotations slightly transposed, we see that Herodotus did not think it inappropriate (nor is it, in his manner of narration)

[1] Long. IV 7, Herod. V 18.

[2] Herod. IX 16. See my *Bacchants of Euripides*, pp. 309 ff.

that his barbarians should use Greek literature in this fashion.

'Then we have Plato again (usually so divine) writing *περὶ δὲ τειχῶν, ὦ Μέγιλλε, ἐγὼ ξυμφεροίμην ἂν τῇ Σπάρτῃ τὸ καθεύδειν ἐᾶν ἐν τῇ γῇ κατακείμενα τὰ τείχη καὶ μὴ ἐπανίστασθαι*[1], when he means simply that a city should not have walls.'

This 'frigidity' is not to be condoned; it arises, we are told, like other such ugly and parasitical growths, 'from a single cause, that pursuit of novelty in the expression of ideas which may be regarded as the fashionable craze of the day[2].'

About 'the day' of Longinus, we may possibly judge when we know what it was. Meanwhile it is certain that in this passage of Plato the departure from the author's ordinary style does *not* arise from 'the pursuit of novelty in expression,' but from the very opposite cause, the modest and natural desire, common to all writers who know their business, to commend new thoughts by old expressions, by clothing them partly in the language of some admired predecessor. Here again one wonders whether the critic can have read Plato. For Plato in the very next words actually mentions 'the excellent and much-quoted speech of the poet on the subject of walls,' and paraphrases a sentence of it: *τῶν δὲ εἵνεκα καλῶς μὲν ὁ ποιητικὸς λόγος ὑπὲρ αὐτῶν ὑμνεῖται, τὸ χαλκᾶ καὶ σιδηρᾶ δεῖν εἶναι τὰ τείχη μᾶλλον ἢ γήϊνα*, 'bronze and iron,' that is,

[1] Long. IV 6, Plato, *Laws* 778 D (ἐπανιστάναι Baiter).

[2] Long. V 1 (Rhys Roberts).

weapons, 'make better walls than earth.' The mention of 'earth' makes clear what even without it would naturally be assumed, that the poetical metaphor of the preceding sentence, that walls 'should be let lie and sleep in the earth,' comes from the same source. The play cited does not seem to be known, but was later in date than the celebrated attempt of the Lacedaemonians, after Plataea, to make the Athenians adopt Spartan principles and refrain from rebuilding their fortifications[1]. The speaker, we notice, refers to the 'restoration' (*ἐπαν-ιστάναι*) not to the mere erection of walls, a fact which alone would show that the language is not Plato's own, for he is concerned only with building. The dramatist apparently found or invented a heroic parallel to that historic situation, and put the argument of 'Sparta' into the mouth of a Spartan. The *disiecta membra* are visible enough,

ἐν γῇ καθεύδειν ταῦτ' ἐᾶτε κείμενα
καὶ μὴ 'πανίστατ(ε) κ.τ.λ.

Of course the fault which the critic discusses in this chapter does really exist. There is such a thing, and it is not uncommon, as incongruous language or metaphor adopted without any other motive than the pursuit of novelty, the desire to be strange and striking. Proper examples and safer he might probably have found in his contemporaries. To find them in ancient works was then, and would be now, *ἐπίκηρον*, 'a hazardous business'; we can hardly be sure that we are not committing the error

[1] Thucyd. I 90.

of Longinus and ignoring the effect of some literary association. With a contemporary one may respectfully venture: 'I let myself *flow out to her in a happy weakness*, and looking all about, and before and behind, *saw the world like an undesirable desert*, where men go as soldiers on a march, following their duty *with what constancy they have*, and Catriona alone there to offer me *some pleasure of my days*.' The oddities and contortions here have not, *so far as I can see*, any literary defence. The style is not that of Stevenson's novel as a whole, and still less appropriate to his hero; it seems to be a mere extravagance of diction, and *if it is that*, it is an example of *τὸ ψυχρόν*. But the examples in Longinus, all of them so far as they can be tested[1], are false, and for the same reason: he ignores the effect, the calculated and legitimate effect, of literary association. His merits and just reputation make the insensibility or inattention to this point, which we cannot but attribute to him and his authorities, all the more significant, as showing what sort of perception we are not to expect from Graeco-Roman critics, and how their judgements need to be discounted.

[1] Of the two that remain, one, the ominous significance of the name *Hermocrates* (IV 3), cannot possibly have been a legitimate example. Whether Timaeus defended the superstition or derided it (and we do not know), in neither case did he commit an offence of style. The comparison of Alexander and Isocrates (IV 2) may have been a proper illustration, but without seeing the text we cannot say.

THE LATIN SAPPHIC

An interesting article by Prof. Sonnenschein (see *Classical Review*, vol. XVII, p. 252) proposes a bold answer to the question—Why did Horace fetter the Sapphic verse (1) by the regular caesura after the fifth syllable (in the *Three Books* almost invariable), and (2) by making the fourth syllable invariably long? Prof. Sonnenschein, modifying the views of Prof. Eickhoff, would reply:—Because these rules were necessary to the rhythm intended by Horace, which was not that of the Greek Sapphic, but was identical, or almost identical, with that familiar to schoolboys,

Pérsicos ódi púer apparátus,

the rhythm of the 'Needy knifegrinder.' The Greek verse had five bars of 3-time, thus:

$\frac{3}{4}$ | 𝅗𝅥 ♩ | 𝅗𝅥 ♩ | ♩. ♪ ♩ | 𝅗𝅥 ♩ | 𝅗𝅥 ♩

The Horatian verse, according to this theory, had four bars of 2-time, thus:

$\frac{2}{4}$ | ♪. 𝅘𝅥𝅯 ♩ | ♩ ♩ | ♪ ♪ ♪. 𝅘𝅥𝅯 | ♩ ♩

which is a delicate modulation of Canning's 'Needy knifegrinder, whither art thou going?'

The points in favour of this are plain, and one of them is strong. It accounts for the facts adduced, and in particular for the puzzling fourth syllable. If Horace intended a trochaic rhythm, what motive, it may be said, could he have for excluding absolutely the double trochee? If the caesura excluded such a verse as that of Catullus,

nuntiate pauca meae puellae,

still we might expect, for variety, a sprinkling of the type

ictus incipit; referuntur ictus,

and other types consistent with the Horatian caesura. Why are these prohibited? The 2-time rhythm explains: without a long syllable in the fourth place that rhythm is impossible. It also accounts for the caesura. In the 2-time rhythm a strong beat falls on the sixth syllable

Pérsicos ódi púer apparátus.

This syllable (by Greek rule) must be short. If it were also unaccented, it would not bear the beat[1]. Such a mode of recitation as

laúrea dónandús Apollinári

might be tolerable as a variety here and there, but not as normal. The Horatian caesura secures that the sixth syllable shall have at least some word-stress, and this is *ex hypothesi* necessary[2].

[1] I do not say that the Latin word-accent either originally was a 'beat' or had become such by the age of Augustus. That it then *affected* the beat, is seen in all branches of Augustan poetry. What precisely it was or had been, we shall hardly know until we can hear ancient Romans recite.

[2] Prof. Sonnenschein gives another reason for the caesura

Further, the adaptation of the Greek Sapphic to 2-time might be illustrated, as Prof. Sonnenschein has probably noted, by the parallel case of the hendecasyllable. This also began in Greek as five bars of 3-time.

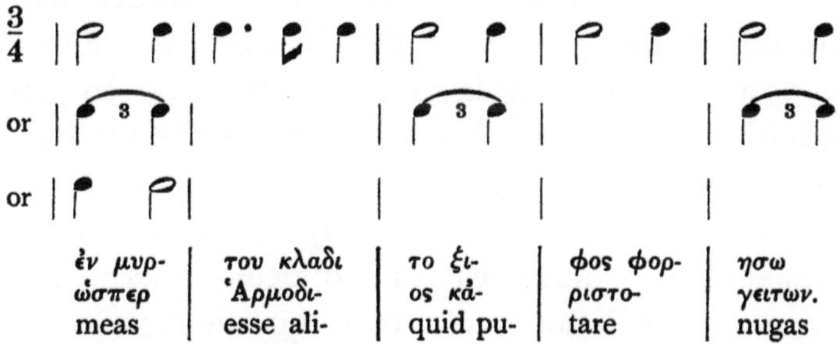

In fact it differs from the Sapphic verse only in the different place of the 'trochaic dactyl,' and in certain consequent rules as to the possible places of the equivalent feet. But the Romans, after some hesitation visible in Catullus, converted it into this,

pőst haec ómnia főrte si movébit
Bắcchus, quám solet, ěsuritiónem.

The Roman rules and practice, especially the invariable spondee at the beginning, absurd and purposeless for the 3-time rhythm, are dictated by the 2-time; the change has some interesting minor results, which we may perhaps follow on another occasion. Now the supposed conversion of the

(p. 253) and quotes from Prof. Eickhoff yet another, both *ex hypothesi* valid, but not, I think, so obvious as the above.

Sapphic, though by no means so easy as that of the hendecasyllable, is analogous, and might well have arisen in the same circumstances.

But though this theory has points of strength and may contain a kernel of truth, it cannot be the whole account of the matter. That Horace had abandoned the 3-time of the Greeks, we cannot suppose. There are facts that cannot be so explained: for example, his treatment of the trochaic caesura, which he allowed throughout as an exception and in his later work largely increased. Prof. Sonnenschein perceives the difficulty here, but proposes a solution more than questionable. He suggests that though the Horatian Sapphic generally was in 2-time, lines having the trochaic caesura were in 3-time, that is to say in plain words, they were *extra metrum*. Thus *Ode* I 25 is in 2-time throughout and has the rhythm of 'Needy knifegrinder,' *except in the eleventh verse*, where this rhythm is to be abandoned, and we are to read,

Thráció baccháante magís sub ínter-.

So in II 6 all is 2-time except the one verse

flúmen ét regnáta petám Lacóni,

but this is 3-time, *extra metrum*. Surely no reader could divine an intention so strange and so contrary to the very nature of metre. If these poems are in 2-time, so must be the verses which have the trochaic caesura, thus,

flű̋men et régnatā̋ petam Lacóni.

The prevalent 2-time rhythm must be supposed

to carry us through these rare exceptions, which, though less suitable to it, are allowed for the sake of variety. This is conceivable; but great difficulties remain. Though such weaker verses may be admitted, there is one place in the poem where the poet would never put them; and that is the beginning. When the rhythm is established, the variety may come in, but we must at all events start right. Yet Horace in his *First Book*, where we most look for direction, and where the trochaic caesura is very rare, nevertheless three times begins a poem with that caesura (*Odes* 10, 12, 30); that is, in such a way as inevitably to suggest that the poem has the Greek rhythm throughout. Still stranger must appear his later work. *Odes* IV 2 seems on this hypothesis unmanageable. Here most stanzas, about two in three, contain verses with trochaic caesura such as

laurea donandus Apollinari,

verses which, if the poem as a whole is 2-time, must either stand outside the metre altogether, or be brought into it by violating the natural run of the words. Surely this is beyond belief. Other difficulties arise as we look further, but this one is enough for the present.

Nor can Prof. Eickhoff's views[1] claim strength from the predominance of the 'Horatian caesura.'

[1] I should say that I know them only through Prof. Sonnenschein. Prof. Eickhoff is, it seems, now prepared to say that the *Greek* Sapphic, the ode ποικιλόθρονε for instance, is 2-time. At present I find this incomprehensible.

They do indeed explain this very well; but it can very well be explained without them. Prof. Sonnenschein says truly that many books of authority do not explain it, but leave us practically to suppose that it was on the part of Horace a mere blunder. But it is explicable nevertheless. It is an application to the Sapphic of the same principles which the Roman imitators applied to those Greek metres which they best succeeded in transplanting, the hexameter and pentameter. It secures a certain *discrepancy* between the rhythmical ictus and the word-accent. Thus in the hexameter the rhythmical ictus is

″́– ⏑ ⏑ | ′́– – | ″́– ⏑ ⏑ | ′́– – | ″́– ⏑ ⏑ | ′́– –,

the heavier beats marking the pairs of feet. The Latin poets, having first decided that, for the purpose of recitation in their language, the two last beats, the fifth and sixth, must regularly *coincide* with a word-accent, and having therefore discarded (rare exceptions apart) the quadrisyllabic ending, next invented rules, inconvenient, stringent, but presumably necessary, to secure that in the earlier part of the verse the beat and the accent should be sufficiently *discrepant.* The most important of all, the predominance of the penthemimeral caesura

impositique rogis | iuvenes ante ora parentum,

secures that, whereas the first of the three heavier beats must always have some word-accent, and the third (the fifth in the verse) always has the full accent, the second (third in the verse) is in the great majority of verses accentless, as here in the last syllable of *rogis*. The other rules, such as that the trochaic caesura shall regularly be followed by the hephthemimeral caesura

et metus et malesuada | fames | et turpis egestas,

are applications of the same principle, namely that *beat and accent shall not too much coincide.* The Latin pentameter developes *mutatis mutandis* in the same way. So also, in respect of the caesura, does the Horatian Sapphic. Words apart, the rhythmical beat is

–̋ ⏑ | –́ ⏓ | –̋ ⏑ ⏑ | –́ ⏑ | –̋ ⏓,

the feet tending here, as always, to fall into pairs. Now of the three chief beats, the third, from the nature of the case, must always have a full word-accent; the first will always have some, and frequently the full. And the 'Horatian caesura'

fronte curvatos | imitatus ignes

simply secures that, in order to oppose a contrast to these two beats, and to prevent the verse from trotting, the second of the chief beats (third in the verse) shall be the final syllable of a word, and therefore accentless. When we see to what embarrassing restrictions Virgil and his successors thought it necessary, for the like purpose, to subject the Greek hexameter, we need not be surprised that Horace in the Sapphic was similarly severe.

The parallel may be carried further; for although Horace does not actually impose on the trochaic caesura in the Sapphic the restriction normally imposed in the hexameter—namely, that it must be followed by an iambic word—yet he shows a strong preference for this arrangement. The rare examples of that caesura in the *Three Books* are all of this type. Thus *Odes* I 10, the only Sapphic poem in those books which uses that caesura in a considerable proportion, gives

> Mercuri facunde | nepos | Atlantis—
> nuntium curvaeque | lyrae | parentem—
> sedibus virgaque | levem | coerces.

In the *Carmen Saeculare*, out of 19 verses with trochaic caesura, 13 have the iambus, as

> Phoebe silvarumque potens Diana.

One is dubious,

> haec Iovem sentire deosque cunctos.

Only five are free[1] allowing the word-accent to fall both on the third beat of the verse and on the fourth, as

> lenis, Ilithyia, tuere matres.

And this one exhibits a Greek word (*Ilithyia*), which, according to the general principles of Latin poetry, would excuse a recurrence to Greek freedom. It is clear therefore that Horace felt such a verse as

> siderum regina bicornis, audi

to be an extreme liberty, and was disposed generally to follow in this matter the track of Virgil.

The view that Horace adopted 2-time, or was even influenced by it, must stand, if at all, on the invariable lengthening of the fourth syllable, this being the only phenomenon for which, with 3-time, it is not easy to account.

[1] vv. 14, 35, 58, 59, 61.

Still this difficulty remains, and it is, in my opinion, serious. A preference for the rhythm –́ ⏑ –́ –, as against –́ ⏑ –́ ⏑, would be intelligible and might be illustrated by other facts in Latin poetry; but not that this preference should be exclusive. The disadvantages are obvious, and Horace cannot have overlooked them. For the rigid caesura we see a compensation, and such as for Roman ears may be supposed adequate. But what was the sufficient compensation here? Horace can write

> plurimum circa nemus *uvidique*
> Tiburis ripas,

that is, he can allow the double trochee at the end of the verse, even where there is no pause to diminish the trochaic effect. Why, then, in spite of the strongest reasons, temptations, and precedents to the contrary, did he abstain altogether from the double trochee at the beginning of the verse? The view that he was influenced by the 2-time rhythm answers this question, and there is so much to be said for it.

But though this were assumed, it would not involve the incredible conclusion that he himself intended his Sapphics to be read with that rhythm. It would be sufficient that he was aware of a prevalent tendency to it among his expected readers. It is easy to conceive such a situation. The metre was foreign. It had no hold yet (if indeed it ever had) upon the Latin language and the Roman ear. Even for those who spoke or read Greek, Sapphics lay out of the common track. Most Romans may be supposed to have known nothing about them. Now Horace, as he tells us, though resolved to satisfy the learned, meant also to conquer a wide public, the whole educated population of the new empire. We know that in one instance (the hendecasyllable) the Romans actually imposed a 2-time rhythm upon a Greek metre made for 3-time. Suppose that they showed a similar tendency in the Sapphic. Suppose it known to Horace by experiment, that, *whatever he intended*, many would take the stanza

> să̋epius véntis ă̋gitatur íngens
> pī̋nus et célsae gră̋viore cásu
> dĕ̋cidunt túrres fĕ̋riuntque súmmos
> fŭ̋lgura móntes

to have naturally the rhythm here given, and would read it so as a matter of course. This would be reason enough for not making it incapable of that rhythm by writing

> sáepiús ventís agitátur íngens
> pínus; áltiór gravióre cásu
> décidít turrís; etc.

Because, although this might please Horace and the learned as well or even, as a variety, better, the only effect of it on such readers as we are supposing would be to make them roll up the book in despair. In such circumstances the *Romanae fidicen lyrae* might well think that, until the *Aeolii modi* should become generally known to his countrymen, the best way to get a hearing for Sapphics was to write them so that people who did not know Sappho, and had no natural disposition for the 3-time rhythm, might at any rate be able to read them.

It is true that, if this was so, the metre could not be expected to take root easily. It was more likely to fail altogether. Well, it is one of the facts to be explained, that the metre, with all its kindred, did fail in Latin; failed, that is, to get a real grip on the language. The *Odes* did not fail: they achieved an immense success. But they did not endow Latin, as Horace hoped that they would, with the metres of Sappho and Alcaeus. Quintilian's remark on the successors of Horace is familiar. The specimens that remain, the Sapphics of Statius for instance, confirm his unfavourable judgement. They are purely academic: stiff, formal, lifeless, foreign, unnatural. And this failure of the Sapphic is explained, if in truth the Romans never could make up their minds how to read it. As a 2-time measure it could not live. In this form it is a hybrid, an unnatural compromise. Unless Latin ears and lips could appropriate the 3-time measure, the Sapphic must wither and die. It did so; and perhaps here was the reason.

The problem of the Horatian Sapphic cannot be separated from that of the Alcaic, to which Prof. Sonnenschein does not refer. Here we have similar puzzles, the regular lengthening of the first and of the fifth syllable,

dūx inquietī turbidus Hadriae,

apparently inexplicable, if the poet meant *and could trust his readers to know* that the rhythm was the trochaic 3-time of Alcaeus, dux | inqui- | eti | turbidus | Hadri- | ae

$\frac{3}{4}$

But this also will be explained if, as a fact, many Latin readers were likely to presume the 2-time rhythm, the schoolboy's rhythm,

dux inqui- | eti | turbidus | Hadriae

$\frac{2}{4}$

To make the verse *possible* for such readers, it must be written as Horace writes it; and this he may have done as a means to the end, while nevertheless himself intending (as for many reasons it is plain that he did) to give the rhythm of Alcaeus, and expecting a time when the Roman lyrist might be on better terms with his public, and have a larger scope.

THE METRICAL DIVISION OF COMPOUND WORDS IN VIRGIL

IN the interesting and almost complete collection of facts and rules respecting the Virgilian Hexameter, published by Mr Winbolt[1], the treatment of the topic above indicated, or rather the want of any treatment, suggests that attention may profitably be called to it.

On the subject of Tmesis (p. 212) it is said in parenthesis that 'We omit a fanciful form discovered by Müller which he says occurs when a part of a compound is separated from the verb by caesura.'

On p. 85 a foot-note to the verse

> navibus, infandum, amissis unius ob iram

says that 'M. Plessis would defend it by counting a caesura by tmesis after the first syllable of *infandum*. Such caesura he says is permissible by tmesis between the prefix of a compound word and the rest of the word: thus *de-* | *torquet*, *im-* | *mensus*.'

Nothing more, so far as I have observed, is said on the topic, and the impression thus suggested is that it has no general importance, and perhaps little reality. This however is not the truth. In Virgil's metre the tmesis of compound words has an importance second only to the division between one word

[1] *Latin Hexameter Verse: An Aid to Composition.* By S. E. Winbolt, M.A. Methuen, 1904.

and another. Without professing to exhaust the subject, we will illustrate it in one very important application, the metrical division of the third foot. For this, the general rule in Virgil may be stated thus:

The third foot of the hexameter, unless contained in a Greek word or a proper name, should be divided either by a caesura *or by a tmesis.*

This is true with exceptions not only rare but almost always explicable by special considerations. But without the last alternative the statement would be wrong.

Take for example the Sixth Book of the *Aeneid.* It contains, if I have counted right, 36 verses which have no caesura (proper) in the third foot. In 11[1] of the 36 the third foot is contained in a proper name, as

in foribus letum Androgeo: tum pendere poenas—
talibus adfata Aenean, nec sacra morantur—
praecipue pius Aeneas. tum iussa Sibyllae—
Aeneas matri Eumenidum magnaeque sorori—

and where this is the case, it seems to be indifferent whether the name is a compound or not: the indivisible name *Aeneas* is so placed in the verse with a frequency almost tiresome. To give exceptional treatment to proper names is the habit of Virgil, and indeed of poets generally. But of the remaining 25 verses[2] all except one exhibit a third

[1] 20, 40, 176, 250, 261, 447, 480, 529, 703, 830, 897.

[2] 99, 100, 143, 149, 186, 197, 213, 222, 236, 254, 345, 382, 408, 414, 415, 428, 465, 571, 607, 614, 684, 698, 781, 831, — 327.

foot divided by tmesis, so that the missing caesura is at least partially represented by the division of a compound :

praeterea iacet ex-animum tibi corpus amici—
coniciunt. pars in-genti subiere feretro—
his actis propere ex-sequitur praecepta Sibyllae—
Tisiphone quatit in-sultans, torvosque sinistra—
en, huius, nate, au-spiciis illa incluta Roma—

and the like. Even the one exception (327) is an exception only apparent—

nec ripas datur hor-rendas et rauca fluenta—

for though the word *horrendas* is not etymologically divisible, there can, I suppose, be no doubt that, for the sake of effect and with a view to its meaning, it is here to be divided, in pronunciation and for the ear, as above indicated, each *r* being separately heard and strongly rolled ; so that the case is only a more subtle application of the general rule.

It need not be said that Virgil uses countless non-divisible words such as *fundabat*, *natorum*, *reginae*, *venturi*, *seminibus*, etc., etc., which, as far as prosody is concerned, might be so placed in the verse. But as a general rule they are excluded in favour of divisible compounds, a preference which can be explained only by supposing that the division of the compound was to the poet's ear significant, and served, by compensating for the caesura, to preserve the balance of the verse.

Thus in

navibus, infandum, a-missis unius ob iram

we should notice, as more important than the divisibility of *infandum* (though that is material), the divisibility of *a-missis*: it is this which brings the verse within the ordinary limits of the poet.

The severity of *Aeneid* VI is, as we might expect, a little beyond the common standard, though the tendency and principle is the same elsewhere. In *Aeneid* I I find the following abnormal verses:

25 necdum etiam caussae *irarum* saevique dolores—
540 permittit patria? *hospitio* prohibemur arenae.

In the following, from the same Book,

180 Aeneas scopulum inter-ea conscendit, et omnem—
224 despiciens mare veli-volum terrasque iacentes—
418 corripuere viam inter-ea qua semita monstrat—

we have tmesis at the trochee, of which Book VI, I think, does not happen to give a specimen[1]. In Book II we have

137 nec mihi iam patriam *antiquam* spes ulla videndi—[2]
222 clamores simul *horrendos* ad sidera tollit—[3]
300 Anchisae domus *arboribusque* obtecta recessit—

In Book IV:

99 quin potius pacem *aeternam* pactosque hymenaeos—
201 excubias divom *aeternas* pecudumque cruore—
405 convectant calle *angusto*; pars grandia trudunt—
431 non iam coniugium *antiquum*, quod prodidit, oro—
538 iussa sequar? quiane *auxilio* iuvat ante levatos—
633 namque suam patria *antiqua* cinis ater habebat—

In Book V:

170 radit iter laevum *interior*, subitoque priorem—

[1] Cf. *Aen.* II 57; IV 291, 464; etc.

[2] But Virgil probably (and perhaps rightly) conceived *antiquus* to be a compound and separable.

[3] Cf. VI 327 above.

250 victori chlamydem *auratam*, quam plurima circum—
316 corripiunt spatia *audito* limenque relinquunt—
468 ast illum fidi *aequales* genua aegra trahentem—
608 multa movens, necdum *antiquum* saturata dolorem.

In most of these it will easily be perceived that the exception is rule-proving: either in the weight of the word, or in the general sense and rhetoric, there is something which justifies to the ear the unusual rhythm. If any may be regarded as a mere licence, it is II 300, not one of the poet's strongest or happiest lines. Those verses which obey the rule and show tmesis are everywhere the vast majority.

It is worth notice, though not strictly within the limits of our subject, that almost every one of the exceptions here quoted exhibits an elision before the exceptional word, and has thus an 'apparent caesura' (in Mr Winbolt's terminology) at the penthemimeral place. And this is usual, though not absolutely universal; see *Georg.* II 5, an interesting case.

Many other applications of the principle may be observed. Thus, although Virgil's

per conubia nostra, per in-ceptos hymenaeos

is partly shaped by recollection of Catullus, it exhibits a Virgilian nicety in the tmesis which marks the place of the hephthemimeral caesura, and thus brings the verse almost within the ordinary Virgilian rules. Catullus, in his similar verse, has the indivisible *optatos* at that place.

Again, a common combination of caesurae in Virgil is this

infandúm, | regina, | iubes | renovare dolorem

occurring, Mr Winbolt says[1], about once in 11 verses. Much more rare, 'about 1 in 400,' is the type having only the two latter of these three caesurae

cornua detorquentque; | ferunt | sua flamina classem.

Now in these circumstances we cannot treat as indifferent the fact that in the much more rare type the missing caesura is represented by a tmesis. Every one of Mr Winbolt's four examples shows this phenomenon, which is scarcely less important for Virgilian metre than the caesurae themselves: add to the above

omnia cor-ripuisse: | metum | iam ad limina ferri—
impulit ef-funditque | solo, | Turnusque secutus—
moenia, sub-limemque | feres | ad sidera caeli.

Whether this rule is universal I have not ascertained, and probably exceptions may be found. But it is manifest that Virgil felt the tmesis, and calculated on its rhythmical effect.

To treat the topic fully is not the purpose of this note, still less to make any complaint against Mr Winbolt. It is the very fulness of his treatise which leads me to suppose that a topic, for which he does not find adequate place, requires some further notice. And indeed I have never seen any treatment answering quite sufficiently to the facts.

[1] p. 83.

A METRICAL JEST OF CATULLUS

THE HENDECASYLLABLE

FEW Latin verses are more familiar than the spirited and humorous piece in which Catullus promises to avenge himself by a return in kind upon the friend who had spoiled his Saturnalia by presenting him with a collection of bad poets. But it has not apparently been observed, or at least the observation has not found its way into editions of authority, that the curse upon those 'plagues of the age,' with which the piece concludes, is enforced and sharpened by an excellent touch of parody. To illustrate the torment of hours spent over their slovenly and inartistic compositions, Catullus, in the act of dismissing them, gives us just one sly specimen of the ignorant, inelegant way in which they would handle his own metre. The point deserves attention not only for its own sake, but for light upon that admirable severity of form, in which the best Romans became the pupils of Athens and Alexandria.

The history of the Greek *hendecasyllable*, the metre of Catullus here, cannot now be perfectly traced. Probably, though not certainly, it was in the first instance one of the numerous varieties, including the Sapphic, Alcaic and many others[1], which by their common quality are to be classed as *trochaic*; that is to say, they were scanned or sung in 3-time, and have for basis the bar ♩ ♪ and its equivalents. It was certainly capable of this treatment, and sometimes was so conceived. Taken as a verse of five trochees, thus,

| maesti- | us lacri- | mis Si- | moni- | deis

the measure is very graceful, and lends itself readily either to stateliness or pathos. Catullus would gladly have naturalized it in this shape, and indeed there are reasons for thinking that some of his poems, notably the famous *Sparrow*, were actually meant to be so sung or so singable;

| luget', | O Vene- | res Cu- | pidi- | nesque

and so on. With this form however we are not here concerned, as the poem now in question, together with almost all Catullus' hendecasyllables and all Martial's, is composed on other principles and in a totally different measure.

It is plain that the notes of the hendecasyllable, though adaptable to 3-time, are equally adaptable to 4-time—thus

| a - rid- | a modo | pumic' expo- | li - tum—

[1] Generically called *iambi*; hence the application of this name to *hendecasyllables*, as by Catullus in *at non effugies meos iambos*

and further that this scansion, perhaps less natural than the trochaic so long as the verses have normally a true trochee for the commencement, becomes not only natural but almost inevitable, if we make the first foot regularly a spondee. The fact that the Roman rulers of the metre adopted this modification, would of itself prove that for them the measure was not five bars of 3-time but four bars of 4-time. And this subordinate form, though far inferior to the other in beauty, and scarcely capable of elevation or dignity, nevertheless, from the acceleration of the verse in its second part, has a singular lightness and smartness. It became perhaps the best of all vehicles for elegant trifling. It is subject however, by its nature, to certain severe conditions, and one of peculiar importance, which is the object of the Catullian parody, and of our present consideration.

In the Roman or 4-time hendecasyllable, then,

| ♩ ♩ | ♩ ♫ || ♪. ♬ ♪. ♬ | ♩ ♩

| Iu - li | iu - gera || pauca Marti- | a - lis

it is manifestly a chief characteristic that the measure is symmetrical and divisible into two equal though different parts, and upon this balance in diversity its effect is chiefly dependent. Four main beats mark the four bars, and two of these, especially strong, mark the commencement of each pair of bars, thus,

Iű̆li | iúgera || paűca Marti- | ális.

In wording the measure therefore attention to these two principal beats is an essential point. The first offers no difficulty. Falling on the first syllable of a word and that a long syllable, it must, without special precaution, almost always fall on a syllable of significance, and will frequently coincide with the natural accent or stress of a word. But the preservation of the other beat requires the most careful handling. To give it the full benefit of stress and significance, that is to say, to divide the verse *invariably* by a caesura after the dactyl, is practically impossible, and if it were done would result in tedious monotony. Manifestly we must admit, as a variety, such verses as the second, third, fifth and sixth of the following,

> Iű̆li iugera paű̆ca Martialis
> *hŏ̋rtis Hesperidū̋m beatiora*
> *lŏ̋ngo Ianiculī̋ iugo recumbunt:*
> lă̋ti collibus ″ĭmminent recessus;
> *″ĕt planus modicō̋ tumore vertex*
> *caĕ̋lo perfruitū̋r sereniore.*

Provided that we keep the true type in view by a liberal admixture of strong verses such as the first and fourth (and this Catullus and Martial are careful to do), we can and must allow the second beat to fall frequently upon comparatively insignificant syllables, mere inflexions and terminations. But shall we go further than this? Shall we allow not only

> hortis Hesperidŭ̋m beatiora

but also

> longo Ianiculĭ̋ iugo recumbunt

or

> solus luce nitĕ̋t peculiari?

The two last verses have a much weaker beat than the first, and for a plain reason. Weight is comparative: the heavy is so by relation to what is light. The final syllables of *Ianiculi* and of *Hesperidum* are equal in weight *per se*; but in *Ianicul″ĭ iugo recumbunt* the beat-syllable has the disadvantage not only of its own weakness but of adverse strength in the following syllable, the first of *iugo*, weighted not only by its significance, but by the *accent of the word*, which falls on it. And in *luce nit″ĕt peculiari* an equal disadvantage, or somewhat more, is produced by the adverse weight of the preceding syllable in *nitet*. But from such disadvantage *Hesperid″ŭm beatiora* is free. How important to Roman ears was the metric effect of the word-accent in such words as *iúgo* or *nítet*, contending as it does against their quantity, is shown by the whole history of Roman metre. We have but to remember how Ovid determined with general approval, that in spite of all inconvenience, the penultimate syllable of a Latin pentameter must always have this accent. To a Roman ear therefore no question in the structure of the hendecasyllable could be more important than this: whether that accent should or should not be normally permitted to fall on either of the syllables immediately preceding and following the chief rhythmical beat of the verse. The decision of the authorities was that in either place it could be so permitted, and that the gain in convenience and in variety more than compensated the weakening of the rhythm. It should be noted, however, that by Martial the indulgence was somewhat carefully watched: his use of such rhythms is less than the vocabulary of Latin would naturally suggest. The rule which could be deduced from his more important and more carefully wrought pieces is that verses like

lapsae per Tiberim *volent* carinae,

or,

et quodcunque *iacet* sub urbe frigus,

are normal indeed, but should be employed sparingly. The poem from which we have been quoting (IV 64) is a specimen of his best workmanship. It contains eight such verses in thirty-six[1]. Catullus, whose manner is in all respects easier, more colloquial, and less academic, than Martial's, admits them generally without reserve. That both poets decided the point with consciousness of its importance, is shown by their treatment of the next question which arises out of it.

Let us have passed, as normal hendecasyllables, (1) verses in which the beat, having itself no natural stress, is preceded by the stressed syllable of an iambic word, and (2) verses in which the beat is followed by such a syllable. What shall we say of verses in which both disadvantages occur together? Let *illuc unde négänt redire quemquam* be good, and also good *quem plus illa ocul'ïs súis amabat.* What of *verum si quid ágës, státim iubeto?* Is this good enough to be passed as normal? Both Catullus and Martial reply emphatically that it is not. By Martial indeed such a rhythm is only just

[1] *v.* 15 *Fidenas veteres brevesque Rubras* must not be counted: by the adherence of *que* the actual accent of *bréves* is displaced, or at least weakened.

not absolutely proscribed. In his Ninth, Tenth, and Eleventh Books the hendecasyllabic pieces amount to about five hundred verses. In all this mass I have noticed this double iambus eight times only[1]. Moreover it is instantly plain in most of these instances, that the breach of rule is not negligent but voluntary. For example, when the poet is regretting the impossibility of putting into Latin hendecasyllables the name of the emperor's favourite *Earinus*, he remarks that a Greek poet could have used *Eiarinus* (Εἰαρινός)—a form which apparently he supposed to have been produced by metrical caprice—but such licentiousness (he says) was not fit for the stricter Muses of Rome (IX 11):

> dicunt Eiarinon tamen poetae,
> sed Graeci, quibus est nihil negatum
> *et quos* Ἆρες Ἄρες *decet sonare*:
> nobis non licet esse tam disertis,
> qui Musas colimus severiores.

The third verse has the double iambus (Ἄρες *decet*), but of course no more signifies approval of that rhythm than of the variation in quantity between Ἀ̄ρες and Ἄ̆ρες. On the contrary, the fact that it is used here, justifies, if need were, the conclusion from its general scarcity, that the author thought ill of it. So again it might be expected that, just because he rejected it from general use, he would occasionally employ it to emphasize a particular point; precisely as in his elegiacs, while observing

[1] IX 11. 15, IX 52. 7, X 19. 10, X 47. 4, X 90. 4, XI 18. 4, XI 24. 7, XI 72. 1. Some I have probably overlooked, but not many.

the Ovidian rule as to the pentameter, he will occasionally *conclude the epigram*, for the sake of a sharper distinction, with the trisyllable or quadrisyllable which that rule rejects[1]. And he does so employ it: we have an instance in IX 52.

> si credis mihi, Quinte, quod mereris,
> natales, Ovidi, tuos Apriles,
> ut nostras amo Martias Kalendas.
> felix utraque lux, diesque nobis
> signandi melioribus lapillis!
> hic vitam tribuit, sed hic amicum:
> plus dant, Quinte, *mihi—túae* Kalendae.

It is of course no harm, but a gain in smartness, that the unelided *túae* has an accent which, by an ear trained in the practice of Martial, is felt to be too heavy for the verse[2]. Elsewhere other reasons may be seen or guessed, but we need not pursue further an inquiry affecting no more than the question, at what point precisely the residuum of bare negligences stands between ½ per cent. and 2. Irregular at any rate and abnormal in the highest degree the thing is, a licence, as above said, which Martial just does not prohibit. In Catullus, as might be expected, the application of the principle is different, but the principle is the same. Suppler and less artificial than Martial in all things, he is so in this. Among his extant hendecasyllables, upwards of five hundred in number, the rhythm in question, the rhythm of

[1] *E.g.* XI. 33, 36, 48, 52, 70 etc.

[2] So in VIII 2. 8 addas, Iane pater, *tuam* rogamus, and elsewhere.

nam castum esse *decet pium* poetam—
a te sudor *abest, abest* saliva—
verum si quid *ages, statim* iubeto—
ride, quidquid *amas, Cato,* Catullum—

will be found about a dozen times[1]. The proportion somewhat exceeds Martial's, but its smallness is in one way even more striking than in his case, from the fact that the *single* iambus is scattered by Catullus with more profusion. Martial, as we have noticed, tends to be sparing even of that; but in the vocabulary of Catullus, which presents words like *boni, meos, pedem, sacrum* either in the second foot or in the third of one verse in every three or rather oftener, it proves an extraordinary vigilance or instinct that with the rarest exceptions we find such words in the second foot *only* or in the third *only,* and not in both. Given the vocabulary of Catullus, lines such as

nam castum esse *decet pium* poetam

must have numbered nearer 30 per cent. than the actual 3, if the poet had not felt them to be dangerous. These exceptions however, so far as they go, do not appear to be much affected, as in Martial, by special motives. They are just irregularities, barely permitted here and there as an extreme concession to variety.

But when we have determined this point, there is yet another important question to be settled,

[1] Those which I have noted are 6. 12 (?), 6. 15, 10. 9, 10. 26 (?), 12. 4, 15. 12, 16. 5, 16. 7, 21. 4, 23. 16, 32. 9, 56. 3, 57. 8. Two are doubtful in reading.

respecting words of this form and so placed in the metre, before we can securely compose. Under what restrictions, if at all, may they suffer elision?

> hesterno, Licini, *die* otiosi—
> si tecum attuleris *bonam* atque magnam—

Are these to be allowed as normal, or not? It is a point for hesitation; not only because the elision adds roughness where there is already some weakness, but also because it increases the weakness itself. The rhythm of

> dum iussus repetit pilos eosdem

is weak, as already explained, because the first syllable of *pilos* is by accent and significance so much weightier than the last syllable of *repetit*, whereas the rhythm demands the contrary relation. Now in

> hesterno, Licini, die otiosi

the first syllable of *die*, stronger in itself than is rhythmically desirable, gains yet a little more strength by slurring or merging of the second syllable. Is this to be? Martial's answer is peremptory. Averse from elision generally, and scarcely ever permitting it in words of this quantity (unless such things as *nequ'*, *datum 'st* are to be counted), he was not likely to select for it a place where it is open to special objections. If there be in his whole works any line like

> hesterno, Licini, die otiosi,

the number of such is at all events not worth counting. Catullus is more facile. With all sorts of cautions, delicacies, and reserves, he allows the elision at this place of both long vowels and short. It is only at this place, we may notice, and only in regard to the 3rd foot of the verse, that our present question can arise. Where such an elision occurs in the 2nd foot—as in

venistine domum | ad tuos Penates—

the beat-syllable (here *ad*) must necessarily have considerable weight of its own; in fact the verse has practically the strong dactylic caesura, which takes it out of our contemplation. For the like reason, where there is the strong caesura, we are not concerned with an elision even in the 3rd foot—as in

visum duxerat | e foro otiosum—
atque id durius | est faba ac lapillis.

Nor, as it happens, have we to do, in the case to which we are leading, with the elision of a word whose full quantities are ◡◡; for which reason, though the quantity of the vowel elided does not much affect the principle of the matter, we will set aside such forms as

sed circumsiliens modŏ huc modo illuc—
quoi primum digitum darĕ adpetenti.

None of these types are very common in Catullus, and in all of them, as will easily be felt and seen by an attentive reader, the poet has been restrained by certain limitations. But the cases which we shall want here are those only which combine the *weak* caesura with an *iambic* word following, and that *elided*:

ut Veraniolum | *meum et* Fabullum—
si tecum attuleris | *bonam at*que magnam—

in re praetereunt | *sua oc*cupati—
qui tum denique habent | *salem ac* leporem—
vos Veraniolo | *meo et* Fabullo—
hesterno, Licini, | *die o*tiosi—
O rem ridiculam, | *Cato, et* iocosam[1].

This, so far as I have observed, is the whole list: seven examples, or, to be safe, about seven, and in five hundred verses.

Let us now sum up Catullus' theory of the hendecasyllable, so far as relates to the present theme. The ideal type of the verse is that exhibited in the only one, or almost the only one, of his hendecasyllabic poems, which by its tone ascends above the level of trifling:

Vivamus mea Lesbia atque amemus
rumoresque senum severiorum
omnes unius aestimemus assis.
soles occidere et redire possunt:
nobis cum semel occidit brevis lux,
nox est perpetua una dormienda.
da mi basia mille, deinde centum,
dein mille altera, dein secunda centum,
deinde usque altera mille, deinde centum;
dein, cum milia multa fecerimus,
conturbabimus illa, ne sciamus,
aut nequis malus invidere possit,
cum tantum sciat esse basiorum.

The rules deducible are (1) that the strong dactylic caesura should be prevalent; here 12 times in 13: (2) that 'iambic rhythms,' as we have called them, may be used, but sparingly: we have an iambic word in the 2nd foot once (*v.* 2), in the 3rd foot not

[1] Catullus 12. 17, 13. 3, 15. 8, 16. 7, 47. 3, 50. 1, 56. 1.

at all: (3) elision, where permitted, should be of short vowels only. Martial agrees in all points, and observes the rules in general more strictly than Catullus, though seldom, if ever, with such splendid severity as we have here. From this type certain deflexions are allowed for the sake of variety, and on common occasions: (1) we may multiply, but not without limit, the weak caesura; (2) we may multiply (according to Catullus without any practical limit, Martial so far dissenting) the number of the 'iambic rhythms.' These variations may be called normal. Further there are certain licences with regard to the iambic rhythm which Martial prohibits or almost prohibits, while Catullus admits them rarely or very rarely: those with which we are concerned are (1) the 'double iambus,' as in *quare quidquid habes boni malique*, and (2) the elision of the long syllable in an iambus, as in *hesterno, Licini, die otiosi.*

And now with these facts before us, let us turn to the words in which Catullus execrates the versifiers to whose compositions Calvus had treacherously made him sacrifice his holiday.

di magni, horribilem et sacrum libellum,
quem tu scilicet ad tuom Catullum
misti, continuo ut die periret,
Saturnalibus, optimo dierum.
non non hoc tibi, salse, sic abibit:
nam si luxerit, ad librariorum
curram scrinia, Caesios, Aquinos,
Suffenum omnia colligam venena,
ac te his suppliciis remunerabor.
vos hinc interea valete, abite
illuc, unde malum pedem attulistis,
saecli incommoda, pessimi poetae.

'*To that same place whence your wretched feet came hither*': *illuc unde malum pedem attulistis!* It is no wonder that Catullus soon had enough of them, if indeed their feet hobbled like this. The verse is miserably bad, in fact mere doggerel, having no other claim to be called a verse, than that there are eleven syllables, and these syllables have the quantities prescribed. Rhythm there is none. The principal beat falls on the last syllable of *malum*, intrinsically as weak a syllable as could be found in the language. Wedged as this is between the accented and significant syllables of *mál*(*um*) and *péd*(*em*), the rhythm is already impaired to an extent which Catullus will very rarely allow and Martial practically never. And then, as if this were not enough, the composer claps on an absolutely needless elision, hard in itself and so placed as to aggravate the weakness already existing. Nor is this the whole of the iniquity. If the reader will look for verses in Catullus which exhibit elision at this point, he will soon become aware that by preference the sense is so arranged that the word elided *coheres closely with those which follow it*: *modo huc modo illuc—in ioco atque vino—bonam atque magnam—novum ac repertum—bene ac beate—salem ac leporem—faba ac lapillis*, such phrases make the majority of examples, some of them, by way of proof that the conditions were not easily satisfied, occurring twice or even thrice. And indeed that such cohesion of sense commends and smooths the cohesion of sound, is perceptible to any ear. Far fewer are the cases where, in point of sense and grammar, the word which suffers elision belongs equally to what precedes and what follows, as in

quoi primum digitum dare adpetenti—

or in

ut Veraniolum meum et Fabullum.

And of cohesion closer with that which precedes than with that which follows I doubt if Catullus exhibits one single instance[1]—except this doggerel,

illuc unde malum pedem attulistis.

Here indeed it is plain enough that the connexion of *pedem* with *malum* is the strongest possible, scarcely less strong than if the two formed one word. Read by the sense, the rhythm is practically the same as, for example, in

vel Praeneste *domate* pendulamque,

a form for which both Catullus and Martial show a marked distaste[2], and which is at any rate inconsistent

[1] Note that this somewhat diminishes the probability of Pleitner's conjecture *quod si non aliud pote ut ruborem* etc. in 42. 16, adopted in the new *Corpus*, though the objection is not decisive.

[2] The reason for the distaste is that this form completely obliterates the typical *bisection* of the verse. The avoidance of it is one of the many proofs that the Roman hendecasyllable was in 4-time. In the primitive hendecasyllable, trochaic or 3-time, *vel Praeneste domate pendulamque* would be an excellent form; whereas on the contrary the favourite form of Catullus and Martial, with the dactylic caesura, would be just the poorest. But all that class of metres the Romans, after the one ominous success of Horace, practically abandoned as contrary to the genius of their language.

with the metrical attachment of *pedem* to *attulistis*. And, what most of all exhibits and emphasizes the humour of the thing, the elision of *pedem*, which makes the worst of the mischief, is so manifestly gratuitous! That the preposition *ad-* is unnecessary to the sense, is duly remarked by Mr Robinson Ellis, who of course also remarks that the *malus pes* signifies *bad metre*. But we ought to add that the preposition is wilfully inserted for the purpose of completing an illustration of that bad metre. It makes the expression somewhat more precise, and for this reason an ordinary speaker, or a writer of prose, would naturally prefer to use it. But a verse-writer who had any taste of his art, would have struck it out, so to speak, before he had time to put it down, writing

illuc unde malum pedem tulistis.

The verse would have been still weak, the sort of thing which a true poet will let pass once or twice in a century. But with *attulistis* it becomes the work not merely of a bungler, but of one who is essentially not a poet at all, who thinks and writes in prose, and has no other notion of verse than that it is prose having certain quantities and cut into certain lengths. Not once, so far as I can observe, has Catullus been guilty of such a trip. Only once has he approached it,

qui tum denique *hábent sálem ac* leporem[1],

[1] 16. 7. We have indeed in 10. 26 a verse which, merely as a verse, is perhaps as bad or a shade worse:

and this is a piece which has other defects besides a rather slovenly versification, and might certainly have been suppressed with little loss to his reputation either as a poet or as a wit. Compositions—and such, we are to suppose, were those of Suffenus and company—of which these 'hobbling feet' were the staple, would be a torment to flesh and spirit, as Catullus found them on that unhappy day of December. He relieved himself, it would seem, by noting down some of the worst horrors.

In conclusion, if the reader has patience, we may illustrate the metrical humour of Catullus by two cognate, though significantly different, examples from Martial.

Quidam me modo, Rufe, diligenter
inspectum, velut emptor aut lanista,
cum vultu digitoque subnotasset,
'tune es, tune,' ait, 'ille Martialis,
cuius nequitias iocosque novit
aurem qui modo non habet Batavam?'
subrisi modice, levique nutu
me, quem dixerat, esse non negavi.
'cur ergo' inquit '*habes malas* lacernas?'
respondi: 'quia sum malus poeta.'
hoc ne saepius accidat poetae,
mittas, Rufe, *mihi—bonas* lacernas[1].

---

hic illa, ut decuit cinaediorem,
'quaeso' inquit 'mihi, mi Catulle, paulum
istos: commodum enim: volo ad Sarapim
deferri.'

But this, for obvious reasons, is to be counted as a sign not of negligence, but of care. If you want to put in verse a bit of casual conversation, the rougher the verse may be, the better for the purpose.

[1] VI 82.

Disagreeable as it is to see such art descending to the office of stimulating the liberality of patrons, the art itself surpasses admiration. It is worth while, with Martial's help, to cultivate 'a better than Batavian ear,' in order to perceive instantly with what apt delicacy the blunt and simple question of the quidnunc is clothed in a verse appropriately inartistic, while at the same time we are prepared for the use of the same exceptional rhythm by way of echo, to emphasize, according to the poet's practice, this concluding point. Better still perhaps is the subtle variety of the piece which relates how, to escape the round of morning visits to great houses, a sore-footed client bethought him of pretending a gout, and acted lameness so faithfully that it threatened to become real:

> Discursus varios vagumque mane
> *et fastus et 'ave' potentiorum*
> cum perferre patique iam negaret,
> coepit fingere Caelius podagram.
> quam dum vult nimis approbare veram,
> et sanas linit obligatque plantas
> *inceditque gradu laborioso,*
> (*quantum cura potest et ars doloris!*)
> desit[1] fingere Caelius podagram[2].

The thing which makes this trifle a work of art, which stamps it, for the 'auris non Batava,' as a 'nequitia iocusque' of Martial, is just simply the definition of the weaker verses. Two only have the full maximum strength, in which the four beats of the four bars all coincide with even accent and there

[1] *i.e.* desiit. [2] VII 39.

is no adverse accent at all[1]: these are the opposed pairs

coe̋pit} fíngere Caélius podágram.
de̋sit}

The slackest in rhythm are those italicized, where a principal beat contends against the adverse accents of *ave*, *gradu*, *potest*; and the penultimate verse, with its *potest et ars*, moves, like Caelius himself, with a 'step laborious.' Though different indeed from the 'wretched foot' of the fellows who plagued Catullus, yet for Martial it hobbles with quite enough pain—and enough art.

[1] This form is the strongest normally attainable. In such a verse as *campus*, *porticus*, *umbra*, *Vírgo*, *thermae* there is indeed an even more complete coincidence of accent and beat, since the subordinate second beat of the 3rd foot has an accent too. But the rhythm is none the stronger for this; it is weaker. The stress on *vírgo* diminishes relatively the much more important stress on *úmbra*, and thus obscures the quadripartite division of bars which is the essence of the metre. Even the absolutely perfect form, *e.g. omnes unius aestimemus assis*, is very little stronger in rhythm than *coepit fingere Caelius podagram*: and it is in practice impossible to achieve such forms except as a rare luxury.

ON A METRICAL PRACTICE IN GREEK TRAGEDY[1]

THERE is a point in the metrical practice of the Greek Tragedians which has not received the attention to which it is entitled, as an aid both to criticism and to the appreciation of their art. The rules which we can tabulate do not of course pretend to state exhaustively the injunctions and prohibitions observed by the native ear and in some degree appreciable by modern observation. But there is still a precept unformulated which, though not a true canon, has such a regular and extensive influence as to require an explicit recognition. The common rules for elision, in Greek and other verse, take account only of the elided syllable. A rule

[1] Throughout this paper account is taken, in statistics and elsewhere, of extant tragedies only, exclusive of fragments. The inclusion of the fragments would have made no difference to the result, but the nature of the questions investigated is such that disturbance in the order of words vitiates for the present purpose the authority of a text. The fragments are peculiarly open to the suspicion of such disturbance; and if on these questions their testimony disagreed with that of the extant plays, it would be to that extent impeachable. It seemed, therefore, more logical not to cite it in proof.

established on this basis is for the Greek Tragedians very far from complete; and it is proposed to give here a more accurate view of the remarkable principles which govern the elision of *dissyllabic words having the penultimate syllable short.*

Before stating the facts it will be useful to call to mind the relation between words of this quantity and the common metre of tragedy, the iambic senarius. It is obvious that for this metre no restriction could be more inconvenient than one limiting the free elision of words having this form. The effect of such a restriction must be in the senarius of Aeschylus, and we might almost add of Sophocles, to confine the word, except when followed by a double consonant, to the last part of the verse; for the true tribrach, that is, a tribrach which cannot be reduced to an iambus by the consonantal pronunciation of a vowel (*synizesis*), is almost unknown in Aeschylus and even in Sophocles unfrequent. On the other hand, if the word be elided, it has six places open to it, the thesis in the six feet. *A priori* therefore we should expect elision to be far more frequent than non-elision: not indeed six times as frequent, for there are several conditions which curtail the freedom even of the elided form besides the necessity of finding an initial vowel to follow it. Thus a word standing first in its clause, such as ἵνα, cannot occupy the third thesis without producing an unfrequent and not very pleasing pause,

⏑ – ⏑ –, | ⏑ – ⏑ – ⏑ – ⏑ –

Again, when an elided dissyllable stands in the fourth thesis, it must, if the line is to have the normal caesura, be preceded by a monosyllable. In the fifth thesis it introduces a cretic caesura, with its attendant disadvantages, while in the sixth it is subject to still more obvious practical limitations. The following examples from Sophocles of an elided μέγα will exhibit the working of these conditions better than a detailed discussion—

> μηδὲν μέγ' εἴπῃς—
> νῦν δ' ἐγὼ μέγ' αὖ φρονῶ—
> ξὺν τῷ δικαίῳ γὰρ μέγ' ἔξεστιν φρονεῖν—
> μέγ' ἄν τι κομπάσειας ἀσπίδ' εἰ λάβοις—
> φρονεῖν μέγ' ὅστις δοῦλός ἐστι τῶν πέλας—
> τὸ μηδὲν ἄλγος ἐς μέγ' οἴσετε—
> μέγ' ἂν λέγοις δώρημα τῆς συνουσίας—
> αὐτῇ μέγ' εὑρεῖν κέρδος—
> κακὸν μέγ' ἐκπράξασ' ἀπ' ἐλπίδος καλῆς.

But with every allowance for restrictions merely metrical, it is clear that elision will prevail. What the exact proportion is in words which can be elided at pleasure, such as ὅδε, τόδε, τάδε, it does not seem worth while to ascertain, but a preponderance of elision over non-elision will be found throughout the whole class of the words having this form which, in the *general practice* of Aeschylus and Sophocles, are subject to elision at all. Under this head come the pronouns ὅδε, τόδε, τάδε, τινα, τίνα, the present imperatives λέγε, φέρε, ἄγε, etc., the adverbs and adverbial conjunctions ἔτι, τότε, ποτε, ὅτε, ἵνα, ὄφρα, the particle ἄρα, the numerals δέκα and δύο, and in fact all 'parts of speech' *except substantives, adjectives, the pronoun ἐμέ, the numerals ἕνα, μία and the adverbs in -α.* The aorist imperatives (μάθε, λάβε, etc.) may probably be included upon the analogy of the present imperatives; the balance of examples in Aeschylus is against elision—two cases only in seven (*Prom.* 706, *Eum.* 657)—but the total number is too small to furnish evidence of a separate treatment, and they are subject to elision both in Euripides (which would not be conclusive) and in Sophocles.

But if, bearing these *a priori* considerations in mind, we pass to the treatment of *substantives, adjectives,* etc., we shall find a striking contrast. The *general rules* respecting these are the same, with slight modifications which will appear as we proceed, for Aeschylus and for Sophocles, and may be stated thus—

1. A dissyllabic substantive or adjective having the penultimate short may be elided, if *both* the following conditions are fulfilled, viz. if

(α) it commences a verse, and also

(β) has a strong emphasis.

2. A vocative of this form (*e.g.* ξένε), may be elided, and therefore generally is elided, when it is preceded by the interjection ὦ, but not otherwise.

3. Except under the conditions stated in (1) and (2) such substantives and adjectives are not elided.

4. The adverbs in -α (ἅμα, δίχα, etc.) are

elided in certain familiar combinations, but otherwise follow the rules for substantives[1].

5. The numerals ἕνα and μία are treated as adjectives, except in certain familiar combinations.

The cases of μέγα and of the pronoun ἐμέ will be separately considered hereafter. We may add that

6. πάρα (for πάρεστι) is not elided.

The reasons for separating Euripides from his predecessors will appear in the remarks which will be made in conclusion upon his usage in this matter. We may say here, however, that he follows the same principles, though with more variation, and Euripidean illustrations will be cited when convenient.

It will be seen presently and may perhaps be believed beforehand that these facts are not fully recognized either in the critical treatment of the tragic texts or in the imitative compositions which represent the consciousness of scholars. In a published volume of translations containing several hundred lines of iambic verse, I read many pages without finding a single instance of a 'short' dissyllabic substantive *unelided*, while I found without difficulty five or six cases of φρέν' for φρένα, χθόν'

[1] The adverb μάλα ought perhaps to be regarded as an exception to this rule, as it is elided regularly before the word which it qualifies. This, however, as will be seen hereafter, may be justified on general principles, and it is further uncertain whether most of the phrases in which elision of μάλα occurs were not (some certainly were) familiar combinations.

for χθόνα, and the like. In short, these substantives were made subject to the obvious rule of convenience, and elided as freely as ἔτι or τόδε. We will now see how far this practice accords with that of the native models. I will premise that, although I cannot guarantee the absolute accuracy of observations extending over upwards of twenty-two thousand lines, I have made a complete study of twenty plays for the express purpose of this paper, and believe that my statements are fairly trustworthy. The positive part of the evidence may be stated briefly. In the extant plays of Aeschylus occur the following words which fall within the above rule[1] :—

ἅλα, βοτὰ, γάλα, Δία, ἕνα, κακά, καλά, κύνα, λίβα, μία, ξένε, ὅπα, πλάκα, πλέα, πόδα, πτάκα, στόμα, τέκνα, τρίχα, φίλα, φίλε, φλόγα, φρένα, χέρα, χθόνα, ἅμα, δίχα, πάρα (πάρεστι).

The examples of these used *without elision* number collectively upwards of *one hundred and twenty*.

Sophocles uses most of the above and also the following—

ἄνα (*O king*), ἐμά, ζυγά, ἴσα, κενά, Λίχα, μόνα, νέα, ὅπλα, πικρά, σοφά, σταθμά, Ὕπνε, Φρύγα.

The examples of these used *without elision* number collectively upwards of *two hundred and ten*. It is scarcely necessary to confirm these totals by a page of references; the *Indices* will supply a ready means of verification.

[1] Excluding σάφα and τάχα, as to which see below.

Of elisions after the first syllable of the verse with strong emphasis (Rule 1) the following are examples; from the nature of the case they are not numerous, but they are sufficient to show a principle.

Soph. *O. T.* 1180.

(Oedipus is making inquiries of the servant who should have exposed him, when an infant, but spared him and delivered him instead to the man by whom he was conveyed to the house of Polybus.)

ΟΙ. πῶς δῆτ' ἀφῆκας τῷ γέροντι τῷδε σύ;
ΘΕ. κατοικτίσας, ὦ δέσποθ', ὡς ἄλλην χθόνα
δοκῶν ἀποίσειν, αὐτὸς ἔνθεν ἦν· ὁ δὲ
κάκ' ἐς μέγιστ' ἔσωσεν· εἰ γὰρ οὗτος εἶ
ὅν φησιν οὗτος, ἴσθι δύσποτμος γεγώς.

Here the emphasis signifies the strange disappointment of the benevolent intention, by which an act of humanity procured misery to the object of it and resulted not in *ἀγαθά* but in *κακὰ μέγιστα*. A similar antithesis is marked in the same way in Soph. *O. C.* 796,

τὸ σὸν δ' ἀφῖκται δεῦρ' ὑπόβλητον στόμα
πολλὴν ἔχον στόμωσιν· ἐν δὲ τῷ λέγειν
κάκ' ἂν λάβοις τὰ πλείον' ἢ σωτήρια.

Similarly in *O. C.* 48 *δίχα* is elided in the first thesis when it forms part of an emphasized phrase.

ἀλλ' οὐδ' ἐμοί τοι τοὐξανιστάναι πόλεως
δίχ' ἐστὶ θάρσος, πρίν γ' ἂν ἐνδείξω τί δρῶ.

The prominent notion of these lines, individual action without public authority, is expressed by the stress upon *ἐμοὶ...πόλεως δίχα*. So also *ἴσα* is elided in *O. T.* 409, 544, where the point lies in the claim of a just equality—

> εἰ καὶ τυραννεῖς, ἐξισωτέον τὸ γοῦν
> ἴσ' ἀντιλέξαι.—
> οἶσθ' ὡς πόησον; ἀντὶ τῶν εἰρημένων
> ἴσ' ἀντάκουσον.

In Aesch. *Cho.* 94 the reading ἴσ' is conjectural for ἐστ'—

> ἢ τοῦτο φάσκω τοὔπος, ὡς νόμος βροτοῖς
> ἴσ' ἀντιδοῦναι τοῖσι πέμπουσιν τάδε;

but ἔσθλ', the conjecture of Elmsley, appears to be better justified by the context. We shall presently see that this use is, as might be expected, frequent in the case of ἐμέ, which has always some emphasis and generally a strong emphasis. Other instances may be found in Euripides, *e.g. Hipp.* 327

> κάκ', ὦ τάλαινά, σοι τάδ', εἰ πεύσει, κακά.—

Phoen. 890 (Teiresias is about to disclose to Creon that the salvation of the city demands the sacrifice of his son Menoeceus)

> ἐπεὶ δὲ κρεῖσσον τὸ κακόν ἐστι τἀγαθοῦ
> μί' ἔστιν ἄλλη μηχανὴ σωτηρίας.

where μία signifies *one and one only*. Cf. Eur. *Hel.* 815 μί' ἐστὶν ἐλπίς, ᾗ μόνῃ σωθεῖμεν ἄν.

Rule 2 is exemplified chiefly in the vocatives ξένε and τέκνα. We find

Aesch. *Cho.* 680	ἐπείπερ ἄλλως, ὦ ξέν', εἰς Ἄργος κίεις.
ib. 220	ἀλλ' ἢ δόλον τιν', ὦ ξέν', ἀμφί μοι πλέκεις;
Eum. 436	τί πρὸς τάδ' εἰπεῖν, ὦ ξέν', ἐν μέρει θέλεις;
Soph. *O. T.* 931	αὔτως δὲ καὶ σύ γ', ὦ ξέν', ἄξιος γὰρ εἶ.
O. C. 62	τοιαῦτά σοι ταῦτ' ἐστίν, ὦ ξέν', οὐ λόγοις κ.τ.λ.

Soph. *O. C.* 75 οἶσθ', ὦ ξέν', ὡς νῦν μὴ σφαλῇς;
ib. 492, 834, *El.* 662, 671, 797, etc., etc.

But on the other hand,

Soph. *O. C.* 161 ξένε πάμμορ', εὖ φύλαξαι·
ib. 668 εὐίππου, ξένε, τᾶσδε χώρας κ.τ.λ.
El. 678 σὺ μὲν τὰ σαυτῆς πρᾶσσ'· ἐμοὶ δὲ σύ, ξένε, τἀληθὲς εἰπέ.
ib. 1182 οὔτοι ποτ' ἄλλην ἢ 'μὲ δυσφημεῖς, ξένε.
ib. 1206 μὴ δῆτα πρὸς θεῶν τοῦτό μ' ἐργάσῃ, ξένε.
Phil. 557, 575, etc., etc.

And again,

Soph. *O. T.* 1484 ὃς ὑμίν, ὦ τέκν', οὔθ' ὁρῶν οὔθ' ἱστορῶν κ.τ.λ.
ib. 1501 οὐκ ἔστιν οὐδείς, ὦ τέκν', ἀλλὰ δηλαδὴ κ.τ.λ.
ib. 1511 σφῷν δ', ὦ τέκν', εἰ μὲν εἰχέτην ἤδη φρένας κ.τ.λ., etc., etc.

But on the other hand,

ib. 6 ἀγὼ δικαιῶν μὴ παρ' ἀγγέλων, τέκνα, κ.τ.λ.
ib. 1493 τίς οὗτος ἔσται, τίς παραρρίψει, τέκνα; etc., etc.

In Soph. *Phil.* 827,

Ὕπν' ὀδύνας ἀδαής, Ὕπνε δ' ἀλγέων κ.τ.λ.,

it will be observed that the vocative is elided when the penultimate is long but not elided when it is short. Trochaic substantives, it is needless to say, are elided freely.

We will now turn to the negative side of the evidence and examine the real or apparent exceptions. I have noticed the following—

Aesch. *P. V.* 139 τοῦ περὶ πᾶσαν εἱλισσομένου
χθόν' ἀκοιμήτῳ ῥεύματι παῖδες.

(So the MSS. Hermann πᾶσαν θ' εἱλισσομένου.)

ib. 339 αὐχῶ γὰρ αὐχῶ τήνδε δωρεὰν ἐμοὶ
δώσειν Δί', ὥστε τῶνδέ σ' ἐκλῦσαι πόνων.

Sept. 628 δορίπονα κάκ' ἐκτρέποντες γᾶς
ἐπιμόλους.
ib. 782 δίδυμα κάκ' ἐτέλεσεν.
Ag. 907 μὴ χάμαι τιθεὶς
τὸν σὸν πόδ', ὦναξ, Ἰλίου πορθήτορα.
Eum. 901 τοιγὰρ κατὰ χθόν' οὖσ' ἐπικτήσει φίλους.
ib. 971 ὅτι μοι γλῶσσαν καὶ στόμ' ἐπωπᾷ.
Soph. *O. T.* 957 τί φής, ξέν'; αὐτός μοι σὺ σημήνας γενοῦ.
ib. 1250 ἐξ ἀνδρὸς ἄνδρα καὶ τέκν' ἐκ τέκνων τέκοι.
O. C. 824 χώρει, ξέν', ἔξω θᾶσσον.
ib. 877 ὅσον λῆμ' ἔχων ἀφίκου, ξέν', εἰ τάδε δοκεῖς τελεῖν.
ib. 1130 κἀμοὶ χέρ', ὦναξ, δεξιὰν ὄρεξον, ὡς κ.τ.λ.
ib. 1206 μόνον, ξέν', εἴπερ κεῖνος ὧδ' ἐλεύσεται.
El. 633 ἐῶ, κελεύω, θῦε· μηδ' ἐπαιτιῶ
τοὐμὸν στόμ', ὡς οὐκ ἂν πέρα λέξαιμ' ἔτι.
Phil. 423 κείνων κάκ' ἐξήρυκε, βουλεύων σοφά.
ib. 664 ...... ὃς χθόν' Οἰταίαν ἰδεῖν κ.τ.λ.
ib. 1137 ὃς ἐφ' ἡμῖν κάκ' ἐμήσατ', ὦ Ζεῦ.

I have some confidence that this list is almost if not completely exhaustive for the extant plays of the two elder tragedians. The balance, then, stands thus[1]—

Cases of non-elision 330 (at least).
Cases of elision ...... 17 (about, say for safety 30).

If now we compare these figures with the average exhibited by words elided freely, in which, as has been said, the proportion is decidedly *in favour of elision*, it will be evident that we have in these substantives, adjectives, etc., no casual divergence, but a principle, and a very powerful principle, since it could contend so successfully against the strongest

[1] I make here a wide allowance for inadvertence on my part, and difference of opinion on particular cases. The true figures are approximately 360 to 10.

prompting of convenience. The instinct which forbade elision in this class was plainly imperious; and where it is or appears to be neglected, we are impelled to seek a countervailing cause to explain the irregularity, or in the alternative to scrutinize with some attention the proof of its existence. *At the same time we must carefully observe that the rule, general as it was, was certainly not absolute, and that we cannot expect fully to understand the qualifications of it. The occurrence of an exception, therefore, by no means raises the strong adverse presumption which lies, for example, against a breach of the cretic pause. It is merely a very rare phenomenon, and as such, invites us to scrutinize the evidence and to seek the explanation for it. The remarks here made upon such cases are to be taken as attempts in this direction and not, for the most part, positive conclusions.*

Now, upon examining the above catalogue of exceptions it will at once appear that some of them at least are quite untrustworthy. In Aesch. *Sept.* 782 and Soph. *Phil.* 1137 the corrections κακὰ τέλεσεν, κακὰ μήσατο are obvious (cf. *Cho.* 604). Again in Aesch. *Sept.* 628 the only thing certain is that the line is *in some way* incorrect. In the corresponding strophe the MSS. reading is

τριχὸς δ' ὀρθίας πλόκαμος ἵσταται
μεγάλα μεγαληγόρων κλύων
ἀνοσίων ἄνδρων κ.τ.λ.

565–6 correspond or should correspond to 628–9,

δορίπονα κάκ' ἐκτρέποντες γᾶς
ἐπιμόλους κ.τ.λ.

Apart from the metre, the sense offers difficulties in both places, and all editors present emendations either in one or in both. As evidence upon a doubtful point they are therefore useless, and we can only add the elision of κακὰ to the other grounds of suspicion.

Upon *Phil.* 423, again,

> οὗτος γὰρ τά γε
> κείνων κάκ᾽ ἐξήρυκε, βουλεύων σοφά,

the scholia exhibit the strange comment γράφε κἀξεκήρυξε. However this note should itself be read, or whatever it may have meant, it does not tend to quiet the doubts suggested by the baldness of the word κακὰ itself; nor is it irrelevant to observe that this verse is in the immediate neighbourhood of the absurd

> Ἀντίλοχος αὐτῷ φροῦδος ὅσπερ ἦν γόνος,

of which I believe no satisfactory correction has been proposed. It is not improbable that the whole passage has suffered from some local accident. The joint authority of these four examples will scarcely convince us that κακὰ was not subject to the rules under discussion when we find that it occurs without elision in the two poets upwards of fifty times.

Four of the exceptions infringe the general rule as to the elision of vocatives—Soph. *O. T.* 957, *O. C.* 824, 877, 1206. If our tastes in the matter of sound were all alike, I should ask with some confidence whether

> τί φής, ξέν᾽; αὐτός μοι σὺ σημήνας γενοῦ

is likely to be the verse of a man with an ear. It is

at all events to be noticed that the context equally admits

τί φησιν; αὐτός μοι σὺ σημήνας γενοῦ.

If the tragedians were indifferent to the elision *ξέν'*, why did they take so much pains to avoid it? We may surmise, and shall presently find reason to believe, that there was something in the circumstances, or form of the sentence, whether we can detect it or not, which justified the variation to the instinct of the poet[1]. Such a 'something' is not always beyond the perception even of a foreigner and a modern, as may be seen in one at least of the above examples, Soph. *O. T.* 1250,

γοᾶτο δ' εὐνὰς ἔνθα δύστηνος διπλοῦς
ἐξ ἀνδρὸς ἄνδρα καὶ τέκν' ἐκ τέκνων τέκοι.

Instinct declares at once in favour of this—but why? Deferring for the moment the answer to this question, we will pass by way of contrast to Aesch. *P. V.* 339,

ΩΚ. αὐχῶ γὰρ αὐχῶ τήνδε δωρεὰν ἐμοὶ
δώσειν Δί', ὥστε τῶνδέ σ' ἐκλῦσαι πόνων.

The ill effect of the curtailed appellation here should be apparent to any one who has read the Greek Tragedians with his ears. But it may be seen from the context that the appellation itself is unnecessary, not to say out of place. Zeus is the subject of the whole dialogue between Prometheus and Oceanus, and is mentioned immediately before without name by Prometheus (332),

καὶ νῦν ἔασον, μηδέ σοι μελησάτω·
πάντως γὰρ οὐ πείσεις νιν· οὐ γὰρ εὐπιθής.

[1] See note on p. 288.

To this the words of Oceanus directly refer, and no one else but Zeus has been mentioned in the interval. We should therefore be warranted, *on the assumption that* 339 *is a genuine verse of Aeschylus*, in suspecting a trivial corruption from

δώσειν νιν ὥστε τῶνδέ σ' ἐκλῦσαι πόνων.

It must be noted, however, that the whole of the line except the words δώσειν Δί', required to complete the sense of the previous verse, is closely copied from 326,

ἐὰν δύνωμαι τῶνδέ σ' ἐκλῦσαι πόνων.

The repetition is weak, and if this were a play of Euripides, we might almost affirm that we had in 339 one of those stop-gaps which abound in the Euripidean MSS. (*Med.* 943 is a good specimen), patched up from fragments of the context and inserted to 'explain' a sentence really left unfinished for dramatic effect. The passage would then run

ΩΚ. ὁρμώμενον δὲ μηδαμῶς μ' ἀντισπάσῃς.
αὐχῶ γὰρ αὐχῶ τήνδε δωρεὰν ἐμοὶ—
ΠΡ. τὰ μέν σ' ἐπαινῶ κοὐδαμῇ λήξω ποτέ·
προθυμίας γὰρ οὐδὲν ἐλλείπεις. ἀτὰρ κ.τ.λ.

The offer of Oceanus has been urged already once, and the interruption well suits the decisive manner of this second rejection. Whether it suits the style of Aeschylus, or can be confirmed by Aeschylean evidence, I am not so sure, but in any case the elision of Δία is here suspicious.

As the result, then, of this first scrutiny we find that of the seventeen examples cited above, six are so far uncertain as to be scarcely ponderable, viz

Aesch. *P. V.* 339, *Sept.* 628, 782, Soph. *O. T.* 957, *Phil.* 423, 1137. Of the remaining eleven, which are at least *prima facie* unimpeachable, the majority admit of reasonable explanation. But for the further examination of these we require a fresh instrument.

The *general* rule against these elisions cannot of course give us a measure of the comparative probability of different exceptions to it. For this purpose we require to know, what is much more difficult of ascertainment, the cause of the rule. Upon such a point it is necessary for a modern student to speak with the utmost caution, but we are not without some indications. These must naturally be sought in what may be called the *regular exceptions* falling under rules 1 and 2. From these we see that either (1) emphatic position both in the sentence and in the verse or (2) the close connexion of the substantive with a word having no independent meaning (ὦ before a vocative) were held grounds sufficient to dispense with the ordinary prohibition. We should infer, therefore, that the rule depended in some way upon the brevity of such forms as κάκ' or χθόν', as they would have been pronounced in the thesis of the five last feet, which did not seem to afford space enough, if we may so say, for the proportions of the word. Or to put the same thing in another way, elision after a short penultimate is permitted in

κάκ', ὦ τάλαινά, σοι τάδ', εἰ πεύσει, κακά,

because the emphasis and consequent pause upon the syllable κάκ' prevents it from being felt as short, and in ὦ τέκν', ὦ ξέν', ὦ φίλ', because in these cases the 'word' for rhythmical purposes is not τέκνα but ὦ τέκνα, etc. and therefore obeys the ordinary rule as to a dactyl. We might therefore expect to find that casual exceptions to the rule would resemble these cardinal exceptions; and we might look for occasional elision either (1) with emphasis in the third or the fifth thesis, or (2) where the elided word is very closely bound up with other words, so that the phrase may be regarded as for rhythmical purposes indivisible. Of the first sort I have noticed no example among substantives or adjectives[1], and this is not surprising, for a little consideration will show that the analogy is not really satisfying. We may compose, by way of illustration, variations upon Eur. *Hipp.* 327,

κάκ', ὦ τάλαινά, σοι τάδ', εἰ πεύσει, κακά,

writing either

ὅσ' ἀγγελῶ κάκ', ὦ φίλ', εἰ πεύσει, κακά,

or again

οὐ κεδνὰ πεύσει· τἀμὰ γὰρ κάκ', ὦ φίλε,

which have elision with emphasis in the third and fifth thesis respectively. The reader will probably agree that neither rhythm is worthy of imitation. No such practical objection prevents the occasional occurrence of the second class of exception, elision in a closely connected phrase, and we have, as I think, a good instance of it in Soph. *O. T.* 1250,

ἐξ ἀνδρὸς ἄνδρα καὶ τέκν' ἐκ τέκνων τέκοι.

[1] See however what is said below as to ἐμέ.

It would be a strange ear indeed that would find any fault in the rhythm of this. But if the reader should allow that the effect of the elided τέκνα in this fine verse is altogether different from that of the elided Δία in

δώσειν Δί', ὥστε τῶνδέ σ' ἐκλῦσαι πόνων,

and will consider in what the difference lies, he will perhaps also accept the explanation, that by the antithesis of ἐξ ἀνδρὸς ἄνδρα and τέκν' ἐκ τέκνων these two sets of words are marked off as each an undivided whole, more especially the latter, the form of which is so far determined beforehand, that if τέκνα were not followed by ἐκ τέκνων, the ear would be sensible of the disappointment. For rhythmical purposes, therefore, as we said in the case of ὦ ξένε, the phrase τέκν' ἐκ τέκνων is the ultimate subdivision, and τέκν' is felt to be not unduly brief simply because it produces no *separate* impression at all. Rhythmical rules are observed for the very purpose of being broken on occasions like this.

More light will be thrown upon the subject by the uses of ἐμέ. That ἐμέ, a word emphatic by nature and terminating with an inflexion, should in the matter of elision follow χθόνα, φλόγα, πόδα, rather than ὅδε, τόδε, τάδε, is to be expected. According to the rules, two places in the iambic senarius are open to it, the beginning and the end, and, as a fact, these are its positions in a very large majority of cases. I have counted in Sophocles alone 45 instances of ἐμὲ not elided, chiefly in iambic verse, and they are numerous also in Aeschylus. Again we have examples of Rule 1 in

Soph. *Phil.* 623 ἔμ' εἰς Ἀχαιοὺς ὤμοσεν πείσας στελεῖν;
ib. 629 τὸν Λαερτίου
ἔμ' ἐλπίσαι ποτ' ἂν λόγοισι μαλθακοῖς
δεῖξαι, κ.τ.λ.
ib. 984 ἔμ', ὦ κακῶν κάκιστε καὶ τολμίστατε,
οἵδ' ἐκ βίας ἄξουσιν;

where, as will be seen from the context, the pronoun is even more than commonly emphatic. To the same influence which has produced Rule 2 may be ascribed the elision of the phrase εἰς ἐμέ, not, so far as I have noticed, in Aeschylus or Sophocles, but in Euripides regularly, *e.g.*

Med. 584 ὡς καὶ σύ· μή νυν εἰς ἔμ' εὐσχήμων γένῃ.
Hipp. 21 ἃ δ' εἰς ἔμ' ἡμάρτηκε τιμωρήσομαι
Ἱππόλυτον.

So also ἐμὲ more than once suffers double elision in the phrase ἄλλον ἢ ἐμὲ, *e.g.* Soph. *Phil.* 347 τὰ πέργαμ' ἄλλον ἢ 'μ' ἑλεῖν. Of the contrary instances in our texts (which in Sophocles are certainly under ten; those which I have observed are noticed here) some are obvious errors, the unemphatic με being admitted both by sense and metre and often required: such are

Aesch. *Ag.* 1537 ἰὼ γᾶ, γᾶ, εἴθ' ἔμ' ἐδέξω

(so Dindorf with the MSS., but Hermann, Paley and others rightly εἴθε μ' ἐδέξω),

Soph. *Ant.* 806 ὁρᾶτέ μ', ὦ γᾶς πατρίας πολῖται.

So in Soph. *Phil.* 1016

καὶ νῦν ἔμ', ὦ δύστηνε, συνδήσας νοεῖς
ἄγειν

the emphasis on ἐμὲ perverts the sense, for there is no comparison between the treatment of the speaker and that of other persons, but a parallel between the former and the present behaviour of the person addressed. We should probably read καὶ νῦν δέ μ', ὦ δύστηνε κ.τ.λ., the καὶ νῦν having the same force as αὖ in 1007,

οἵ αὖ μ' ὑπῆλθες, ὅς μ' ἐθηράσω λαβὼν κ.τ.λ.

And again in Soph. *O. T.* 441

ΟΙ. ὡς πάντ' ἄγαν αἰνικτὰ κἀσαφῆ λέγεις.
ΤΕ. οὔκουν σὺ ταῦτ' ἄριστος εὑρίσκειν ἔφυς.
ΟΙ. τοιαῦτ' ὀνείδιζ' οἷς ἔμ' εὑρήσεις μέγαν,

we should read, not less for sense and syntax than for metre,

τοιαῦτ' ὀνείδιζ' οἷς μ' ἐνευρήσεις μέγαν.

There are, however, exceptions not so questionable. Thus we find

Soph. *O. T.* 462 κἂν λάβῃς ἐψευσμένον,
φάσκειν ἔμ' ἤδη μαντικῇ μηδὲν φρονεῖν.
O. C. 646 ἐν ᾧ κρατήσω τῶν ἔμ' ἐκβεβληκότων.
ib. 784 ἥκεις ἔμ' ἄξων οὐχ ἵν' ἐς δόμους ἄγῃς κ.τ.λ.
ib. 800 πότερα νομίζεις δυστυχεῖν ἔμ' ἐς τὰ σά,
ἢ σ' ἐς τὰ σαυτοῦ μᾶλλον ἐν τῷ νῦν λόγῳ;
Trach. 469 σοὶ δ' ἐγὼ φράζω κακὸν
πρὸς ἄλλον εἶναι, πρὸς δ' ἔμ' ἀψευδεῖν ἀεί.
ib. 921 τὸ λοιπὸν ἤδη χαίρεθ', ὡς ἔμ' οὔποτε
δέξεσθ' ἔτ' ἐν κοίταισι ταῖσδ' εὐνάτριαν.

To the first of these examples the emphatic form is unnecessary, in the third it is scarcely right, and the authority of both is therefore not very good[1].

[1] Both admit of the very simplest corrections—ἐμῇ δὴ—ἥκεις σύ μ'.

In the last we have an instance of elision with emphasis in the fifth thesis, noted already as a possible extension by analogy from Rule 1. It is not beautiful and we cannot regret that it is rare. The πρὸς ἔμ' of *Trach.* 469 may perhaps be classed with the εἰς ἔμ' allowed by Euripides. More interesting, however, than these mere licences are the cases from *O. C.* 646, 800, for in these, taken in connexion with some others, we may perhaps discern a principle. If we consider the pronunciation, for instance, of this from the *Aias* (1293)

> οὐκ οἶσθα σοῦ πατρὸς μὲν ὃς προὔφυ πατὴρ
> ἀρχαῖον ὄντα Πέλοπα βάρβαρον Φρύγα;
> Ἀτρέα δ', ὃς αὖ σ' ἔσπειρε, δυσσεβέστατον κ.τ.λ.,

or again of *O. C.* 800

> ἔμ' ἐς τὰ σά,
> ἢ σ' ἐς τὰ σαυτοῦ μᾶλλον,

we find this difficulty. The difference between the emphatic σε and the unemphatic σε was indicated first by the change (of tone or whatever it was) represented by the accentuation, and also, as the whole phenomena of the language tend to prove, by the modern way of stress. How can either of these have been made perceptible in a monosyllable whose only vowel is lost by elision? It is important, therefore, to observe that in these examples the elision of σέ is *an elision only to the eye and not to the ear.* As far as the sound is concerned, it is as easy to give the pronoun its full and emphatic form in εμεστασα (ἐμὲ ἐς τὰ σά) as in εμοιστασα (ἐμοὶ ἐς τὰ σά), or in σεστασαυτου, σεσπειρε (σὲ ἐς τὰ σαυτοῦ, *σὲ ἔσπειρε*) as in *σουσταςαυτου, σουσπειρε*[1]. To write *ἐμὲ 'ς τὰ σά* and *σὲ 'ς τὰ σαυτοῦ* would offend against *graphic* symmetry, but that does not affect the question of sound. So in *O. C.* 646 the apparently irregular elision is in reality no elision at all, and this applies also to Eur. *Med.* 749, where the same 'graphic' elision occurs before the same verb:

μήτ' αὐτὸς ἐκ γῆς σῆς ἔμ' ἐκβαλεῖν ποτε.

I had intended to treat here in full the elision of *σέ, σά*, and *τὰ σά*, but as these do not strictly fall within the subject, and there is still much to be said, they shall be postponed to another occasion.

If now we return to our list of elided substantives, and consider them in the light of the above, we shall see that among those which have sufficient authority there are differences in the degree of their irregularity. In Soph. *Phil.* 664, as in *O. T.* 1250, the elision may at once pass unchallenged—

ὅς γ' ἡλίου τόδ' εἰσορᾶν ἐμοὶ φάος
μόνος δέδωκας, ὃς χθόν' Οἰταίαν ἰδεῖν,
ὃς πατέρα πρέσβυν, ὃς φίλους κ.τ.λ.

χθόν' Οἰταίαν is here treated as rhythmically indivisible, a treatment which suits both the meaning of the words and the form of the whole period. Three of the remaining cases have a strong resemblance to one another, and must be considered together.

Aesch. *Ag.* 907 ἔκβαιν' ἀπήνης τῆσδε, μὴ χαμαὶ τιθεὶς
τὸν σὸν πόδ', ὦναξ, Ἰλίου πορθήτορα.

[1] Three, perhaps the only three, elisions of *ξένε* (Soph. *O. C.* 824, 877, 1206) are followed one by *ἔξω*, the others by the conjunction *εἰ*. Perhaps the final vowel was not quite elided but merged in the succeeding vowel or diphthong. [Add *O. T.* 957.]

Soph. *O. C.* 1130 καί μοι χέρ', ὦναξ, δεξιὰν ὄρεξον, ὡς
ψαύσω, φιλήσω τ' εἰ θέμις τὸ σὸν κάρα.
El. 633 ἐῶ, κελεύω, θῦε· μηδ' ἐπαιτιῶ
τοὐμὸν στόμ', ὡς οὐκ ἂν πέρα λέξαιμ' ἔτι.

Considering the extreme rarity of these elisions, it is probably something more than an accident that two should be in the same place of the verse before the same form ὦναξ, though why this should have any effect I am unable to see[1]. In the resemblance of the first and third in the above trio there is more instruction. It will be noticed that in each case there is a strong emphasis upon the preceding possessives τοὐμὸν and τὸν σὸν—*Set not to ground* thy *foot, the foot of Troy's conqueror—Blame not* my *lips, for I have done,* and we may well suppose that it was this which commended the elisions. Emphasis is relative, and what is lost by curtailment to the substantives is gained by the possessive adjectives, which here carry the substantives as mere appendages. This explanation might appear inconsistent with what has been said upon Rule 1, but is not so. In the cases under Rule 1, it is not the elision which gives the emphasis,—it would naturally have the opposite effect,—but it is the emphasis which, by increasing the weight of the penultimate syllable, makes the elision permissible. In the three remaining passages (see the list, pp. 276 f.), two in anapæsts

[1] I may perhaps add that I feel nothing harsh in the second example, the reason being, if I do not mistake, the slight importance of the substantive χέρα when combined, as here, with an adjective (δεξιάν) which could stand without it. It will be observed that this explanation applies also to Soph. *Phil.* 664.

(Aesch. *P. V.* 139, *Eum.* 971) and one in iambics (Aesch. *Eum.* 901), I see no speciality of rhythm, and should register them in this respect simply as irregularities, subject only to the general doubt which in the condition of our MSS. must attach to any phenomenon observed to be highly exceptional[1]. But in the iambic passage there are circumstances which justify further inquiry[2]. The scene is the reconciliation of Athena and the Eumenides, and the context runs thus:—

XO. *ἄνασσ' Ἀθάνα, τίνα με φῂς ἔχειν ἕδραν;*
AΘ. *πάσης ἀπήμον' οἰζύος· δέχου δὲ σύ.*
XO. *καὶ δὴ δέδεγμαι· τίς δέ μοι τιμὴ μένει;*
AΘ. *ὡς μή τιν' οἶκον εὐθενεῖν ἄνευ σέθεν...*
XO. *θέλξειν μ' ἔοικας καὶ μεθίσταμαι κότου.*
901. AΘ. *τοιγὰρ κατὰ χθόν' οὖσ' ἐπικτήσει φίλους.*
XO. *τί οὖν μ' ἄνωγας τῇδ' ἐφυμνῆσαι χθονί;*
AΘ. *ὁποῖα νίκης μὴ κακῆς ἐπίσκοπα,*
καὶ ταῦτα γῆθεν ἔκ τε ποντίας δρόσου
ἐξ οὐρανοῦ τε κἀνέμων ἀήματα
εὐηλίως πνέοντ' ἐπιστείχειν χθόνα κ.τ.λ.

The metrical irregularity of 901 is not more remarkable than its meaning. The context requires that *κατὰ χθόν' οὖσα* should mean *dwelling in the*

[1] Neither *P. V.* 138–9 nor Aesch. *Eum.* 971–2 are given in the MSS. without *any* flaw. The corrections usually adopted are extremely slight, but a small error on the surface is often the sign of a deeper disturbance.

[2] [It is clear that the author was unaware that Weil had in his 1st edition of the play, 1861, proposed the correction *κατᾆσον οὓς*. In his own edition, 1908, where it is again defended, he assigns it to Weil, characteristically making no claim to independent authorship. Weil does not discuss the correction either in his 1st or 2nd (1884) edition. The present essay was first published in 1883.]

land; the correct translation is *being about the land*, or *over the land*. Further there is no proper connexion between 901 and 902. Surely something is required to bridge the transition from the confession of the Eumenides that their anger is passing, to the question, *What then dost thou bid me chant over this land?* This want of connexion would alone suffice to raise suspicion. I will not waste time in trying to estimate the exact weight which should be attached to it, but will simply point out that all objections might be removed at once by a minute alteration:

ΧΟ. θέλξειν μ' ἔοικας καὶ μεθίσταμαι κότου.
ΑΘ. τοιγὰρ κατᾆσον οὓς ἐπικτήσει φίλους.
ΧΟ. τί οὖν μ' ἄνωγας τῇδ' ἐφυμνῆσαι χθονί;

Athena has been offended (see 827 and compare 970) at the obstinacy of the Eumenides in resisting her propitiations, and she now consults the dignity of herself and her city by suggesting that if they mean to be friends, they should earn the reconcilement by converting their threats into blessings. *Win, therefore*, she says, *with a good spell those whom thou art to make thy friends*. To which they appropriately answer, *What incantation then dost thou bid me chant over this land?* κατᾴδειν is a term of witchery and signifies to *chant a good spell*; see Eur. *Iph. T.* 1337

ἀνωλόλυξε καὶ κατῇδε βάρβαρα
μέλη μαγεύουσ', ὡς φόνον νίζουσα δή,

and Herod. 7. 191 ἔντομά τε ποιεῦντες καὶ καταείδοντες †γόησι τῷ ἀνέμῳ οἱ Μάγοι. The last citation proves the association of the word with spells to bind the forces and elements of nature, such as the Eumenides are here invited to pronounce and subsequently do pronounce in favour of the land, the city, and the people of Attica (*Eum.* 903 ff., 916 ff.). With a personal object καταᾴδειν signifies to *soothe* or *charm by a spell.* The examples of this construction cited in the Lexicon *s. v.* are not classical, but it is completely warranted by the analogous use of κατεπᾴδω, καταυλέω etc., *e.g.* Plato *Meno* 80 A γοητεύεις με καὶ φαρμάττεις καὶ ἀτεχνῶς κατεπᾴδεις. It would be easy to misread the first part of the unfamiliar KATAICON as the preposition κατά or καταί, after which nothing could well be made of the rest but what the MSS. actually give us.

But whatever may be our conclusions respecting the irregular elisions of this kind presented to us in the MSS., one thing is clear, we must not increase the number of them by conjecture. If we cannot determine with completeness the conditions which justified the licence where it actually occurs, still less can we prove that those conditions are satisfied by an invention of our own. Commentators have not always observed this consideration, and I have noticed one or two proposals which should be reconsidered from this point of view.

In *Ag.* 1172 ἐγὼ δὲ θερμόνους τάχ' ἐν πέδῳ βαλῶ Mr T. Miller has suggested the reading ἐγὼ δὲ θερμὸν οὐ στάγ' ἐν πέδῳ βαλῶ (see Mr A. Sidgwick's edition *ad loc.*). No verse with such a rhythm as this occurs in Aeschylus. If the poet used the accusative of στάξ, he placed it, we may be tolerably sure, as he places other words of the kind, at the end of the senarius. Whether the conjectural verse has anything in its movement to condone for the breach of a law, each will judge for himself. In Aesch. *Supp.* 896 Mr Paley's later conjecture ἔχιδνα δ' ὥς μέ τις πόδα δάκνουσ' ἔχει has a decisive advantage over his earlier πόδ' ἐνδακοῦσ' ἔχει (MSS. τί ποτ' ἐνδαχοσέχ). Certainty cannot be looked for among such wretched ruins as the MSS. here preserve. There is more interesting material in Aesch. *Cho.* 854

AI. ἰδεῖν ἐλέγξαι τ' αὖ θέλω τὸν ἄγγελον,
εἴτ' αὐτὸς ἦν θνήσκοντος ἐγγύθεν παρών,
εἴτ' ἐξ ἀμαυρᾶς κληδόνος λέγει μαθών.
† οὔτοι φρένα κλέψειαν ὠμματωμένην.

Here the reading commonly received is Elmsley's

οὔτοι φρέν' ἂν κλέψειεν ὠμματωμένην.

Others prefer

οὔταν φρένα κλέψειεν ὠμματωμένην,

and in support of this it may be said that this is the *regular* position of ἂν in a sentence following οὔτοι. But the lengthening of the α is very unsatisfactory, and I would suggest[1] as better than either

οὔταν φρένας κλέψειας ὠμματωμένας.

[1] [At a later date the author found reason to defend the MS. text. The note *ad loc.* in his edition of the play is as follows: "Cf. Hom. *Od.* 14. 122 ὦ γέρον, οὔ τις κεῖνον ἀνὴρ ἀλαλήμενος ἐλθὼν | ἀγγέλλων πείσειε γυναῖκά τε καὶ φίλον υἱόν, | ἀλλ' ἄλλως κομιδῆς κεχρημένοι ἄνδρες ἀλῆται | ψεύδοντ', οὐδ' ἐθέλουσιν ἀληθέα μυθήσασθαι, 'No one, offering news of Ulysses (as alive), *will convince* his wife and son: vagabonds tell lies *to procure entertainment* and will not keep to the truth.' That passage so entirely

Seeing minds, 'tis said, cannot be cheated. The plural φρένας and the use of the second person (for the indefinite *one*) are both appropriate to a proverbial sentiment (τοι), and may be illustrated by Soph. *Ai.* 154

> τῶν γὰρ μεγάλων ψυχῶν ἱεὶς
> οὐκ ἂν ἁμάρτοις.

In Soph. *Phil.* 201 εὔστομ' ἔχε, the scholiast proposes, wrongly on every ground, the alternative εὖ στόμ' ἔχε.

There are a few words whose peculiarities need a separate treatment. μέγα is both an adjective and an adverb. The elision of the adverb where it immediately precedes the word which it qualifies, might always be justified on general principles by the close connexion of the two. It is so elided in Aeschylus twice:

> *P. V.* 647 ὦ μέγ' εὔδαιμον κόρη.
> *Cho.* 311 τοὐφειλόμενον πράσσουσα Δίκη μέγ' ἀϋτεῖ.

μέγ' εὐδαίμων is almost as truly one word as εὐδαιμονεστάτη. The adjective is elided by Aeschylus twice with the justification described in Rule 1:

> *Ag.* 1102 τί τόδε νέον ἄχος [μέγα]
> μέγ' ἐν δόμοισι τοῖσδε μήδεται κακόν;

coincides with the sense of this, while illustrating the archaic grammar, that it was probably in the mind of Aeschylus. It is the traditional character of the phrase which justifies both the syntax and the metre (φρενᾶ κλέψειαν) which, though rare in Attic poetry, would be regular in other poets, and is here to be regarded as an archaism. The whole verse may well be a proverb or quotation."]

P. V. 251 μέγ' ὠφέλημα τοῦτ' ἐδωρήσω βροτοῖς[1]—

and once at least irregularly:

Pers. 119 μὴ πόλις πύθηται κένανδρον μέγ' ἄστυ Σουσίδος.

Considering the convenience of free elision, it might be expected that where it once obtained it would quickly encroach[2], and the example set by the elisions of the adverb appears to have produced this effect upon the adjective, for in Sophocles we have, beside more numerous cases without elision, the following elided:

Aias 386 μηδὲν μέγ' εἴπῃς. οὐχ ὁρᾷς ἵν' εἶ κακοῦ;
2. *ib.* 424 ἔπος
ἐξερῶ μέγ', οἷον οὔτινα, κ.τ.λ.
3. *ib.* 1088 ....νῦν δ' ἐγὼ μέγ' αὖ φρονῶ.
ib. 1122 μέγ' ἄν τι κομπάσειας ἀσπίδ' εἰ λάβοις.
5. *ib.* 1125 ξὺν τῷ δικαίῳ γὰρ μέγ' ἔξεστιν φρονεῖν.
Ant. 479 φρονεῖν μέγ' ὅστις δοῦλός ἐστι τῶν πέλας.
ib. 836 ......μέγ' ἀκοῦσαι.
8. *O. T.* 638 καὶ μὴ τὸ μηδὲν ἄλγος ἐς μέγ' οἴσετε.
O. C. 647 μέγ' ἂν λέγοις δώρημα τῆς συνουσίας.
ib. 1746 μέγ' ἄρα πέλαγος ἐλαχέτην τι.
El. 830 μηδὲν μέγ' ἀΰσῃς.
12. *ib.* 1305 αὐτὴ μέγ' εὑρεῖν κέρδος.
13. *Trach.* 667 κακὸν μέγ' ἐκπράξασ' ἀπ' ἐλπίδος καλῆς.

It will be seen that the second, third, fifth, eighth, twelfth and thirteenth of these are irregular, that is about one fifth of the cases in which the word occurs;

[1] Cp. Soph. *Ai.* 1122, *O. C.* 647, 1746, afterwards cited.

[2] We may compare the case of the adverb μάλα, which is almost always elided. Nearly all these elisions are before a verb, or adjective, or adverb with which μάλα enters into combination, and many occur in set phrases, such as μάλ' αὖ, μάλ' αὖθις. οὐ μάλα is elided in Aesch. *Pers.* 384.

a small proportion, but sufficient to show a yielding to the pressure of convenience.

Why the adverbs ἅμα, δίχα, etc., should, as stated in Rule 4, be treated like substantives, and classed for the purpose of elision with χθόνα and κακά, it is not easy to say; but the fact is beyond dispute. ἅμα occurs in the two elder tragedians together upwards of twenty times. It is elided in

Soph. *Ant.* 436 ἅμ' ἡδέως ἔμοιγε κἀλγεινῶς ἅμα

(but this is justified by the position and emphasis), and also once in combination with ἕπομαι,

Soph. *Ai.* 814 τάχος γὰρ ἔργου καὶ ποδῶν ἅμ' ἕψεται,

and twice in combination with the dative of αὐτός,

Soph. *Phil.* 983 ἀλλὰ καὶ σὲ δεῖ
στείχειν ἅμ' αὐτοῖς, ἢ βίᾳ στελοῦσί σε.
ib. 1026 ἔπλεις ἅμ' αὐτοῖς.

The elision before ἕπομαι is admitted by Euripides even in a play of which the metrical treatment is notoriously severe, and which exemplifies perfectly the rules deduced in this paper,

Med. 1143 στέγας γυναικῶν σὺν τέκνοις ἅμ' ἑσπόμην[1],

and that before αὐτὸς several times, *e.g.* *Phoen.* 174. Similarly we have in Euripides three times the elision ἅμ' ἠγόρευε καὶ κ.τ.λ. *while he was speaking*, etc. (*Phoen.* 1177, *Bacch.* 1082, *El.* 788). These elisions are similar to the elision of ἐμὲ in the phrases εἰς ἐμὲ, ἄλλον ἢ ἐμὲ, and have doubtless a similar origin. By familiarity of use the phrases ἅμ' ἕπεσθαι, ἅμ' αὐτῷ, ἅμ' αὐτοῖς, ἅμ' ἠγόρευε coalesced into

[1] This example is subject, however, to some doubt as to the reading. See the *Addendum* to my larger edition.

indivisible wholes, so that, ἅμα being no longer felt as an independent word, the curtailment of it ceased to offend. I have noticed two elisions of ἅμα introduced into the text of Aeschylus by conjecture—*Suppl.* 991 καὶ ταῦθ' ἅμ' ἐγγράψασθε, Hermann, for the MSS. καὶ ταῦτα μὲν γράψεσθε, and *Ag.* 1267 ἅμ' ἕψομαι for the MSS. ἀμείψομαι. The second is metrically justifiable, though, as I think, erroneous[1]; the first would be doubtful in metre, even if it were otherwise desirable. If any change is required (as to which see the commentators) I should prefer καὶ ταῦτά μοι γράψεσθε. The case of δίχα is very similar: the word occurs in the two poets twenty times, and is elided twice. In Soph *O. C.* 48 (cited p. 274) the elision is justified by position and emphasis; not so, however, in Soph. *Ai.* 236

τὰ δὲ πλευροκοπῶν δίχ' ἀνερρήγνυ.

In Euripides we have (I depend here upon the *Index*) *Hec.* 119

δόξα δ' ἐχώρει δίχ' ἀν' Ἑλλήνων
στρατὸν αἰχμητήν.

Beside these I would place the one elision of θαμά in Sophocles (Aeschylus does not apparently use the word; Sophocles has it without elision three times) *El.* 1144

οἴμοι τάλαινα τῆς ἐμῆς πάλαι τροφῆς
ἀνωφελήτου, τὴν ἐγὼ θάμ' ἀμφί σοι
πόνῳ γλυκεῖ παρέσχον.

It will be observed that in all these three the elision takes place before a preposition commencing

[1] [See author's note *ad loc.*]

with α, and therefore may be what in the case of ἐμέ we have termed 'graphic'; it is therefore likely that it was so, and that *the pronunciation* would be more nearly represented by δίχανερρήγνυ, δίχαν' Ἑλλήνων, θαμὰμφί σοι, the vowel serving to the ear for both words. We must note, however, that in the only example of θαμά cited by the *Index* to Euripides (*Iph. T.* 6) we have an elision which cannot be 'graphic,' and is not justified by phrase-connexion or otherwise,

ἀμφὶ δίναις, ἃς θάμ' Εὔριπος πυκναῖς
αὔραις ἑλίσσων κυανέαν ἅλα στρέφει.

The usage of Euripides in these elisions is, as will presently be seen, somewhat less regular than that of the other two tragedians, and his prologues in particular are notorious for irregularities of all kinds, not only of metre but of syntax, whether from carelessness of composition, or much more probably from interpolation and other injury. The adverb σφόδρα occurs in tragedy too rarely to establish any rule or tendency respecting it; it is not elided in Soph. *Ai.* 150, but elided in Soph. *El.* 1053

οὐδ' ἢν σφόδρ' ἱμείρουσα τυγχάνῃς.

We have no proof that σφόδρ' ἱμείρειν was a set phrase, but on the other hand no reason for thinking that it was not. σάφα is almost always elided, because it rarely occurs except in the familiar combinations σάφ' οἶδα, σάφ' ἴσθι, σάφ' εἰδέναι, etc. In the same way τάχα is elided frequently in τάχ' ἄν, τάχ' εἴσομαι, but otherwise has almost always its full form. In Soph. *Ai.* 334 we have

τάχ', ὡς ἔοικε, μᾶλλον· ἢ οὐκ ἠκούσατε
Αἴαντος οἵαν τήνδε θωΰσσει βοήν;

The emphasis upon τάχα here (Tecmessa desires to rouse the sailors to interfere by urging the near danger of a catastrophe) would justify the elision according to the usual practice.

With respect to ἕνα and μία the case stands thus: μία is not, I think, elided either in Aeschylus or in Sophocles, occurring in the two together thirteen times. It is elided several times in Euripides, and one or two of the instances appear to be purely arbitrary, *e.g.* *Tro.* 660

καίτοι λέγουσιν ὡς μί' εὐφρόνη χαλᾷ
τὸ δυσμενὲς γυναικός.

Of ἕνα there are in Aeschylus and Sophocles only two certain elisions, both in the phrase εἷς ἀνήρ or ἀνὴρ εἷς,

Aesch. *Pers.* 763 ἕν' ἄνδρ' ἁπάσης 'Ασίδος μηλοτρόφου
ταγεῖν κ.τ.λ.

Soph. *O. T.* 846 εἰ δ' ἄνδρ' ἕν' οἰόζωνον αὐδήσει, σαφῶς κ.τ.λ.

The elision both before and after ἄνδρα occurs several times in Euripides. In Soph. *O. T.* 62 we read

τὸ μὲν γὰρ ὑμῶν ἄλγος εἰς ἕν' ἔρχεται
μόνον καθ' αὑτόν, κοὐδέν' ἄλλον, ἡ δ' ἐμὴ
ψυχὴ πόλιν τε κἀμὲ καὶ σ' ὁμοῦ στένει.

If this is correct, it is an example of the rare elision with emphasis in the fifth thesis which we have noticed before in ἐμέ. But the many peculiarities of these lines—the dubious expression εἰς ἕνα ἔρχεται, the verbosity of μόνον καθ' αὑτὸν κοὐδέν' ἄλλον, the abrupt substitution of the singular σὲ for the plural (ὑμεῖς) of the rest of the speech, the elision of σὲ where it should be emphatic, etc.—may raise a doubt whether all three are not an interpolation.

τρίτα occurs in Soph. *O. T.* 283 and is elided,

εἰ καὶ τρίτ' ἐστί, μὴ παρῇς τὸ μὴ οὐ φράσαι.

The treatment of ὅσα in Sophocles is particularly instructive. At first sight elision seems to be quite unrestricted. In senarii the balance stands thus—

ὅσα (not elided) occurs *four* times at least—*Ant.* 688, 712, *O. T.* 1228, *Trach.* 580.

ὅσ' (for ὅσα elided) occurs *fifteen* times at least—*Ant.* 684, *O. T.* 77, 1122, 1285, *O. C.* 53, 74, 1582, 1634, *El.* 896, *Trach.* 664, 1150, *Phil.* 64, 362, 1072, 1224.

But of these fifteen examples thirteen are made up as follows—three in ὅσ' ἔστι, two in ὅσ' ἦν, two in ὅσ' οἶδα, and six in ὅσ' ἄν, that is, they occur in what we may safely affirm to have been familiar and fixed combinations, and to this class we may add *O. C.* 150 ὅσ' ἐπεικάσαι. The comparative weight of the scales is thus reversed, and there remain as evidence of free elision some four or five cases at most—*O. T.* 1298 πάντων ὅσ' ἐγὼ προσέκυρσ' ἤδη, *O. C.* 223 ὅσ' αὐδῶ, *Trach.* 664 ὅσ' ἀρτίως ἔδρων, *Phil.* 1224 ὅσ' ἐξήμαρτον. Whether these exceptions had any special justification to the poet we are not in a position to say, but that the elision, speaking generally, was not arbitrary is clear enough. I have not noticed an example of the word in Aeschylus, nor is any cited in the *Index*, but it may be presumed that his rule would have been the same. He has τόσα in *Pers.* 786

οὐκ ἂν φανεῖμεν πήματ' ἔρξαντες τόσα.

In Soph. *Ai.* 277 we have elision of δὶς τόσα,

ἆρ' ἔστι ταῦτα δὶς τόσ' ἐξ ἁπλῶν κακά;

This would of course by no means prove the elision of τόσα, and it seems probable that the practice was the same for all the three adjectives of quantity.

It remains to consider the point hitherto postponed, how far the practice of Aeschylus and Sophocles in the matter we have been considering is followed also by Euripides. To examine the statistics of the later dramatist with the same fulness as the earlier would double the length of this essay, a result as little desirable to the reader as to the writer. It will be sufficient to indicate summarily the result, which is, that the general rules are still the same, but the exceptions are rather more numerous in proportion and, as far as I can judge, more arbitrary. The seventeen hundred and fifty lines of the *Phoenissae* contain nearly as many clear violations as the fourteen plays of Aeschylus and Sophocles together. Thus we have

Phoen. 541 καὶ γὰρ μέτρ' ἀνθρώποισι καὶ μέρη σταθμῶν
ἰσότης ἔταξε.

ib. 1191 κἀς μέσ' Ἀργείων ὅπλα
συνῆψαν ἔγχη.

ib. 1274 A. οἳ 'γώ, τί λέξεις, μῆτερ; I. οὐ φίλ', ἀλλ' ἕπου.

ib. 1285 τρομερὰν φρίκᾳ τρομερὰν φρέν' ἔχω.

ib. 1300 μονομάχον ἐπὶ φρέν' ἠλθέτην.

ib. 1454 ἄμφω δ' ἅμ' ἐξέπνευσαν ἄθλιον βίον.

ib. 1465 οἱ δ' εἰς ὅπλ' ᾖσσον.

ib. 1713 πομπίμαν ἔχων ἔμ' ὥστε ναυσίπομπον αὔραν.

This list does not include the elisions of εἰς ἐμέ, which must be called in Euripides regular. The examples in the same play which support the rules number about sixty, again not including the elisions of εἰς ἐμέ. In the *Hippolytus* the proportion is much the same. Against nearly forty examples *pro* we find the following *contra*,

Hipp. 315 φιλῶ τέκν'· ἄλλῃ δ' ἐν τύχῃ χειμάζομαι.
ib. 610 τά τοι κάλ' ἐν πολλοῖσι κάλλιον λέγειν.
ib. 847 ἔρημος οἶκος καὶ τέκν' ὀρφανεύεται.
ib. 1120 οὐκέτι γὰρ καθαρὰν φρέν' ἔχω.

(Note the close resemblance of the last to *Phoen.* 1285.)

Hipp. 327 falls and has been cited under Rule 1. One more exception appears in *Hipp.* 450

φοιτᾷ δ' ἀν' αἰθέρ', ἔστι δ' ἐν θαλασσίῳ
κλύδωνι Κύπρις, πάντα δ' ἐκ ταύτης ἔφυ.
ἥδ' ἐστὶν ἡ σπείρουσα καὶ διδοῦσ' ἔρον,
οὗ πάντες ἐσμὲν οἱ κατὰ χθόν' ἔκγονοι,

but I should hardly care myself to cite the last two lines, which spoil with their prosaic specification the climax of πάντα δ' ἐκ ταύτης ἔφυ: the sentiment ἐκ τοῦ γὰρ γένος ἐσμέν was one of the most notorious commonplaces of later Greek literature, and has, I suspect, been thrust in here without permission. We may observe by the way that the lines, by whomsoever written, exhibit a correct use of the phrase κατὰ χθόνα (οἱ κατὰ χθόνα = literally *those over earth*), which may be usefully contrasted with the supposed use of the same in Aesch. *Eum.* 901. The proportion of irregularities in the *Hippolytus* and *Phoenissae* will be found, I believe, fairly representative. In the *Alcestis* where the total of instances *pro* and *contra* is unusually small, the proportion of exceptions is rather higher; in the *Bacchae* it is much lower. In the *Medea*, which is perhaps in merely technical finish the most perfect of extant Greek tragedies, there is, I believe, no exception at all. In *Med.* 1411 the editors or most of them (including myself) have followed the MSS. of the Vatican family (S′) in reading

τέκν' ἀποκτείνασ' ἀποκωλύεις
ψαῦσαί τε χεροῖν θάψαι τε νεκρούς.

But the MSS. of the other family (S), the Laurentian and Palatine, have preserved the correct reading τέκνα κτείνασ' ἀποκωλύεις. In *Med.* 1254 the MSS. have

τέκνοις προσβαλεῖν χέρ' αὐτοκτόνον

which corresponds exactly to the antistrophic

πετρᾶν ἀξενωτάταν ἐσβολάν.

But the correspondence of dochmiac *strophae* is not by syllables but by feet, as this very chorus signally proves, and we should probably restore the form χεῖρα, which is of course elided freely. Between these two the MSS. vary incessantly; see *e.g.* the same chorus 1283, where, as observed in my note, the choice is indifferent[1].

As a point of curiosity, we may note that the *Auctor Rhesi* is a very purist in these matters. Not only, if my observation is accurate, does he preserve without fail the full forms of χέρα, τρίχα, φλόγα,

[1] The *Medea* affords good illustrations of Rule 2. Contrast 901, 969, 1029, with 89, 118, 1000.

πόδα, χθόνα, στόμα, φίλα, σταθμά, πυρά, κακά, μέσα, τὰ σά, τέκνα, ἕνα, μία, πάρα (πάρεστι), δίχα, but he extends the same protection to *μόλε* (226), *ἴδε* (383) and *κλύε* (384). In 685 an elision of *ἴθι* is introduced by some editors on conjecture; the true reading is uncertain. The adverb *μέγα* is elided once (452 *μέγ' αὐχοῦντας*) where the reading is scarcely open to doubt, though the best MSS. give, by a common sort of error, *μεγαλαυχοῦντας*, with an anapaest in the fourth foot. At 821, where Hector, on learning the disaster of his Thracian allies, threatens the chorus of soldiers with punishment for having quitted their watch, they give (in the MSS.) the nonsensical reply

821 μέγας ἐμοὶ μέγας, ὦ πολιοῦχον κράτος,
τότ' ἄρ' ἔμολον, ὅτε σοι
ἄγγελος ἦλθον, ἀμφὶ
ναυσὶ λόχον πυραίθειν[1].

Dindorf writes conjecturally *μέγ' ἄρ' ἐμοὶ μέγ', ὦ π. κ., κακὸν ἔμολεν, ὅτε κ.τ.λ.*, and the elision of the adjective would be justified by its position, according to the Aeschylean principles. But the total change in 822 is great, and unnecessary, for I think we may restore more closely and better,

μετά σε μὴ μετά σ', ὦ πολιοῦχον κράτος,
τότ' ἄρ' ἔμολον, ὅτε, κ.τ.λ.;

Then perchance I came not to summon thee, sovereign, to summon thee, etc. They appeal (by an ironical question) to Hector's knowledge of the circumstances which called them from their ordinary duty; the

[1] The passage is apparently not strophic.

apology thus accords exactly with the opening of the play: see especially 17, 23, and 49

σοὶ δ' ὑποπτεύων τὸ μέλλον
ἦλυθον ἄγγελος, ὡς
μήποτ' ἐς ἐμέ τινα μέμψιν εἴπῃς.

The adjective μέγα occurs in 198 not elided, and the adverb in 69. In the last line of the preceding citation the MSS. give μήποτέ τινα μέμψιν εἰς ἔμ' εἴπῃς. The transposition (Bothe) is required by the corresponding metre of 32. The author might have justified εἰς ἔμ' abundantly from Euripides, but it is not clear that he would have thought the authority sufficient[1].

How far the irregularities of Euripides are mere irregularities, or how far they have special justifications or exhibit the working of subtler principles, cannot be shown without unduly protracting our inquiry. Such incompleteness as necessity or inadvertence may leave in the statement of detail will not affect the general truth of the principles which were laid down for investigation.

[1] ὅτ', τότ', ποτ', τιν', τίν', ἴν', and τάχ' ἂν (138, 561) are admitted even by the *Auctor Rhesi*. ἔτ' has been introduced by conjecture in 464.

THE NAME *LAMIA* IN HORACE

THE name *Lamia*, if we include the description *vetusto nobilis ab Lamo* in *Od.* III 17, occurs in Horace five times. Among the various kinds of name which are introduced in the *Odes*, *Lamia* belongs to a peculiar class—it is both a Greek word and name and, by adoption, a Roman name, like *Grosphus* (*a javelin*), for example, or *Musa* in the names *Pompeius Grosphus* and *Antonius Musa* respectively. In Greek the Λάμια was a kind of vampire-snake supposed to suck the blood of men. Like Μόρμω, Ἔμπουσα, and other such, the word was a suitable nickname for a certain class, and was in fact best known as the name of the too notorious beauty, who spent the plunder of Demetrius Poliorcetes[1]. In a Roman writer it might, like Μοῦσα or *Musa* itself, be the name of a real person of either sex, belonging to the servile or freedman class. It may also, of course, in Horace be a fictitious Greek name chosen either at hazard or, as is often the case[2], for its history or signification, to designate a purely imaginary personage whom the reader is not

[1] See Smith's *Dict. Biog.* Keats's poem *Lamia* is founded on a similar use of the word. Cf. *Ars Poet.* 340.

[2] See Wickham's edition of the *Odes*, *Appendix* I.

intended to identify. But besides these there is another possibility, which, as it happens, seems to have had hitherto exclusive attention.

Lamia, like many words both Greek and Latin as little or less elegant in original signification, was the cognomen of a Roman family; whether the family was widely diffused does not appear, nor at what time it first became notorious; but in the first two reigns of the empire one member of it rose to the highest rank, a L. Aelius Lamia, who ten years after the death of Horace became consul, and later still, under Tiberius, praefect of the city. How the family came by the addition, whether, as so used, the word had any connexion with the Greek Λάμια, we cannot say. There is evidence that these *Aelii* were of good position in the last days of the republic. Tacitus ascribes to the praefect *decorum genus*; and it may be inferred from Horace, that the pedigree had even been traced to the Homeric *Lamos*, the mythical king of the Laestrygons. But Tacitus and Horace are not plain folk, and do not always say what they mean. The notoriety thus given to this tradition probably counted for something in causing the selection of the family cognomen by Juvenal as a type of antique nobility[1]. It is none the less possible, as may be seen by a glance at the amusing discussion of the *Vitellii* in the beginning of Suetonius' life of the emperor so named, that this or that 'Aelius' had no more to do with *Lamos* or with the antiquities of the *Lamiae*, whatever they really

[1] Juv. IV 154, VI 385.

were, than Thackeray's *Muggins* with *Hogyn Mogyn*, and that the nobility of the house, or of some who claimed its dignity, may have dated, and at no great distance, from the ambition and success of a Greek freedman. The Augustan 'peerage' was no more authentic than those of modern times. At all events, the name was Roman and respectable when Horace wrote, and we must therefore add to the former alternatives the chance that he uses it as Roman, either to designate a real person who bore it, or by arbitrary choice. And it is important to remember that each occurrence of the name is severally open to all these interpretations, as the identity of name is no proof of personal identity[1]; from the several contexts only can we judge, whether the same person is intended throughout, and what character or characters are to be supposed. External evidence as to the relations of Horace with any Lamia there is, I believe, none at all.

This said, let us consider simply upon the internal evidence the familiar poem *Carm.* III. 17.

> Aeli vetusto nobilis ab Lamo—
> quando et priores hinc Lamias ferunt
> denominatos, et nepotum
> per memores genus omne fastos
>
> auctore ab illo ducit originem[2],
> qui Formiarum moenia dicitur

[1] See Wickham's *Appendix* just cited, and compare II 4 with IV 11, II 5 with III 15 etc.

[2] On the punctuation and reading see the commentaries. The correction *ducit* (MSS. *ducis*), which is fortified by the strongest possible consensus of critics, is defended as a corollary from the

princeps et innantem Maricae
litoribus tenuisse Lirim,

late tyrannus—cras foliis nemus
multis et alga litus inutili
demissa tempestas ab Euro
sternet, aquae nisi fallit augur

annosa cornix. dum potis, aridum
compone lignum: cras Genium mero
curabis et porco bimestri
cum famulis operum solutis.

It has been already remarked that, in assigning a character to the *Lamiae* whom we meet in Horace, one only of the possible suppositions seems to have been considered. For instance, it has been assumed here, that in *Lamia* we are to see a member of the family which produced the *praefectus* of the year A.D. 32, perhaps the *praefectus* himself. What aid has this assumption given to a satisfactory understanding of the poem before us? So little, that some have thought it necessary, if the poem is to be held genuine, to restore it to a form worthy of Horace by some excision, which method itself has proved so difficult of application that a bolder and 'more consistent' critic has pronounced the whole spurious. 'The purpose of the poem can only be guessed.' Rather, upon the current assumption, it

required punctuation. But it is perhaps possible that *memores genus omne fastos* means 'a recording calendar of all kinds' or 'classes.' For the adjectival use of *hoc genus*, *id genus* etc. see the Dict. *s.v.* genus. Such a phrase would very well suit the purpose, as I conceive it, of the poet, and with this construction the punctuation does not require an alteration of the text.

cannot be guessed, as appears from the fact that scarcely any two commentators agree in their opinion. Nearly half the poem is occupied with a parenthesis on the mythical origin of the *Lamiae*, and the importance of this parenthesis, already great from its proportion to the whole, tells more from the triviality of the remainder. The digression, then (so infer some and not unreasonably), contains the point, the rest 'merely supplying an imaginary reason for addressing Lamia at all.' The object is to compliment the noble friend upon his long descent. But this object is so ill pursued, that more than half the modern readers of the poet seem to be in doubt whether the genealogical statement is to be taken seriously. 'The introductory passage seems very much as if it were playful.' 'Simulata autem, ni fallor, huius digressionis gravitas admodum festive opponitur reliqui carminis hilaritati.' And it would certainly be difficult to ridicule a piece of false history more keenly than by the contrast between this pompous invocation, with its allegations in proof, and the bathos of the sequel—'it will be wet to-morrow; stack dry wood while you can; to-morrow you shall make yourself comfortable on pork and wine with the servants.'

On the other hand, let us follow Orelli and accept the 'simulata gravitas,' and let us suppose, as then we must, that the Lamia addressed is a sensible man, who knows the true value of his own pedigree and would enter into the joke about his legendary forefather. How then is he rewarded for his sympathy with the poet's humour? By a couple of verses so empty and purposeless as to be in themselves an additional impertinence. The poem contains nothing but the jest, not even a proof or intimation of the poet's friendship.

We are assured indeed very positively by some that in the picture of the next day's feast we are to see a delicate invitation given by Horace to himself, to join the noble master and the reposing servants over their wine and their sucking-pig. But the suggestion only proves how strongly those who make it have felt the inanity of what is actually said, and the need of something which is not said, to explain the poet's drift. The 'Selbsteinladung' is simply not there. The honour of an 'Ode' may have been great, may have proved much greater than the most far-seeing critic could have anticipated; but 'Lamia' must indeed have been a man superior to vulgar prejudices and covetous to a fault of literary notice, if he was likely to be grateful for such notice as this. Perhaps there is not a commentator who does not either say or show that he has wondered why the poem was ever written. Some, who express admiration of it, remark in the same breath that it might be better if it were otherwise than it is. Macleane himself (to whom few things are difficult) twits the critics, and the poet too, rather more gaily than usual,—which is perhaps only another way of making the general admission. Nor has it gone well with emendation. To diminish the 'simulata gravitas' (and to smooth the construction), it has been proposed to strike out lines 2–5, leaving only

> Aeli, vetusto nobilis ab Lamo,
> qui Formiarum etc.

But except that what is not good is the better for being shorter, it is difficult, as many have replied, to see how we gain by this somewhat arbitrary proceeding—arbitrary, because there is no apparent motive for the supposed interpolation. The commencement remains grandiose, the sequel remains inept; and indeed a piece of verse which is objectionable chiefly because there is too little in it, cannot be rectified by excision.

In these circumstances it is permissible to suggest that the method of interpretation which leads to so much disagreement, has not improbably taken a false start, and that the true road is already left when it is assumed that the person intended is really one of the noble *Aelii* who distinguished themselves from other *Aelii* by the cognomen *Lamia*. The pedigree has seemed to many like a jest;—only, addressed to a real *Aelius*, and unsweetened by any graceful addition, such a jest is too like an insult. But is it addressed to a real *Aelius*? If we had the conclusion of the poem by itself, as a fragment, and were restoring the whole conjecturally, we should scarcely prefix an address to a friend of the poet, and that friend a nobleman. An order to lay in wood to-day, and a promise of wine and pork with the servants for to-morrow, would make us look a little lower than the curule seats. The language is surely that of a superior to an inferior, of a master to a servant, neither more nor less. Nor is this inconsistent with the invocation actually prefixed; on the contrary it is upon this supposition only, as I think, that the invocation, with the whole poem, acquires a point and a purpose. That the name of a country gentleman's servant might well be *Lamia*, I hope to show very sufficiently in a moment. Of course no such person would bear the name of *Aelius*, or any gentile name at all; but neither did the person here addressed. The appellation *Aelius* is part of the jest. The slave's name is *Lamia*, and *Lamia* only. The accident that a family, pretending to a prodigious antiquity, bore the same as a cognomen, suggests to the speaker, the master, the pretended inference that his *Lamia* too must doubtless be an *Aelius* and, doubtless, a descendant of the Laestrygonian prince; and he gives him his title accordingly. As a jest between master and servant, it is a fair bit of humour, and as proof of kindly feeling and easy intercourse, not unworthy of a little vignette to itself. If the use made of the family legend is not profoundly respectful, nothing could be more like Horace than to give such vanity a quiet pinch; rudeness of course there is none, when it is once understood that no veritable Aelius is in the view of the poem.

If this were the limit of our evidence, if we could carry matters no further than to say that the speaker here is a master, the person addressed a slave named Lamia, this interpretation would have claims to preference. The difficulties so often signalized disappear. The disproportionate length and dubious tone of the address, the triviality of the sequel, become at once intelligible, become in fact the point and substance of the piece. The poem presents a little scene from household life in the country, containing exactly the touches required and nothing besides. But the evidence does not end here, for we know a country servant named Lamia, and this Lamia was no other than the *vilicus* or steward at the poet's own farm. The reader will perhaps be surprised, but I will submit the evidence. To the steward on the poet's farm is addressed the fourteenth Epistle of the First Book—

Vilice silvarum et mihi me reddentis agelli etc.

The Epistle consists, it will be remembered, of an argument in favour of the country against the town, for which the steward, formerly a town-slave, is supposed to have a mistaken preference. This 'thorn in the mind,' this morbid dissatisfaction with the present, his master professes to extirpate by philosophy, and will prove himself, if possible, a more skilful 'weeder' in the moral field than the steward in the material. There is a circumstance which makes the discussion somewhat *mal à propos*, but Horace is disposed to push it nevertheless.

certemus spinas animone ego fortius an tu
evellas agro et melior sit Horatius an res—
me quamvis Lamiae pietas et cura moratur
fratrem maerentis, rapto de fratre dolentis
insolabiliter, tamen istuc mens animusque

> fert et amat spatiis obstantia rumpere claustra—
> rure ego viventem, tu dicis in urbe beatum; etc.

Who is this *Lamia*, the thought of whose grief for the loss of a brother makes the poet pause for a moment before urging upon his steward the commonplaces of his moral discourse? Surely it can be no other person than the steward himself. What other person's grief could have any bearing on the situation, or could occur to the mind of Horace in connexion with it? Here again the unfortunate intrusion of the 'consul and praefectus' seems to have sent explanation astray. Let us consider the matter fairly. Let it be supposed that this rising Aelius Lamia, or some member of his family known to Horace, had lost a lamented brother, and that the poet desired to record his sympathy. What a form of condolence is this! He represents himself writing a little lecture to his own servant, in the tone of a kindly patron, upon a matter of private difference between them, and into a parenthesis he puts the suffering of his noble friend, observing that it might but shall not prevent his intended communication. Why should it? Or what gratitude was the surviving Aelius likely to feel for the publication of the fact that the recollection of his mourning made Horace half indisposed for a moment to chatter philosophy to his steward—though on second thoughts he determined to do so forthwith all the same? Horace is so much affected by Aelius' fraternal sorrow that—he does *not* postpone a letter to his slave which has no connexion with the subject, and for which any other time would have done as well. There is, I submit, notwithstanding the tradition which has so long protected this view, but one way of giving the passage a connected sense, and that is to take *Lamiae pietas* as an equivalent for *pietas tua*. The rhetorical figure, the change of person, is common enough, particularly in epistolary forms; the way is prepared for it here by the similar use of *Horatius* for *ego* in the previous line[1]; and what is more important, there is good reason for it in the ethical situation. In the substitution of the *Lamiae* for the *tua* there is something like respect; the third person is and always has been a less familiar form of address than the second. The humane feeling which prompts the writer, even in the act of scolding good-humouredly a discontented slave, to avoid the appearance of forgetting a deep sorrow, not new but not exhausted,—this same humanity finds expression in the slightly ceremonious form of speech. It is a true touch. Grief and affection are in themselves respectable.

I said that this was the only way of giving connexion to the passage. Strictly speaking, it would meet the bare demands of the context if we supposed *Lamia* to be some person connected,

[1] So in Shakespeare *Mids. N. D.* II 2 54 Hermia to Lysander,

> Now much beshrew *my* manners and my pride
> If *Hermia* meant to say Lysander lied.

But there is scarcely need of illustration: every literature and even the language of common life supplies examples. Cf. *Odes* III 9 6, IV 10 5.

though not identical, with the *vilicus* and likely therefore to be associated with him in thought—some other slave, for instance, in the household of Horace. But though this might do well enough in a real letter, where the correspondent has the key to the meaning, in a literary 'epistle' it is not intelligible without a note giving the facts. If, on the other hand, the steward and *Lamia* are one and the same, the passage is, as it should be, self-explanatory.

In either case this epistle shows us a *Lamia* who belongs to the household of Horace, and thus proves the personages of the ode to be real. The *Lamia* addressed is the slave of the epistle, the master is the poet himself. Between the master who jests and the master who condoles it is not difficult to find the resemblance, nor to see the suitability of both characters to the humane temper which in all relations Horace professes and probably maintained[1].

But because two of the references to the name *Lamia* designate no Aelius at all, but only a humble and melancholy namesake of the Aelii, it does not

[1] The chronological bearing of these passages is worth a moment's notice. Without the epistle the ode loses some of its point, as, except from the epistle, very few could know the name of a servant in the poet's house. We should naturally suppose, therefore, that when the Three Books were finally put in shape, the epistle, if not 'out,' was at all events written and intended to appear immediately. Now I think it will be generally admitted that this is, to say the least, not likely to have been the case in the year 23.

follow that every *Lamia* is to be so identified. Pope names his footman John, but not every John whom Pope knew was his footman. As before, the context must decide; and let us consider next the *Lamia* of *Odes* I 36.

> Et ture et fidibus iuvat
> placare et vituli sanguine debito
> custodes Numidae deos,
> qui nunc Hesperia sospes ab ultima
> caris multa sodalibus,
> nulli plura tamen dividit oscula
> quam dulci Lamiae, memor
> actae non alio rege puertiae
> mutataeque simul togae.

Apparently[1] the character here supposed is that of an *ingenuus*, nor is there at first sight any reason why this *Lamia* should not be an actual friend of the poet, an Aelius of the distinguished family. He might of course have an old school-fellow called Numida, whose return from the West (from the Cantabrian war, it is suggested) might be the subject of these rejoicings. This might be actual history; but there is one circumstance against it. The names in the poem, or at least three of them,

[1] 'Apparently,' for I do not think it honest to suppress my belief that this *Lamia* simply is what *her* name implies, a *meretrix*, the mistress of *Numida* when a lad. For the point of the masculine designation and attire in *vv.* 8, 9 see a Dictionary or Dictionary of Antiquities s. v. *toga*. The character is quite in keeping with the whole scene (see *vv.* 17–20), and the equivocal description of course designed. Had it not been designed, the name *Lamia* would have made it ridiculous.

are *significant*. *Numida*, a form rudely Latinized from the Greek Νομάς, Νομάδος, signifies *The Wanderer*. Considering that Horace is fond of significant names[1], it is scarcely supposable that when he celebrates the return of a *Numida* from distant lands, the meaning of *Numida* was forgotten. This indeed is no proof that 'Numida' was not a real person, for Horace plays upon the consular name of *Bibulus* (III 28 8) as well as on the probably fictitious Γλυκερά. But then again in the subsequent lines,

> neu multi Damalis meri
> Bassum Threicia vincat amystide,

accident (or choice?) has again furnished a name suitable to the context. What is the true origin of *Bassus* as a Latin name, from what dialect even it came, may be doubted. When the *Odes* were in writing, and for long after, it was a very famous name and conveyed to every ear the thought of the greatest *parvenu* in republican history, the slave who had lately (B.C. 38) achieved the honours of a triumph (the *bâton de maréchal* in modern language) to the disgust of the *pur-sang* appropriators of the national honour who had no triumphs to show[2]. It became proverbial, as Pliny tells us, for a *parvenu*, and in its Latin aspect may throw some light on the ideas of Horace about the ancestry of *Lamia*. But the language in which Horace is thinking here is

[1] See Wickham's *Appendix* I.

[2] See Smith's *Dict. Biog.*: P. Ventidius Bassus.

Greek[1], and from a Greek point of view *Bassus* (cf. *βάσσων, βαθύς, βαθειᾶν κυλίκων τέρψις, βαθὺς κρητήρ* etc.) is no ill name for the deeper drinker who is not to be beaten at the 'Thracian draught.' *Damalis* (*The Wench*, by original meaning *Heifer*) upon any theory would seem a mere Greek fiction; it is one of the numerous names derived from animals which Horace bestows by choice upon his female personages, *Lyce, Lycoris, Pholoe* (cf. *φολίς*) etc. With all this, as we have no independent evidence for any Numida or Bassus connected with the poet, and there is not a touch in the poem which suggests reality—the very region of *Numida's* travels is 'ultima Hesperia,' that is, anywhere or nowhere—it would seem a safe supposition that the whole picture is fictitious, Numida, Bassus, Damalis, and Lamia all puppets dubbed with names for convenience. As for the name *Lamia*, we know that it lay near to the poet's hand.

The fourth and only other use of the name occurs in what is apparently the most careless and trivial piece in the collection[2]. As it has but three stanzas, I subjoin it entire:

Musis amicus tristitiam et metus
tradam protervis in mare Creticum
portare ventis, quis sub Arcto
rex gelidae metuatur orae,

[1] In addition to the half-Greek vocabulary, note the imitation of the Greek *ἡ πολύοινος* by the peculiar genitive (of quality) *multi meri*; that this is the construction the position of the words decides. Cf. III 9 7, IV I 15 etc. Martial also plays upon *Bassus*, XI 98.

[2] I 26.

quid Tiridaten terreat, unice
securus. O quae fontibus integris
  gaudes, apricos necte flores,
    necte meo Lamiae coronam,

Pimplea dulcis! nil sine te mei
prosunt honores: hunc fidibus novis,
  hunc Lesbio sacrare plectro
    teque tuasque decet sorores.

From the accident that the political events alluded to were uncertain in date, the poem has been the subject of a discussion which does not here concern us. Written earlier or written later, it is not without its small difficulty as to 'the point of connexion between the first and last parts' of it, the question why *Lamia* should be so emphatically pronounced a proper theme for the Muse and her friend in their singular indifference to political anxieties. Without professing a positive answer, I think that here again the consul and praefectus with his possible relations have been of little service. It is not enough to say that he or some Aelius Lamia known to Horace may have been a somewhat melancholy youth who would benefit by the contagious example of gaiety. This fact is neither likely to have been generally notorious nor given by the poem, which indeed determines scarcely anything except perhaps that Horace in his true and proper person is the speaker. Believing the key to the poem to be at present lost and very likely not recoverable, I would only note that there may be a certain significance in the phrases *fidibus novis*...

Lesbio plectro. If these words are not idle, and neither the style of Horace nor the brevity of these verses would make us suppose so, it is *the example of Alcaeus* and the Greek Ἐρωτικοὶ which suggests the recommendation of *Lamia* to the Muse. Long ago the internal evidence of the metre led a great critic to the conclusion that this piece was probably among the earlier attempts of the poet in imitation of the Alcaic stanza[1]; and it may be conjectured that our difficulties might disappear, if we knew, as the Roman reader probably knew, the precise original which Horace has in view. Was it one of those poems which Horace elsewhere describes as typical of the Lesbian soldier and singer, poems in which Alcaeus charmed away the distresses of his adventurous life with singing the praises of the beautiful young page who seems to have played Patroclus to this lyric Achilles?—

> qui ferox bello tamen inter arma,
> sive iactatam religarat udo
> litore navim,
>
> Liberum et Musas Veneremque et illi
> semper haerentem puerum canebat,
> et Lycum nigris oculis nigroque
> crine decorum[2].

Certainly such a poem would not admit of serious translation from the conditions of Alcaeus to those of Horace. It would scarcely have suited the

[1] See Lachmann's argument, cited by Orelli and Wickham. The word *novis* itself assists the inference.

[2] I 32. 6.

humour of the retired clerk of the treasury at his quiet farm to pose in the old-fashioned armour of such a fighting troubadour as the exile of Lesbos. But the very contrast of characters might give piquancy to an imitation which was something of a parody; and if the *Lamia* for whom Horace twines the lyric wreath must be a real person, I see no reason why he may not be the only real Lamia—as I have tried to show—to whom Horace introduces us, his slave and (the Epistle justifies the word) his friend, the Lamia in his own household. Doubtless this not very gay personage is an odd representative of 'beauteous Lycus, black of hair and eye,' but Horace, when he wrote the *Odes*, was at least as odd a representative of Alcaeus; the Sancho and the Quixote seem not ill matched, and the parallel very much in the spirit of the jesting touch, borrowed from the life of the Greek master, with which the Roman Alcaeus adorns the recollection of his own military career—

> tecum Philippos et celerem fugam
> sensi *relicta non bene parmula.*

Moreover, thanks to the fidelity with which Demetrius Poliorcetes continued to fling the spoil of cities into the lap of his 'Vampire' long after her wrinkles were visible to every eye but his, the name of *Lamia* was of as high fame in the literature of 'erotica' as *Lais* or *Phryne* itself, and the coincidence with that of the slave adds a fresh touch of humorous incongruity.

There is thus a point in the insistent emphasis

of *hunc fidibus novis*, *hunc Lesbio plectro*, and a meaning in the assurance that to celebrate *Lamia* is a 'becoming' task. 'If you take me for your Alcaeus,' the poet would say to the erotic Muse, 'my attendant—whose name at least is known to you—must do for your Lycus, and then together we will forget politics as the old Greek forgot war.' This he may have meant; whether he actually did, it would be rash to pronounce till a roll of Alcaeus shall be found in some library of the Levant.

A VEXED PASSAGE IN HORACE

Carm. I 6.

Scriberis Vario fortis et hostium
victor Maeonii carminis alite,
quam rem cumque ferox navibus aut equis
  miles te duce gesserit.
nos, Agrippa, neque haec dicere, nec gravem
Pelidae stomachum cedere nescii,
nec cursus duplicis per mare Ulixei,
  nec saevam Pelopis domum
conamur, tenues grandia, dum pudor
imbellisque lyrae Musa potens vetat
laudes egregii Caesaris et tuas
  culpa deterere ingeni.
quis Martem tunica tectum adamantina
digne scripserit? aut pulvere Troico
nigrum Merionen? aut ope Palladis
  Tydiden superis parem?
nos convivia, nos proelia virginum
sectis in iuvenes unguibus acrium
cantamus; vacui, sive quid urimur,
  non praeter solitum leves.

ALTHOUGH what I have to say at present of this poem refers chiefly to the last stanza, a few words on the whole of it will be useful by way of preface. The general meaning is clear and simple, nor, until the last stanza, is there any difficulty of detail which is significant from a literary point of view. '*Heroic exploits require a Homer to sing of them*, says Horace, and so gives Agrippa the lyric glory that (it would seem) he has asked for, while preferring to leave the task of celebrating such exploits to the epic genius of Varius' (Wickham). Passing over the grammatical dispute on the first stanza, the interest of which is purely scientific, we find in the second two points of a different importance. (1) Here and throughout the poet naturally speaks in the plural (*nos* 5, *conamur* 9, *nos* 17); naturally, because he speaks not of his personal character, but of the lyric genius as contrasted with the epic, and what is said is to be understood as true of himself and his class. This is of course obvious and has not escaped notice (see *e.g.* Wickham on *v.* 17), but for reasons which will presently appear it is desirable to bear it in mind. (2) The scholar Charisius (*circ.* 400 A.D.; see Wickham on *v.* 6) notes the word *stomachum* 'as an instance of intentional ταπείνωσις,' which he defines *rei magnae humilis expositio*, the use of a term beneath the dignity of the subject. Mr Wickham does not lay much stress on this, and even seems not to be sure whether Charisius was right. But we should surely require very strong evidence on the other side to justify us in disputing the judgement of a great native scholar on the question whether a word was or was not poetical; and in this case the evidence supports the judgement, for it does not appear that *stomachus* (*anger*), or any of the words derived from it, are used in dignified writing. Horace himself has the word in the lines (*Carm.* I 16. 13)—

> fertur Prometheus addere principi
> limo coactus particulam undique
> desectam et insani leonis
> vim stomacho apposuisse nostro—

but in its proper sense as a part of the body, and moreover in a humorous poem by no means demanding the exclusion of terms below the dignity of the epic. We may assume then that in describing the epic wrath of Achilles as *gravis stomachus*, Horace intends to illustrate the ridiculous failure which awaits the writer who would soar above his natural level; and it is probable that if we had the advantages of Charisius, we should perceive other traces of the same intention. One such may even now be perceived in *v.* 13, where Horace has been blamed for rendering χαλκοχίτωνα by '*tunica* tectum adamantina.' To prove that the common-place name of the garment *tunica* would not have an odd sound when transferred to the mail of Ares (and the negative evidence of extant poetry goes to show that it would), Orelli can only adduce the fact that Varro (*L. L.* 5. 24) describes a *lorica* of ring-mail as *ferream tunicam*. But unless there is reason to suppose that Varro meant his description to be poetical, the evidence is scarcely to the point; nor, if we consider the style of Varro and the style of Horace, would it prove very much if it were. These humorous touches enforce the intended comparison, which, let us repeat, is between the warlike theme and lofty language of the epos and the humbler ambition of the erotic lyre.

With this preface we may come to the consideration of the last stanza. The general sense of this also is certain—'The subject of the lyric poet is love.' But the difficulties of detail have long been notorious; and they go to the very essence and effect of the whole poem. 'The *proelia virginum*,' says Horace, 'which we sing are not the battles of the Παρθένος (contrast *v.* 15), but those which they wage *sectis in iuvenes unguibus acres*.' What are these *proelia*, and why do the virgins who are to wage them cut their nails? The 'battles,' it is said, are the struggles or scuffles such as will often occur, we know, between young men and young women, at a banquet for example, says Orelli, 'inter pocula et ioculares rixas.' This seems to be more or less agreed, but as to the cutting of the nails opinions differ. Most think they were cut from amiable motives, that they might not hurt; others (Ritter) on the contrary that they were cut 'to a point' (though the poet omits to say so), and to make them more formidable as weapons. Bentley proposed to clear up the matter by reading *strictis*, but the expedient has not pleased. Mr Wickham declines to decide the question of motive, and we may leave it ambiguous, noting it however as a sign that we have not yet got on to firm ground.

But many have no doubt thought, without saying, —for commentators like lawyers have a maxim against the 'awaking of doubts,'—that the ambiguity of *sectis unguibus* is a very small part of the difficulty. The description of the *proelia* must in some way be a general description of amatory themes. This being considered, it is obvious that if we had been dealing with a modern poet, or any one but an ancient Roman, the above explanation would have been regarded as too absurd for serious discussion. It would have been remarked long ago that young women are not all, or even mostly, romps or viragoes, and that 'a predestinate scratched face,' like that of Beatrice's husband, is decidedly exceptional. But the difference of ancient manners and the coarseness of Roman manners in particular are supposed to remove all objections of this kind. To save time and narrow the question, we will assume this to be so far true that a fight between the sexes at a feast or elsewhere would have seemed to Horace altogether a pleasant and amusing performance. But surely it is going rather far to assume that it was not only a natural incident, but so common as to be *typical* of the relations between young men and young women, and of the subjects proper to the writer of amatory verse; or so common—to put the thing another way—that the *virgines* would naturally prepare for it beforehand by cutting their nails, blunt or sharp as their feelings disposed them. Once or twice in his own lyrics Horace describes a scene of violence, distantly resembling these supposed *proelia*, once with an express indication that the persons engaged in it are not of a high class[1]. But it will be hard indeed to show that *battles of virgins* in this or any like sense bore or could be supposed to bear a relation to the lyric poetry of love as general as that of the heroic battles to the poetry of Homer or Varius; and nothing less than this will satisfy the context.

But though the Roman *virgo* did not habitually pare her nails for an encounter with a *iuvenis*, there was an occasion on which she did; and this was no other than her marriage. In Greek and Roman religion, as in many religions, all operations connected with the purification of the body were matters of ritual importance, the bath, the combing and cutting of the hair, and among others the cutting of the nails. Hesiod, it will be remembered, lays it down that during a religious feast the nails must not be cut, or in mystic phrase 'the dry must not by the iron be severed from the quick off the thing of five branches':

μηδ' ἀπὸ πεντόζοιο θεῶν ἐν δαιτὶ θαλείῃ
αὖον ἀπὸ χλωροῦ τάμνειν αἴθωνι σιδήρῳ.

From Ovid we learn that the Romans had a similar practice, and, which is more important for the present purpose, that there was a special connexion between it and the performance of a marriage. 'Having,' he says (*Fasti* 6. 218), 'a daughter to marry, I made inquiry as to times suitable and unsuitable for the ceremony'—

[1] Uxor *pauperis* Ibyci, *C.* III 15. See also III 20, which, to judge by the internal evidence, does not describe contemporary manners at all, but is a mere imitation from the Greek.

Tum mihi post sacras monstratur Iunius Idus
  utilis et nuptis, utilis esse viris;
primaque pars huius thalamis aliena reperta est.
  nam mihi sic coniunx sancta Dialis ait:
donec ab Iliaca placidus purgamina Vesta
  detulerit flavis in mare Thybris aquis,
non mihi detonso crines depectere buxo,
  non ungues ferro subsecuisse licet,
non tetigisse virum, quamvis Iovis ille sacerdos,
  quamvis perpetua sit mihi lege datus.
tu quoque ne propera: melius tua filia nubet
  ignea cum pura Vesta nitebit humo.

(*Fasti* 6. 223–234.)

The Flaminica, the wife of the Flamen Dialis, a priest of Jupiter, informed Ovid that the latter half of June was an auspicious time, the first half specially unfavourable; and alleged as evidence that until the fifteenth of the month, when the temple of Vesta was annually purified and the sweepings (*purgamina*, καθάρματα) cast into the Tiber, she herself was not permitted to cut or to comb her hair, to cut her nails, or to have intercourse with her husband. 'Thou also,' she concluded, 'be not hasty; it will be better for thy daughter to marry when fiery Vesta (*i.e.* the fire on the sacred hearth which represented the goddess) shines upon a clean floor.' Now it will be seen that the whole point of these directions rests on the parallel between the cases of the Flaminica and the bride (tu *quoque* ne propera). After the fifteenth, but not before, the Flaminica cuts her nails, combs her hair, and becomes a wife. After the fifteenth, but not before, the maiden should become a wife. And as we know that the parallel extends to the combing of the hair (an important act in the marriage ceremony), it would, I think, be unreasonable to doubt that it extends also to the 'cutting of the nails,' which if it had nothing to do with the matter, would of course not have been mentioned at all. And this being so, it is not too much to say that to Roman ears a *virgo sectis in iuvenem unguibus*, 'a maiden when her nails are cut for a young man,' could not mean anything but *a bride*. But what then are the *proelia*? For this we must go to a poem of Propertius, the resemblance of which to this of Horace has been noted by others[1]; though not, at least in the books before me, the bearing of the parallel on the present question. In that poem Propertius (II I) excuses himself to Maecenas for not taking as a theme the exploits of Caesar and Maecenas (II I. 17), as Horace to Agrippa for not taking those of Caesar and Agrippa[2], and on similar grounds,—the unsuitability of an *elegiac* writer to an *heroic* subject (*ib.* 39). As Horace, so Propertius likens the prohibited theme to those of the Greek epos (*ib.* 17 ff.), with only this difference, that while Horace says he will not essay either one or the other because he is not fit, Propertius says that if he were fit for either, he would prefer the exploits of Caesar. Horace deprecates the injury which the

[1] See Paley on Prop. II I. I.

[2] Even the form of the phrase is similar, cf. *laudes egregii Caesaris et tuas* with *bellaque resque tui memorarem Caesaris, et tu | Caesare sub magno cura secunda fores.*

praises of Caesar would sustain from the defect of his genius (*culpa ingeni*); Propertius explains that his genius comes not from Calliope (the epic muse), but only from his mistress (*ingenium nobis ipsa puella facit*, *ib.* 4). Both Propertius and Horace say that their proper subject is love, and as we shall immediately see, they express it in closely similar terms. The two pieces are so precisely parallel in form, and their coincidences of expression are so many, that here, as in some other passages of the two poets, we cannot but suppose either imitation of one by the other, or imitation by both of the same or similar Greek originals. Now the antithesis which we are considering, between the *proelia* which are not the proper subjects of the writer and the *proelia* which are, is reproduced in Propertius,—and in this manner. 'You ask me,' he says, 'why I write of nothing but love. It is because my genius depends wholly upon my love. I praise her every act, her dress, her walk, her music,—

> seu nuda erepto mecum *luctatur* amictu,
> *tum vero longas condimus Iliadas* (*ib.* 13).

If I were equal, Maecenas, to celebrating heroic war, I would not follow Hesiod, Homer, or Ennius, but I would sing of Philippi, Naulochus and Actium. But I am an elegiac poet, a follower of Callimachus, and must keep to my theme':

> Navita de ventis, de tauris narrat arator,
> enumerat miles volnera, pastor oves;
> *nos contra angusto versantes*[1] *proelia lecto*:
> qua pote quisque, in ea conterat arte diem.

[1] sc. *narramus*, if this is the right construction. The question

Considering the closeness of the parallel throughout, we can scarcely be wrong in using Propertius here as a commentary on the briefer expression of Horace, and Propertius is perfectly clear. The *proelia* which he contrasts with those of the epos are the *proelia Veneris* or union of the sexes, the comparison of which to a wrestle or combat is 'a most established figure' in ancient literature[1]. I see no reason to doubt that Horace, using an exactly similar expression in a context precisely parallel, meant the same thing, and that the *proelia virginum sectis in iuvenes unguibus acrium* are simply the pleasures of the wedding-night. The ambiguity of *proelia* is sustained, it will be noticed, by *acrium*; for *acer* (*eager*) is applied to love as well as to other passions, and is to be so understood here, though at the same time it is accommodated to the metaphor. For *virgo* of the bride, see *C.* II 8. 23 *miseraeque nuper virgines nuptae*, and the famous *in omne virgo nobilis aevum, Surge quae dixit iuveni marito* etc. (*C.* III 11. 35); for *iuvenis* of the groom, see the last passage and the *epithalamia* of Catullus, *e.g. tu fero iuveni* in manus | floridam ipse puellulam | dedis, O Hymenaee, etc.[2]

is not here material. In *nos* (Propertius, Callimachus, and the elegiac poets: see the context) we have another parallel to Horace.

[1] I need but refer to the passage in Lucretius (4. 1049), where the metaphor is worked out with grotesque minuteness. See Munro, *ad loc.*

[2] The doubt about the construction of *in iuvenes* disappears with this explanation. The words affect both *proelia* and *acrium*;

It may be noticed that, given the meaning of *sectis unguibus*, there is still another interpretation possible for the *proelia*. We *may* understand them of the feigned resistance which it was absolutely essential that a bride should offer to the feigned violence of the ceremony of abduction. I think that Horace was aware of this ambiguity and counted on it. The style of the *Odes* is far removed indeed from the outspoken freedom of Propertius, and the possibility of this latter interpretation makes the expression here the more discreet. One more word only on this part of the subject, with respect to the *convivia*. 'The subjects of the lyric poet are feasting and the joys of love.' This is a simple sense, but in one respect the mention of the *convivia* here may be thought out of place. I mean that they have nothing to do with the antithesis between heroic and lyric themes. There is plenty of feasting in the epic narratives. Without laying stress on the point, which is of no importance to the general question, I think it worth while to suggest that there may be in *convivia* an error of one letter for *convicia*, which would of course be joined, as well as *proelia*, with *virginum*. 'The only *railings*, the

the bride meets the bridegroom and is eager to meet him. At the same time they belong primarily, as their position indicates, to *sectis unguibus*, in the sense *when they have cut their nails for the bridegroom*, *i.e.* at their marriage. That the nails were cut to prevent the bride from resisting was very likely a popular explanation of the ritual practice, though it is very unlikely to be the true one. It seems to be suggested, perhaps only in joke, by the language of Horace.

only *battles* which we sing are those of brides,' etc. In the battles of the *Iliad*, such as those of Diomede mentioned in the fourth stanza, the angry speeches are almost as prominent as the actual fighting; and on the other hand the *convicia virginum* are equally to the point, the 'railing' being as essential as the struggling to a properly conducted marriage. As the text stands, we must separate *convivia* from the antithesis. '*We* sing not of battles but of feasting, or if of battles at all, then only of the battles of virgins,' etc. And there is nothing objectionable in this; only, if authority for *convicia* could be found, I think it would be better and simpler.

We will now pass to the concluding words—*vacui sive quid urimur non praeter solitum leves*—on which again there is much difference of opinion. The questions raised may be divided thus:—

(1) What is the meaning of *leves*? Is it *inconstant*, *changeable* (in affection)? This is undoubtedly the natural meaning of the word as an epithet of persons, and is taken here by Orelli and others. But in that case the conclusion has no bearing on the poem, for the constancy or inconstancy of the love-poet does not affect his unfitness, as a love-poet, for the celebration of heroic themes. Or is it *fanciful*, *light* (in the themes which we treat)? This interpretation (taken by Wickham and others) avoids in part the difficulty of the other,—only in part, for we do not hear in the preceding verses of any *gravitas* proper to the epic. But no authority has been given, and I doubt if any will be found, for

describing a person as *levis* when it is meant that his themes are *levia*.

(2) How should we construct the words *non praeter solitum*? This difficulty is even more serious than the other. The majority take together *non praeter solitum leves*, understanding these words somewhat as Mr Wickham, 'light-hearted much after my wont.' But *non praeter* ('not beyond') is not the same thing as 'according to.' Surely the only legitimate meaning of 'non praeter solitum levis' is '*levis* not beyond my wont' or 'not more than my wont': but this, whatever sense we give to *levis*, the context will not admit, and perhaps it has never been defended. There is also a disagreeable ambiguity in *solitum*, for there is nothing to determine us between 'my wont' and 'the common wont.' Both of these objections are avoided by the alternative punctuation (recommended, I think, by Professor Kennedy at a meeting of the Cambridge Philological Society)—*vacui, sive quid urimur non praeter solitum, leves*, 'loveless, or if we feel a moderate flame, not too serious,' literally 'not exceeding the wont' or 'our wont.' This accounts fairly for the negative form *non praeter solitum*, and the ambiguity of *solitum* ceases to be important. But this punctuation, notwithstanding the difficulties of the other, has against it a great majority, and we may easily conjecture why. To close the sentence and the verse (here also the stanza and the poem) upon such a word as *leves* with a stop before it, gives to the word such an extreme sharpness of emphasis

as only a very peculiar occasion can justify. The very few examples in Horace show better than any description what the effect is, and why it is so parsimoniously used:—

at tibi
ne vicinus Enipeus
plus iusto placeat, *cave*. (III 7. 24.)
tu nisi ventis
debes ludibrium, *cave*. (I 14. 16.)
quod spiro et placeo, si placeo,—*tuum est*.
(IV 3. 24.)

The case of III 16. 44 is of course not really an example of this rhythm:

cui deus obtulit
parca quod satis est manu.

It may be a convenience to the eye to stop off the words *quod satis est*; but to the ear there is no stop at all. There is nothing, I think, to justify us in classing the present case with these rare exceptions; and the contrary presumption is very much strengthened by the fact that *levis* is an adjective. But of this hereafter.

In this puzzle we may perhaps again find help in the fortunate disposition of the Latin poets to be always imitating themselves and each other, and to repeat themes and phrases which have been proved useful, a habit which Henry Nettleship has noticed as characteristic of the literature. We have just seen Horace and Propertius supplying commentaries to each other. Here Horace may supply us with a note upon himself. Going back for a moment to the first stanza, we see that the main thought of the poem, that only a heroic poet is equal to a heroic theme, is expressed by a natural metaphor taken from *flight*. The poet who shall celebrate the achievements of Agrippa must be one who, like Varius, can *soar with the wing of Homer* (*Maeonii carminis ales*). Now many years after the publication of the *Three Books*, when Horace, at the instance of the emperor, reluctantly resumed his *operosa carmina* with the express commission to do what he here deprecates, to celebrate the achievements of Caesar, he seems to have bethought himself of this figure—the comparison of different poetical powers to different flights—as one which was suitable to express his feelings and would bear a little more working out. At any rate he did work it out in the well-known opening of *Pindarum quisquis* (IV 2. 1–32), which *mutatis mutandis* bears much analogy with our poem. Pindar, 'the Dircaean swan,' takes the place of Varius 'the bird of Maeonian song'; Horace is only the Matinian bee, hovering industriously around the banks of thyme. If the bee should attempt to soar with the swan, if Horace were to essay Pindaric ἐπινίκια, it would be a rash 'flight of Icarus,' which would end in the natural failure.

> multa Dircaeum levat aura cycnum,
> tendit, Antoni, quotiens in altos
> nubium tractus: ego, apis Matinae
>   more modoque
> ...... operosa parvus
>   carmina fingo.

Applying this analogy to the poem before us, we see that what we should expect at the conclusion, to bind the whole together and finish the point, is a description of the lyric poet, not as *fickle* (in his affections) nor as *light* (in his themes), but as *humble* or *low* in his range. But this, I venture to think, is exactly what Horace has written:

> nos convivia, nos proelia virginum
> sectis in iuvenes unguibus acrium
> cantamus, vacui sive quid urimur:
> *non praeter solitum leves.*

We are not to be lifted beyond (or *above*) *our wont*, literally *you cannot lift us.* Here *leves* (second person subjunctive) is used in the familiar way for the English *one*; of course the general term includes Agrippa who is trying to do what cannot be done. For *levare* we have a precise parallel in *levat aura cycnum* of the passage just quoted[1]. The accusative *nos* is readily supplied from the emphatic pronouns just preceding. In common prose Latin the accusatives of *is* are often omitted under such circumstances 'especially when a short antithesis is emphatically subjoined to what goes before' (Madvig, *Lat.*

[1] Cf. Columella, 9. 12 *apis confestim se levat sublimius*, and other examples in the Dictionaries. Having cited this passage from the 4th Book, I may take occasion to remark that the complaint sometimes made against the expression *more modoque* as tautological seems to arise from misunderstanding: *modo* means *limit* or *limitation* (not *manner*), and the addition of it is necessary to the point. 'I fly as the bee, and with the same limit of flight'; or, dropping the metaphor, 'My manner of working sets a limit to my attempts.'

Gramm. § 484 a, Eng. trans.); the treatment of *nos* here is analogous to the common treatment of *is*, and should perhaps be regarded as a slight extension of Latin Grammar in the direction of the Greek, so well known as a quality of Horace's style. Probably, however, even a prose writer would not have felt any difficulty in this particular case.

I think it will be found that by this interpretation all the difficulties are instantly removed. The stanza and the poem conclude with the proper point. There is no longer any possible ambiguity of construction, and the ambiguity of the word *solitum* ceases to be troublesome, for both senses, '*our* wont,' and 'the general wont' or 'common life,' are equally appropriate and in fact merge together. And it is in itself not a slight reason for our view that it converts *leves* from an adjective into a verb. It is well known how sensitive are the Latin writers about the use and position of adjectives, and how careful are the best poets in this matter. In the lyrics of Horace, when the sense closes, as it generally does, with the stanza, the last word of the stanza is in an immense majority of cases a verb or a substantive; and the exceptions show (like those at the end of the Virgilian hexameter) a great caution. We have a few participles or adjectives of participial or verbal form (*e.g. acuto* I 9. 4, *arrogantem* III 26. 12, *pertinaci* I 9. 24, *minaces* III 26. 8), here and there a specially sonorous adjective of the rhythm – ∪ – ∪ at the end of the Alcaic, such as *aestuosis*

II 7. 16, *luctuosae* III 6. 8, a few comparatives or superlatives, and a very few, such as *cote cruenta* II 8. 16, which cannot be specially classed. Adjectives of the quantity ∪ – hardly ever occur, nor in spite of their convenience, the similar pronominal adjectives *meus, tuus* etc. Both in III 13—

me dicente cavis impositam ilicem
saxis unde loquaces
lymphae desiliunt *tuae*—

and in III 19—

puro *te* similem, Telephe, Vespero
tempestiva petit Rhode;
me lentus Glycerae torret amor *meae*—

the emphasis is carefully justified by the relation to the other opposed pronouns[1]. It is to be noticed that the stanza preceding that which we are discussing has one of the weakest endings to be found in Horace—*Tydiden superis parem.* We have already seen that this stanza is not meant to be wholly satisfactory, and shows reason against rather than for the supposition that *leves* is an adjective too. Equally against it is the very remarkable ending of III 3—

non hoc iocosae conveniet lyrae:
quo, musa, tendis? desine pervicax
referre sermones deorum et
magna modis tenuare *parvis.*

The poet is there descending with intentional bathos from one of his longest and highest flights. Here there is no flight from which to descend.

[1] The first raises the suggestion of a talk (note *loquaces*) between the poet and the spring.

It is possible that the change of interpretation here given to the first and last parts of the stanza may indirectly affect the exact sense we should put on *vacui, sive quid urimur*. This is generally understood to mean 'sometimes loveless, sometimes a little in love.' But of course the words in themselves do not mean this: *vacuus* means simply *unoccupied*[1], whether by love or anything else; *uri* is a word of equally wide scope, meaning *to be distressed, hurt, or galled*, and applied to all sorts of more or less painful feelings, not to *love* only or even chiefly. The limitation *amore* must be supplied, if at all, from the context. And it is not clear that it can be or ought to be so supplied. In the first place there is no word from which to supply it; secondly, whether the lyric poet is not in love at all, or a little in love, has very little to do with the description of wedding raptures; and thirdly, an objection perhaps more easily made palpable, *vacuus* and *uri*, if antithetical, are surely not well-chosen words. There is no natural contrast between being unoccupied and being burnt. For these reasons I take *vacui sive quid urimur* to have, at any rate in the first place, their full and simple sense, *when unoccupied or when something galls us*[2]. 'We love-poets,' the meaning will then be, 'are not equal to a

[1] See I 5. 10 *qui semper vacuam* (*te*), *semper amabilem sperat* (cited by Mr Wickham), 'who trusts to find thee ever unpossessed (by any rival) and open to his love.'

[2] The alternative reading of the MSS. *quod* is still more favourable to this view.

sublime effort; we only write our amatory descriptions to amuse ourselves when we are unoccupied or uncomfortable.' Of course this is not a true description of love-poets, but it must be remembered that writing love-poetry was at Rome in the time of Augustus almost a part of the character of a man of fashion, and there must have been in circulation an enormous mass of scribbling to which the account thus given would most strictly apply. At the same time, I do not deny that the words are *open* to the interpretation, 'some of us not in love at all, some of us perhaps a little,' and I think Horace was quite willing that any one who chose (Propertius for example) should take them so.

In conclusion I would submit that this poem gives a strong support to the view of Horace's love-poetry in the *Odes*, and his intention respecting it, defended in the fifth Essay (*Venus and Myrtale*) of my *Studies in Horace*. The poet here describes by a type the themes of the poet of love. And he is careful to take that type, exactly as the most decorous of modern poets might do, from the love consecrated by religion. At the same time he remarks that writing love-poetry is commonly a mere pastime, with which the feelings of the poet have little or nothing to do. Nothing could be imagined more completely hostile to the licentious element in the contemporary literature. I am certain that this hostility is characteristic, and I do not believe that it was unreal.

AN INTERPOLATION IN HORACE.

Carm. IV 8.

THIS poem, not in other respects very remarkable, has attained an unhappy notoriety in criticism, as presenting almost the only conspicuous difficulty in the text of the *Odes*. I refer of course to the lines

non incisa notis marmora publicis,
per quae spiritus et vita redit bonis
post mortem ducibus, non celeres fugae
reiectaeque retrorsum Hannibalis minae,
non incendia Karthaginis impiae,
eius, qui domita nomen ab Africa
lucratus rediit, clarius indicant
laudes quam Calabrae Pierides; neque,
si chartae sileant quod bene feceris,
mercedem tuleris. quid foret Iliae
Mavortisque puer, si taciturnitas
obstaret meritis invida Romuli?

The problem is briefly this. To a plain understanding the author here clearly implies that the same *Scipio Africanus* who burnt Carthage was celebrated in the poems of the Calabrian Ennius; that is, he confuses the *Major* and the *Minor*. That this is the natural *prima facie* meaning no one has disputed. I do not think it necessary to consider the attempts, some of them very curious, which have been made to show that, if we scan the text like a lawyer rebutting an *innuendo*, the author might conceivably get a verdict. We may take it in the alternative: either (1) he made the mistake, or (2) he did not see, and was not told, that he must seem to have made it, or (3) he saw this, but did not care. It is difficult to say which supposition is least consistent with what we know of Horace and his work. And the strong suspicion that some one else has meddled here, rises to something like certainty when it is observed (as first by Meineke) that every Ode but this (of 34 lines) is divisible into quatrains, although more than twenty others are written in a metre of couplets or single lines. The coincidence is generally allowed to be almost decisive; and we may perhaps assume that if there had been found here *a couplet*, the omission of which would remove the historical error, and for the insertion of which a good plain reason could be given, that couplet would have been pronounced spurious by general consent. But there is no such couplet; and so the question becomes again completely dark. The light which I hope to throw upon it will come chiefly from the side of metre.

An opening in this direction was attempted by Bentley, who rejected, for want of the regular caesura, *v.* 17, *non incendia Karthaginis impiae.* In itself the reason is not adequate: if Horace could write once in a way *dum flagrantia de-torquet ad oscula*, he might once have gone one step further. Nor does Bentley explain why the verse should have been inserted: and besides we now see that the omission of one verse would not satisfy the conditions. But if we look a little further, we shall find that the metre gives a different report, both as to the existence of an interpolation and as to the extent of it.

The Fourth Book of the *Odes*, among its many broad differences from the original Three, exhibits a far more severe treatment of metrical irregularities. To show this contrast, which is little noticed even in the best editions, let us compare the statistics (A)

of the Fourth Book (minus the lines which contain this strange allusion to the Scipios, *vv.* 15—20), in the whole 576 lines,

and (B)

of 576 lines in the same metres taken from various parts of the original Three[1].

And first, as to the admission at the end of the verse of a short syllable *in arsi* (*i.e.* taking the beat of the metre), as for example in

nolis longa ferae bella Numantiae
nec dirum Hannibalem nec Siculum *maré*
Poeno purpureum sanguine *mollibús*
aptari citharae modis:

[1] As the nearest metrical equivalent to IV 7, I took part of I 7. To make sure that no mistake was incurred by the choice of the particular 576 lines, I took also the statistics for the whole of the Three Books and for each separately, and these are of some independent interest. See hereafter.

or as in

> ut barbarorum Claudius *agminá*
> *ferrata.*

For the sake of simplicity we will take no account of anything except the structure of the verses, including, for example, in our list of such licences

> nardo vina *mereberé.*
> *nardi* parvus onyx etc.,

without regard to the full stop and the division of the stanzas. By going into detail we might easily sharpen our contrast, but for the present purpose it is not worth while. Counting thus, we find the numbers to be

A[1]	B
11	30

Secondly, as to hiatus between the lines. Here again for simplicity we will ignore all minor distinctions, such as the quantity of the vowel, the punctuation, etc., and include, notwithstanding the stop and division of stanzas, even such cases as

> procidit late posuitque collum in
> pulvere *Teucro.*
> *ille* mordaci velut icta ferro etc.

This gives the result

A[2]	B
12	27

and even these figures do not represent the true difference. For on looking at the list A (see note 2 below), we see that five examples, that is nearly

[1] IV 4. 9, 4. 14, 4. 54, 5. 6, 5. 10, 5. 35, 7. 22, 9. 25, 12. 16, 12. 19, 14. 29.

[2] IV 1. 16, 1. 18, 1. 20, 1. 24, 1. 27, 4. 4, 6. 12, 8. 24, 10. 2, 11. 12, 13. 1, 15. 10.

half, lie close together in the first poem, the remaining 536 lines of the book having only seven examples between them. This strange inequality of distribution calls for an explanation, and on turning to the first poem the cause is at once apparent. The most striking point in it is the carefully studied elision near the close:

> cur facunda parum decoro
> inter verba cadit lingua silentio?

In this, the only elision of a long vowel between verse and verse in the whole of the *Odes*, the metre of course reflects the sense. The harsh elision is itself a 'parum decorum inter verba silentium.' For this effect it is essential that the elision should appear unnatural, which it will best do if the ear is previously accustomed to the contrary effect of hiatus, as in *vv.* 16 and 27, *e.g.*

> laudantes pede candido
> in morem Salium ter quatient humum.

In this poem therefore hiatus is not a *licence* at all, but a device, and for our present purpose we must subtract from Book IV the first poem, and from the other side equivalent lines in the same metre. The figures then become

A	B
7	25

Thirdly, let us look at elision. Of elision generally the Fourth Book is much more sparing than the Three, and approaches the standard of the *Carmen Saeculare*, in which both hiatus and elision almost vanish[1]. But for the present we are concerned only with an exceptional kind of elision, that at the caesura, as in

> mos et lex maculos*um* edomuit nefas—
> regum timendor*um* in proprios greges—
> Pegasus terren*um* equitem gravatus.

For this elision the figures are

A[2]	B
3	7

Taking now the three figures together, we have as the total of metrical irregularities of all the three kinds

A	B
11 + 7 + 3 = 21	30 + 25 + 7 = 62

or to put the thing in words, the work of the Fourth Book is about three times as severe as that of the first Three; and this, I venture to say after a careful study, will be found, in whatever way the test be taken, certainly not an exaggerated statement of the difference. Now, with these facts before us, let us look at our passage again:

> non celeres fugae
> reiectaeque retror*sum* *Han*nibalis minae,
> non incendia *Kartha*ginis impi*ae*,
> *e*ius, qui domita nomen ab Africa
> lucratus red*ii*t, clarius indicant
> laudes quam Calabrae Pierides; ne*qué*
> *si* chartae etc.

[1] The elision of *que* and the fixed combination of *est* in *vestrum est*, *dictum est* are hardly noticeable. Except these there is but one, *v.* 71 *puerorum amicas*.

[2] IV 5. 13, 5. 22, 11. 27.

Five metrical licences of various kinds (and therefore clearly without purpose) within five lines:—for we must add the hiatus *ii*, of which this is, I believe, the sole example. It will be difficult to show that Horace ever thought such work good enough. When he wrote Book IV he had long utterly renounced such indulgence. If the rest of the Book were so written, our examples would be counted by hundreds. The most irregular pieces in Book I[1] offer no parallel to it, and for the place where it stands it is quite unfit.

As to the language of the passage there is not much new to say. The use of *eius* (here only and in the almost equally suspicious III 11. 18[2]) has been noted by all since Bentley, but not always so as to put the point quite fairly. It is not the use of the *genitive case* which is noticeable, nor is the emphasis material. Nowhere in all his lyrics, the *Epodes* included, does Horace use, with or without emphasis, any part of the common pronoun *is*, easily found in his other writings or in any others. These two places have it, and it is a most remarkable accident. Something might be said on the plural *fugae* and on the poetical quality of *lucrari*. We might wonder to see the poet so pompous in praise of epitaphs, and so very modest in praise of literature. If an

[1] I 3 is much the most irregular of all, at least in appearance. How far this may be intentional we cannot here consider. I will add the approximate proportions of these irregularities for the Books separately; I—17·5 per 100 lines; II—12·5; III—10; IV—4·5; *Carm. S.*—1.

[2] The stanza is declared spurious by almost universal consent.

inscription can restore the dead to life, it is hard to see why the 'gift' of the poet should be particularly precious. Should we express our appreciation of the *Odes* by saying that they contribute to the fame of Augustus 'not less' than the *Monumentum Ancyranum*? Again, we might admire the terseness of 'vita redit *post mortem*,' the felicitous arrangement of 'bonis post mortem ducibus' (meaning apparently 'leaders good after death' or 'good men who become leaders after death'), and above all the riches of the *Gradus ad Parnassum* as displayed in 'Calabrae Pierides.' No doubt *Pierides* is a 'synonym' for *Musae*; but it is none the less a local name. The Calabrian Muses, it might be supposed, were the Muses not of Pieria but of Calabria, and the daughters not of Pieros but of Calaber—or however the eponymous hero of Calabria may have been called. 'Sicelides Musae' is sense: but could Virgil possibly have written 'Pierides Siculae'? It is of course good enough for a writer who confuses the Scipios. However, these are arguments of taste, and we need not press them. Only let the experiment be tried of constructing such an indictment against any equal piece of the Book (or indeed of the *Odes*): and let us abide by the result.

But now let us recall Meineke's 'law of quatrains,' which seemed to suggest that the poem is too long by two lines. To be accurate, we should say in algebraic language 'too long by $4n+2$ lines.' We have seen that the interpolation must be larger than 2 lines. Let us try 6; thus

non incisa notis *marmora* publicis
per quae spiritus et vita redit bonis.
si *chartae* sileant quod bene feceris,
mercedem tuleris? quid foret Iliae
Mavortisque puer, etc.

Not what the people can grave upon marble *is the means whereby the good return to breathing life. If* paper *tell nothing of thy good deeds, wilt thou have had thy reward? What now would be the son of Ilia and Mars etc.* Stones, that is, wear away at last and leave no trace; the 'inscriptions' of Romulus are gone long ago; it is the living speaking page, the literary monument perishable in appearance yet 'more lasting than bronze,' which alone can give a true immortality.—If we ask why into this simple antithesis should have been thrust the wedge we see, the answer is to be found in the importance of the punctuation. Restore the ancient writing by removing the stop at *bonis* and the note of interrogation at *tuleris*, and we can easily understand why to the author of the inserted verses, and indeed to readers much more competent than he, the sense should have seemed incomplete. The poet is not to blame; but it is quite likely that beyond his intimate circle he was scarcely ever correctly understood, and that in the very first 'complete edition' after his death the supposed lacuna was filled up. The editor should have known, however, that not he nor any man could put six undistinguishable lines into the Fourth Book of the *Odes* of Horace.

STARE IN HORACE, *SAT.* I 9. 39.

ventum erat ad Vestae, quarta iam parte diei
praeterita; et casu tunc respondere vadato
debebat, quod ni fecisset, perdere litem.
'si me amas,' inquit, 'paulum hic ades.' 'inteream si
aut valeo stare, aut novi civilia iura,
et propero quo scis.' 'dubius sum, quid faciam,' inquit;
'tene relinquam, an rem.'

THIS passage, with the whole satire on 'the bore' in which it occurs, is so familiar that no long introduction will be necessary in discussing it. 'We had arrived,' says the poet, describing his compulsory walk with the pertinacious intruder, 'at the place and the hour of legal business; it happened that my companion had to appear to a summons, under pain of losing the action. He begged me to support him in court (*adesse*). I pleaded ignorance of law and my previous engagement. After some hesitation, he went on with me.' The language, otherwise simple, presents one obvious difficulty in the words *aut valeo stare.* Prof. A. Palmer, the most recent editor, writes as follows—'*valeo stare*: (1) "if I am able to appear as an advocate in court," *stare* = *adesse*, for which meaning Mr Beare quotes

Plaut. *Men.* 5. 2. 47: *hinc stas, illinc causam dicis.* So also *Rud.* 4. 4. 57: *atqui nunc aps te stat: verum hinc cibit testimonium.* (2) "If I am strong enough to stand so long": so Comm. Cruq. (3) "If I can stop": so Porph., who says *negat se posse eum expectare.*' This simple juxtaposition of the three interpretations seems to indicate that none of them satisfies the editor. In fact, the first and third appear impossible on linguistic grounds, while the second, the only one, as I conceive, which the uses of *valere* and *stare* admit, is almost nonsense. Even if it were clear, which it is not, that *stare* could be used, as in (3), absolutely for *to wait,* still *valeo stare* could only mean 'I have the power in myself to stop,' not 'I am at liberty under the circumstances to stop.' The English 'I can stop' is ambiguous between these meanings, and this ambiguity covers the mistranslation. The first rendering avoids this objection, but only to encounter one equally strong in *stare,* the evidence alleged for *stare* = *adesse* (in the technical sense) being surely inadequate. In neither of the Plautine passages is there any difficulty in translating by the simple *stand.* The context indeed shows that 'stand on that side' and 'stand on your side' probably have in these places a metaphorical meaning, 'be on your side in the dispute,' as well as the literal 'stand by you,' but this is far different from what we require for the passage of Horace. As for (2), there is, in the first place, no reason for supposing that an *advocatus,* in the Roman sense, would necessarily have to stand a long time (it must be remembered that he did not always or commonly make a speech), and further, a man who is met out for a walk and who represents that he is 'hurrying' to a sick friend would scarcely excuse himself on the ground of extreme debility from one of the commonest offices in Roman society.

If, then, the choice lay between these three, I should prefer to give the passage up. But I think we can prove the possibility of something better— '*If you love me,*' *said he*, '*support me for a short time in court.*' '*May I be confounded,*' *said I*, '*if I have either any talent in that way or any knowledge of law.*' Had the MSS. given *ista re* instead of *stare*, the meaning would have been obvious: after *valeo*, *nil valeo* (to which *inteream si valeo* is here equivalent), *multum valeo*, *plus valeo*, etc. an ablative is constantly used to express the sort of power, faculty, or efficacity which is meant. The dictionary will furnish abundant examples, such as *valere equitatu*, *armis*, *ingenio*, *opibus*, etc. Here *ista re* would mean *in the business you mention*, viz. τῷ *adesse*, in the function of an *advocatus*. Further, *ista re* is actually admissible in metre, and if it were certain that Horace would have so written the words, it would not be a very bold correction to restore them. I believe, however, that even this change is not necessary. The MSS. of Plautus contain several examples which show that the contracted forms *staec* for *istaec*, *stac* for *istac*, etc. were at one time actually written, and it is probable that *iste* and its derivatives were in colloquial Latin frequently so pronounced. Now the *Sermones* of Horace are, as might be expected, full of colloquial phrases, for which we can often find parallels, if at all, only in the older colloquial Latin of the comedians. (See Prof. Palmer, *Preface*, p. xxiii, citing among many others *verba dare*, *serva* (look out!), *aufer*, *noster*, *sodes*.) This satire in particular, representing casual talk in the street, abounds with such phrases, as the commentaries will show:—for example, *ut nunc est* 5, *cupio omnia quae vis* ib., *numquid vis?* 6, *sodes* 41, *Maecenas quomodo tecum?* 43, etc. It does not seem unlikely that even in the time of Horace pronunciations like *'sta* for *ista* were often to be heard in careless speech, and they would be likely to hold their place especially in set phrases frequently required, such as the *nil valeo 'sta re* of our hypothesis. And if this was the pronunciation, there could be no reason why Horace, when trying, like Plautus, to reproduce the language of ordinary life, should not do as Plautus did, and write what was actually said.

THE STORY OF ORPHEUS AND EURYDICE IN THE FOURTH GEORGIC.

IT is commonly assumed that according to Virgil, as according to Ovid, the creature which caused the death of Eurydice was a snake, an ordinary snake. I propose to show that this is not so, and that a different conception is necessary, indeed vital, to the sense and connexion of the story as Virgil received it. That a different conception once existed appears from the *Liber Monstrorum*[1], the materials of which are thought to have been drawn largely from commentaries on Virgil. There the offending animal is a fabulous monster, a 'snake in armour' (*armatus anguis*), compounded apparently of serpent and tortoise, which decapitated the nymph and dragged her down into the water. The proof that Virgil, though he touches this part of the tale with reticence and discretion, figured his 'vast water-beast' (*immanem hydrum*) as something of that sort, lies in this,—that the shell of the creature, the tortoise-like part of it, served Orpheus, when he had killed it, for the first making of a lyre.

'Eurydice,' says Proteus to Aristaeus,

[1] 3. 2 (cited by O. Gruppe in Roscher's *Lexicon* 'Orpheus,' § 95, col. 1160).

illa quidem, dum te fugeret per flumina praeceps,
immanem ante pedes hydrum moritura puella
servantem ripas alta non vidit in herba.
at chorus aequalis Dryadum clamore supremos
implerunt montis; flerunt Rhodopeiae arces
altaque Pangaea et Rhesi Mavortia tellus
atque Getae atque Hebrus et Actias Orithyia.
ipse cava solans aegrum testudine amorem
te, dulcis coniunx, te solo in litore secum,
te veniente die, te decedente canebat[1].

We see that the poet, with a noticeable abruptness of transition, overleaps the death (for which he had the more reason if it involved the horrors of the *Liber Monstrorum*), and passes on from the Dryads to Orpheus in a manner which still leaves something untold, something which he assumes to be known. But here, at the second transition, we are directed or reminded how to fill up the gaps:

ipse cava solans aegrum testudine amorem...

What does this mean? Conington, who felt a difficulty, remarks that *cava* is a literary or epic epithet of the lyre; and nothing more illuminating, it seems, has yet been said.

Now, it is the fashion at present to speculate on the particular disadvantages which hamper, in education and otherwise, the study of the classics. Here is one of them, and not the least: that perhaps in no other study, so much as in this field of inanimate tradition, is it permitted or possible to be decorously evasive. To call a word epic sounds very well; but fully set out and in plain English, what does

[1] *Georg.* IV 457 ff.

the comment come to? It comes to this. The sense of Virgil here would have been properly and entirely expressed by *ipse amorem solans lyra*,—by these words in this order. This is all he had to say. His poetical function consisted, first in substituting for *lyra* the 'synonym' *testudine*, next in tacking to each substantive an otiose adjective, *cava testudine*, *aegrum amorem*, and finally in piecing a hexameter together like a Chinese puzzle. The emphasis on *cava* means nothing, the word itself being idle; the junction of *ipse cava* means nothing, *cava solans* nothing, *aegrum testudine amorem* nothing whatever. It is a school-boy verse consisting of words which scan and, when you have got them all, are significant if mentally re-arranged—*ipse amorem aegrum solans testudine cava*. Seriously, this carries the licence of mosaic beyond what can fairly be attributed to Virgil, especially in a narrative so exquisitely finished as this. The words should mean (or to speak more properly, they do mean, whether the writer so intended or not) that 'Orpheus, having hollowed the tortoise, consoled with its hollowness his passion by the tortoise grieved,' that is, embittered, angered, or turned to melancholy. In the power to compress this by pregnant grouping of words lies the very merit of Latin, especially poetical Latin. And the sense is clear enough, for the purpose of a tale retold. Like Hermes in the Homeric Hymn, Orpheus is led to the making of the lyre partly by accident. As Hermes 'bores out the life of the tortoise' in childish malice, to begin with, so

Orpheus here 'hollows out' the fabulous beast in revenge, *cavat testudinem*; the adjective *cava*, placed as it is, has the effect of a participle, *cavata*. The hollow sound of the shell is grateful to his wounded feelings, and prompts his artistic faculty; he adds a string to bring out the resonance,—and the lyre, his consolation, is begun.

It seems not improbable that here the legend originally ended, having for its subject the invention of the lyre. That this was at least part of the subject, appears in the sequel, where the rapt astonishment of the dead and of their gods signifies that they had not heard music before. It is a petty notion, not native to the times of genuine mythical invention, that Hell should be so agitated by the dexterity of a certain *maestro*.

PHILIPPI AND PHILIPPI

(Lucan, *Pharsalia* I 678–694.)

What is the cause of the strange persistence of the Roman poets in making a connexion, which becomes a confusion and even a sort of rhetorical identification, between the far-separated sites of Pharsalia and Philippi? The fact, thanks to the learning of Professor Mayor and others, is familiar. Repeatedly, and by several authors, language is used which implies that since the two battles had in some sort a common scene, described for the most part vaguely as *Emathia* or the like, the later may be regarded as a repetition of the former, as the second and not the first 'Philippi.' Lucan alone offers several illustrations[1] and sufficiently attests that the idea was for some reason popular. But why? Mere error is no explanation. Let it be supposed, though the supposition is, I think, extravagant, that some one actually blundered, and really thought that Pharsalia and Philippi lay close together. Why should the mistake be adopted, and give rise to a train of allusions? Why should a series of writers find poetical satisfaction in what

[1] See Haskins, *ad loc.*

some at least must have known to be not literally true?

In the passage above cited we have a glimpse of what may be the explanation. A Roman matron, inspired by Apollo, rushes into the street, and in a prophetic vision unfolds the successive scenes of the coming contest, imagining herself transported to each. First she beholds the scene of Pharsalia, which she describes however not by its own name, but by those of Pangaeus, Haemus, and *Philippi*; next she is taken to Egypt and the death of Pompeius, then to the region of Thapsus and Utica; then, after a flight within view of Munda, to Rome itself, 'war in the very senate,' and the death of Caesar. Hereupon 'Factions uprise once more, and all round the circle I begin to pass again.' But at this the demoniac rebels and implores: 'O Phoebus, let me see new sea-shores and new earth; Philippi thou hast shown before.'

> consurgunt partes iterum totumque per orbem
> rursus eo. nova da mihi cernere litora ponti
> telluremque novam: vidi iam, Phoebe, Philippos.

Now it would seem that in these expressions, especially in the cry for 'new sea-shores and a new earth,' something more should be signified than mere impatience of repetition. And when we consider that the speaker, being possessed by Apollo, is a kind of Sibyl, and remember how largely, as we see in Virgil, the *Cumaeum carmen* dealt with the notion of cycles, we may not improperly conceive the insinuation to be, that a new, a better, a 'golden' world ought now to begin, because the age of civil war has completed its circle. This is doubtless a conception very different from that of Virgil's Sibylline poem, the Fourth *Eclogue*. There the world's history is supposed to go round in an orbit, upon which view the recurrence of Pharsalia, in the form of Philippi, could warrant only the most dismal expectations. But every prophet, happily for our peace of mind, has his own system, and different systems for different occasions. It does not seem unlikely that, about the time when Virgil was ruminating upon the possible advent of the golden age as prefigured in his 'prophecy of Cumae,' some other poet or poets, or even the popular voice, should have hailed the return of the war to its starting-point in 'Emathia' as a sign that it was over, and upon this assurance should have promised peace to mankind, and the opening of 'new seas and earth' under the allied government of Octavian and Antonius; nor improbable either that this forecast should have been presented as Sibylline. If so, if we may suppose that the Sibyl of Lucan represents an idea once important and popular, there is no longer reason to wonder that it should have left a permanent mark upon poetical rhetoric, and the less reason because, in a certain sense, the prognostic proved to be true.

In a certain sense, Philippi was actually the end of the *bellum civile*; it did terminate the contest as conceived, for example, by Lucan. The party which stood against Julius, the party which, as

Lucan says, sprang to arms again after the death of Julius, the party of the senate and the old government, did not survive Philippi. Actium was, after all, a family and dynastic quarrel; the principles which contended at Pharsalia were at Actium both on the side of Caesar, so far as the defeated of Pharsalia were represented at Actium at all. And this view of things must have gained in attraction when the victors and vanquished of Actium were merged in a single line, and the descendants of Antonius sat on the throne of Augustus.

All this considered, it seems not unlikely that the identification of Philippi as a second Pharsalia owed its origin, impressiveness, and reception to that craving for 'a sign,' that expectation of some world-wide and beneficial change, coming by observation, which appears in Virgil and other witnesses of the age. It was an attempt to give precision to the fulfilment of a literary or popular belief, that the new world should open when the course of the world-war notified its cyclic term by completing the circuit of the Mediterranean and entering once more upon the region of its beginning. In this sort of interpretation desire is the master of fact, and will make little of a few leagues of distance. Our passage of Lucan, which is the most developed example of the idea, may thus perhaps point to the source of it.

STATIUS, *SILVAE* II 7. 8 ff.

(Greek Words in the Latin Poets.)

In restoring defaced passages of the Latin poets, perhaps hardly sufficient use has yet been made of that portion of their vocabulary which they borrow from Greek; to seek Latin words is of course more obvious. The Greek vein has indeed been successfully and brilliantly worked, but it is probably not exhausted. It is to later poets in particular, and to lighter works, that the principle is most applicable. It has led to happy discoveries in Martial, and such a work as the *Silvae* of Statius, if we had a correct copy, might well be found to exhibit a much larger proportion of Greek than we commonly allow for. The language was unknown to the copyists, and therefore specially liable to loss. But to investigate this subject properly would be a large task, involving much technical machinery, and beyond our present scope. I must be content for the moment to call attention to the subject by a single example, taken indeed from the *Silvae* but depending in no way on the date of Statius' poem, or the quality of the MSS. It is a case such as might occur anywhere in Latin poetry, but in this way noticeable, that, unless I am mistaken, the path indicated, the path of looking for Greek rather than Latin, leads with simplicity out of a troublesome maze.

All sources of inspiration, says the ode for the birthday of Lucan, all the givers of song, are to refresh their forces in honour of a festival so poetic,—Hermes and Bacchus, Apollo and the Muses:

> et Paean et Hyantiae sorores,
> laetae purpureas novate vittas,
> crinem comite, candidamque vestem
> perfundant hederae recentiores.
> docti largius evagentur amnes,
> et plus Aoniae virete silvae;
> et si qua †pater aut† diem recepit,
> sertis mollibus expleatur umbra[1].

For the repair of the last couplet no satisfactory materials have been found in native Latin. The correction

> et si qua *patet aut* diem recepit...

is a mere makeshift, scarcely even intelligible. What should stand in the place of *pater aut* is manifestly the subject of *recepit*; and this we may find without difficulty, if we turn to Greek:—

> et si qua *Patareus* diem recepit,...

'And if anywhere Apollo's grove lets in the day, with bending wreaths be the shade filled up.' 'Patareus' is the title of Apollo as possessor of the sacred wood of Patara in Lycia, the place (according to some) of his birth:

[1] *Silv.* II 7. 8 ff.

qui Lyciae tenet
dumeta natalemque silvam
Delius et Patareus Apollo[1].

Statius, with his usual compression of allusive phrase, puts 'the god' for the grove of the god,—just as, to take the nearest instance, 'fertile with olives' becomes in his language *Tritonide fertilis*[2]—and chooses this particular designation of Patareus because, associated with a wood, it was proper to describe the god as possessor, together with the Muses, of the metaphorical forest of poesy. Further, on this supposition, the traditional error explains itself at once. A writer who missed *patareus* read the final *s*—which in its long form is a constant source of danger—as a *t*[3], and out of *patareut* made, very naturally, *pater aut.*

[1] Hor. *C.* III 4. 62. [2] *Silv.* II 7. 28.
[3] Cf. *Silv.* I 6. 38 *nescit* for *nescis.*

INDEX.

For EU product safety concerns, contact us at Calle de José Abascal, 56–1°, 28003 Madrid, Spain or eugpsr@cambridge.org.

www.ingramcontent.com/pod-product-compliance
Ingram Content Group UK Ltd.
Pitfield, Milton Keynes, MK11 3LW, UK
UKHW042142130625
459647UK00011B/1151
9781107643000